Where to watch birds in the

London area

Dominic Mitchell

Illustrated by Jan Wilczur

D1806205

Christopher Helm

A & C Black · London

Christopher Helm (Publishers) Ltd, a subsidiary of
A & C Black, 35 Bedford Row, London WC1R 4JH

0-7136-3868-0

A CIP catalogue record for this book
is available from the British Library

Typeset and designed by D & N Publishing
Membury Business Park, Lambourn Woodlands, Hungerford, Berkshire

Printed and bound by Redwood Books, Trowbridge, Wiltshire

*Dedicated to the memory of my brother Laurence,
whose early interest in birdwatching inspired my own*

CONTENTS

Contents

FOREWORD

London is my city, for I was born and raised there. I have never been at a loss to find something of wildlife interest, including birds, even in the most unpromising places. My own discovery of where to watch birds in the London area began before I was three years old. I removed a baby Blue Tit from a low nest in Ladbroke Square – the largest private square in the capital. Both parent birds had just left so that I had time to take the little bird into the house to show my mother and then return it before the adults came back. Later I noted over 60 species in the square, and of these 13 bred. In 1937, in nearby Holland Park, I watched fledged Marsh Tits, nesting Jays and found the first recorded Chiffchaff's nest in Inner London. I made regular counts in the central Royal Parks, on Hampstead Heath and Wimbledon Common, and I saw my first Redstarts, Wood-larks, Hawfinches and Goosanders in Richmond Park. I cycled out to Staines Reservoirs before school in quest of divers, wading birds and Long-tailed Ducks. I made expeditions to Beddington Sewage Farm for warblers and wagtails, and the Surrey woods for their dawn choruses. From a green but eager schoolboy learning the rudiments of birdwatching, I was ultimately able to turn my hobby into a lifelong professional career. I am grateful for what I learned in London.

As the BBC's director of its wildlife sound recording projects I made the first recordings of Little Ringed Plovers on the site of the William Girling Reservoir. Later I directed several films about the wildlife of the capital. From 1951 to 1980, I carried out at Dollis Hill, in northwest London, what was almost certainly the longest continuous study of the birdlife of a sub-urban area. I was privileged to help in setting up the Parkland Walk in north London and am a founder member of the Welsh Harp Conservation Group. To me London was and still is one of the most fascinating and rewarding birding areas, and there are many who would subscribe to that view.

Of course, there have been changes over the 70 years. There have been losses of breeding species such as Wryneck, Red-backed Shrike and Cirl Bunting and gains such as Cormorant, Common Tern, Ring-necked Parakeet, Collared Dove and Cetti's Warbler. The ornithological picture is a dynamic one and the changes are always full of interest. As the Song Thrush has gone into decline, Blackbirds in suburban gardens may breed at 10 times the density that they achieved in the woodlands from which they first came.

It was in 1957 that I was invited to review the seminal volume *The Birds of the London Area since 1900*. I described this book as 'a great step forward in the treatment and presentation of the birds of the region.' Now, 40 years later, appears this book – the ultimate *vade mecum* (companion guide) for birdwatchers in London. Firmly based on his own wide experience and the countless observations of others, Dominic Mitchell has provided an incomparable guide to London's birds and where to find them. For the spectacle of roosting gulls in winter go to Hilfield Park Reservoir, and for Water Rails to Brent Reservoir. For observers seeking Cormorants, Grey Herons and wildfowl there are Walthamstow Reservoirs, while there is Epping Forest for Mandarin Ducks, Foot's Cray Meadows for Ring-necked Parakeets, Rainham for waders and perhaps even Thorpe Park for the delightful and elusive Smew. These are just few from a vast range of possibilities.

I welcome Dominic Mitchell's meticulously researched, deeply detailed and attractively presented essential itinerary. It covers more than 70 major sites and many minor ones, with accounts of their history and habitats, bird species, times to visit shown as a calendar and, last but not least, any conditions of access and availability for birdwatchers. I am confident that *Where to watch birds in the London area* will have a wide appeal, stand proudly on the shelf alongside other volumes in the series and richly deserve the success among birdwatchers that it will undoubtedly enjoy.

Eric Simms
January 1997

ACKNOWLEDGEMENTS

The idea for this guide to birdwatching in London was first suggested to me by David Lindo, who also supplied information on some locations in the western half of the capital. Keith Betton helped refine the original choice of sites, provided contact points for a number of local observers and made comments on the final draft. Mark Hardwick contributed useful background information on many areas and gave valuable feedback on draft site accounts, as well as advice and encouragement at various stages during the writing of this book. Tim Harris gave much useful input on sites in west London and commented on extensive batches of drafts, as did Roy Beddard, Margaret Mitchell, Andrew Moon, Stephen Moss, Ken Osborne and Brian Slyfield. I am particularly grateful to Robert Kirk at Christopher Helm for patiently keeping the book on course through thick and thin.

Many others assisted by contributing or checking information on various sites or by providing help in other ways, including Neil Anderson, Sacha Barbato, Leo Batten, Ken Barrett, Alan Bell, John Birkett, Neil Bowman, Martin Boyle, Steve Carter, Derek Coleman, Mike Dennis, Richard Drew, Gary Elton, Peter Gann, Jeremy Gaskell, Steve Harrington, Tim Hill, Ron Kettle, Mick O'Malley, Tony Morris, Doug Napier, Pete Naylor, Mike Netherwood, Nick Pope, Bill Rutherford, Steve Spooner, Bob Watts, Nigel Wheatley and Jan Wilczur. My apologies to anyone else whose name I may have inadvertently omitted from this list. Jan Wilczur's delightful illustrations also enrich this book and help bring the capital's locations, as well as its birds, to life. John Mather produced the excellent maps that accompany the site accounts.

Thanks are also due to Mike Brophy at Thames Water for facilitating access to the company's sites during the research for this guide, and to other organisations including Birdline South East, the Lee Valley Regional Park Authority, the London Natural History Society and the London Wildlife Trust for providing information and assistance in various ways.

Last but not least, special thanks to Hazel Green for unrelenting encouragement and support during the writing of this book, and to her and our son Eddie for their patience while the task was being completed.

INTRODUCTION

To the uninitiated birder, a site guide to the London area might seem like an unlikely addition to this *Where to watch birds* series covering Britain and Ireland. Yet to the hundreds of active birders who live in and bird this capital city and the thousands more who regularly visit its sites, London's ornithological attractions are enough to rival those of any inland English county. River valleys, reservoirs, gravel pits, marshes, parks, woods, heaths, farmland, even tidal foreshore – the mix of habitats in such a vast metropolitan sprawl is truly unique. This fact is amply illustrated by the capital's bird list of an impressive 345 species; it is also noteworthy that more than 220 species are recorded annually.

The London area, for this purpose of this guide, constitutes the city and adjacent land to the outer limit of the M25 peripheral motorway. This definition, which includes the fringes of the neighbouring counties of Essex, Kent, Surrey, Buckinghamshire and Hertfordshire, is slightly less extensive than the recording limits defined and used by the London Natural History Society, which encompass the entire area within a 20-mile radius of St Paul's Cathedral in the city centre. However, most other outermost 'London' sites falling just outside the M25 limit (for example Wraysbury Gravel Pits in Buckinghamshire and the upper Lea Valley in Hertfordshire and Essex) are covered in other guides in this series and need not be duplicated here.

The main purpose of this book is to guide the reader around the foremost birding sites in London. Some of these are well known and nationally important habitats which clearly demand inclusion, while others are less visited, but nonetheless productive, birding sites which also deserve attention. In arriving at this final selection I have tried to strike a balance between the birding 'value' of a particular area and its geographical location, so that coverage is spread more evenly across the area and not unduly weighted towards the major reservoirs, river valleys and parks. In a small number of instances reservoirs for which there is currently no general public access have been included; this has been done not only for the sake of completeness, but also because entry restrictions or site ownership can change without notice and lack of accessibility may not always be a problem in the future.

There are doubtless other worthwhile sites which will not have found their way into this edition, in some cases simply through lack of space, but in others because they have yet to be brought to wider attention. As everywhere, London has its fair share of 'local patches' which provide stalwart observers with rewards through regular or intensive coverage, but whose reputations have not reached a more public audience. In particular, southeast London and its greener outer suburbs must surely have more to offer birders: I would be happy to receive information on these or other areas for consideration in future editions of this book.

Equally, I hope this guide might also inspire readers to strike out in search of new sites of their own. There are still a great many unwatched or underwatched parts of London which must have their fair share of good birds, and every discovery made helps to plug another gap in our knowledge of the capital's avifauna. A few of the sites included here have

11

come to prominence only recently, and there surely must be others await-
ing 'discovery'. By reporting records to the London Natural History
Society (see Useful Addresses, page 226) and participating in survey work
in the capital, birders can add directly to existing knowledge of bird status and distribution in the area and, in the long term, help others to get
more enjoyment from their birding in London too.

The face of the capital is constantly changing and its bird habitats are
more fragile than most, largely due to pressures of development and
intensive public usage. As this book was being written, construction
crews began bulldozing a dual carriageway road across the regionally-
important Rainham Marshes, inflicting another permanent scar on the
landscape. So that such dramatic changes do not mask the history and
value of London's sites, I have tried wherever relevant to indicate how
bird status and land use have changed over the years. In common with
many other parts of Britain a number of the capital's formerly common
breeding birds are in decline, and efforts to monitor these species are
every bit as important as recording rarer visitors.

Despite such ups and downs, however, London remains an important
area for a wide range of species. Resident woodland birds, breeding warblers in summer, passage waders, wintering wildfowl, even a fair sprinkling of national rarities – there is much to see across the city throughout
the year, and I hope that this book will help you to enjoy it to the full.

Dominic Mitchell
London, November 1996

USING THIS BOOK

This guide has been designed to incorporate all the information you need to get the most from birdwatching in the London area. The sites have been grouped together geographically by chapter in a 'circular' order, beginning with the natural dividing line of the Lea Valley in northeast London and running clockwise through east London, the lower Thames, the southeast and southwest, the Thames reservoirs, the Colne Valley and west London, the northwest and north London, and finally central London.

The main site accounts comprise sections dealing chiefly with habitat, species, timing, access and calendar; the content of these are covered in more detail below. A number of minor sites have also been included and are dealt with in less depth, but still include the most important information about location, habitat, species and access. For those who feel inspired to broaden their horizons further still and investigate other locations in the London area, a complete list of ornithological sites within 20 miles of St Paul's Cathedral can be found in the *London Bird Report,* published annually by the London Natural History Society (see Useful Addresses, page 226).

Habitat

This introductory section aims to give a feel for each site by outlining location and basic habitat types. Where relevant, some historical information on land use, long-term importance to birds and conservation significance has also been included – this is especially important background for urban sites which are often in a constant state of flux and subject to development pressures and heavy public usage. Where known, details of local bird lists are also given.

Species

The key information concerning birds to be found at a particular site is contained in this section. Species are often discussed in systematic order for the more important sites or for those with a range of habitats, but for some locations, such as small woodlands or wetlands, a different treatment may have been adopted if this seems more suitable; this flexible approach is designed to give the most appropriate balance to the birding merits of each site. As well as details of what birds may be expected to occur, reference is also often to made to past records, especially of rare birds, so that a particular site's history and potential can be more fully assessed.

Timing

This section gives an indication of daily and seasonal factors which may affect birding at certain sites. For the most part daily timing concerns vary little from site to site in London, and a good rule of thumb would seem to be the earlier in the day that a visit is made, the better – especially at weekends. Where particular local conditions are important, such as tidal ebb and flow on the lower Thames for wildfowl and wader roosts, these details are also given in this section.

Access

Details of local access arrangements, permit requirements and so on are followed by directions for birders travelling by road or on foot. Because of the vast network of roads in the London area this can be a very complex task, so in general the route is specified from the nearest major road. These directions are then followed by details of relevant bus, underground and rail routes. For some very well-served sites, such as those in central London, it has not always been possible to list every bus route, but in each instance the information given will be more than adequate. When travelling by public transport, bear in mind that timetables and routes are liable to frequent change, and also that large areas of south and southeast London are not served by the tube system.

Calendar

This at-a-glance reference details the species of interest which occur at each major site throughout the year. In many cases it is unlikely that any one observer will succeed in seeing all the species listed for a site in one visit at a particular time of year, but very often at least a good proportion should be feasible. Conversely, other species not listed may also be seen; these will usually comprise a wide range of common birds which occur throughout the London area and elsewhere and which in their own right are unlikely to merit a specific bird-finding trip. Importantly, remember also that success in looking for particular species will depend partly on weather conditions prior to and during a visit to any site. Winds with an easterly component in spring or autumn will increase your chances of finding migrants in London, for example, whereas cold northerly winds with rain in the summer months will often reduce the number of passerine species you might see or hear.

The bird names used in the guide, like most (but not all) other guides in this series, follow those in common general usage, although in a very small number of cases they include minor modifications as recommended by *Birdwatch* magazine in its *Complete Checklist of the Birds of Britain and Ireland*. The 'new' names recommended by the British Ornithologists' Union have not gained wide acceptance among birders or publishers and seem unlikely to do so in the immediate future.

Key to maps

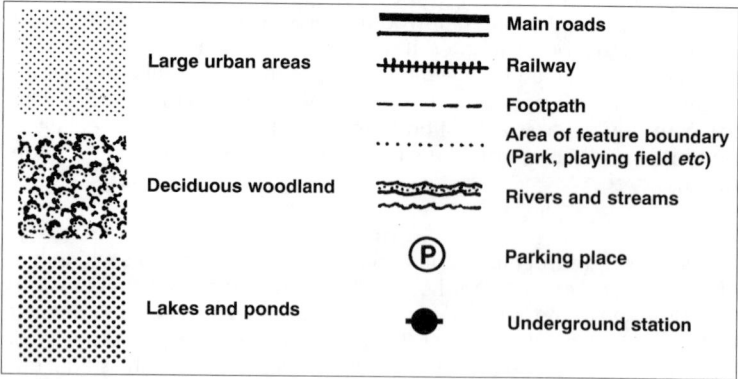

Large urban areas	Main roads
	Railway
	Footpath
	Area of feature boundary (Park, playing field *etc*)
Deciduous woodland	Rivers and streams
	ⓟ Parking place
Lakes and ponds	Underground station

THE LEA VALLEY

1 KING GEORGE V RESERVOIR
OS ref. TQ 374964

Habitat

This huge body of water, the most northerly of the Lea Valley reservoirs, comprises two raised basins just south of the M25 between Enfield and Chingford. Collectively known with William Girling Reservoir to the south as the Chingford Reservoirs, they have together been notified as a Site of Special Scientific Interest. Along with the Walthamstow complex to the south and an extensive network of gravel pits and watercourses in the upper Lea Valley to the north, the whole area constitutes an important wetland habitat for resident species and a major attraction to birds moving through the northeastern sector of the London area.

Both basins of King George V prove attractive to wildfowl, though the southern basin is home to a sailing club and is therefore more prone to disturbance. The northern basin is the larger of the two, and for both of these reasons also the area where many birders concentrate their efforts. The large surface area of water, a lure visible to over-flying birds for some distance, attracts a good variety of dabbling and diving ducks for feeding and roosting. However, the concrete-sided margins are less attractive to waders, which often drop in for relatively short stays in migration periods or during hard-weather movements. Gulls are present in good numbers outside the breeding season and there is a large winter roost, but it is overshadowed by the massive nightly gathering at the neighbouring William Girling Reservoir.

The reservoir banks and adjacent land are largely rough pasture, in places grazed by sheep, with scattered hawthorn hedgerows. The fringes of the River Lea and the Lea Navigation Channel offer cover in the form of willows and other bankside vegetation, but otherwise the landscape is uninterrupted with views across farmland to the north and east and, in contrast, the industrial landscape of Brimsdown and Enfield to the west.

Species

Divers occur annually in the Lea Valley and this reservoir is as good a place as any to look for them. All three species have been recorded here and Great Northern has appeared in several recent years, though birds may sometimes commute between different waters in the area. Up to 100 or so Great Crested Grebes can be present from autumn, the peak time, through to late winter, and there is always a chance of at least one of the three scarcer grebes: Black-necked are more likely in autumn and

Goosanders

Slavonian and Red-necked in winter, all typically occurring singly, but multiple occurrences have been known.

Flocks of several hundred Mallard and Teal comprise the bulk of dabbling duck in winter, but Shoveler can also reach three figures and both Pintail and especially Wigeon may drop in. Rafts of Tufted Duck may number more than 1,000 in midwinter, with between 100 and 200 Pochard and perhaps 50 or so Goldeneye present. Goosander is the only regular sawbill, with scattered parties sometimes totalling 40 birds ranging between here, William Girling and other nearby sites; both Red-breasted Merganser and Smew are erratic visitors during winter. Other wildfowl stragglers worth searching for through the thousands of waterfowl present at peak times are Scaup and Common Scoter, the former mainly in winter but the latter also in spring and summer, when inland movements across Britain may bring birds to the area – such as the 25 males seen together here in June 1993.

Waders can also provide surprises, with the concrete margins typically hosting only the odd Redshank or Lapwing but with a wide variety of species dropping in during the course of a year, especially if drainage work is underway and more mud is revealed. The spring and autumn migration periods are most productive, with occasional Ringed Plover, Ruff, Greenshank and Common Sandpiper, and less frequent records of normally coastal species such as Oystercatcher, Turnstone and Knot. London's third Spotted Sandpiper clearly found the site to its liking during a 12-day stay in autumn 1988, often being seen in company with Common Sandpipers. Hard-weather movements in winter may also produce shorebirds of note, as demonstrated by recent records of Purple Sandpiper and Grey Phalarope: the latter has also occurred after strong southwesterly winds in autumn, most notably after the 'Great Storm' of October 1987 when up to three were present.

Gulls are a dominant feature of the reservoir in winter, with large numbers of all five commoner species sometimes reaching 25,000 roosting birds in total. Glaucous and especially Mediterranean Gulls are the most likely additional species in winter, best looked for in the afternoon as birds arrive from outlying areas to roost, and Iceland has also been recorded. Most exceptional were the four Sabine's Gulls here following the severe southwesterly blow in October 1987. In contrast, appearances of Little Gull and Kittiwake are near-annual in spring, when good numbers of Common Terns and Black Terns also appear, the latter sometimes in double figures. This species is regular in August too, though the other terns are less predictable in their appearances and only Arctic is at all likely. Remarkably for a scarce seabird so rare inland, juvenile Long-tailed Skuas have put in prolonged appearances here in two recent autumns.

Although waterbirds are the prime attraction, other species should not be ignored. Ospreys are almost annual on migration in the Lea Valley, and in autumn 1989 one lingered around here and William Girling Reservoir for almost a month. Autumn 1993 brought Marsh Harriers moving through on two dates, emphasising the area's use as a fly-way for more than just wildfowl and waders, and resident Kestrel and Sparrowhawk are frequently seen in the area. Other breeding birds include a pair of Red-legged Partridges, notable in an area where this species is surprisingly scarce, and Little Owls also breed nearby.

Such is the pulling power of this prominent river valley site that passerine migrants can also prove interesting. Hirundines and Swifts congregate in large feeding flocks when passage movements are underway, notably in May for the latter, when numbers sometimes exceed four figures. Rock and Water Pipits are occasionally found foraging along the shoreline during passage periods or in winter, perhaps mostly lingering when the water level drops to expose a richer food supply. In spring and autumn the rough pasture holds good numbers of Meadow Pipits, with wagtails on shorter turf or the banks of the basins themselves: Pied, Yellow and the occasional White may be present and gather in small flocks, and Blue-headed has been recorded in two recent springs. Rarer still was London's second-ever Citrine Wagtail, an all-too-brief bird on the causeway between the two basins in August 1994. Grey Wagtails are best searched for along the Lea Navigation Channel on the west side of the reservoir or around the river itself along the eastern boundary, these watercourses also being the most likely spot for Kingfisher.

Passage periods can bring chats to the environs of the reservoir: look out for Stonechat, Whinchat and Wheatear on suitable perches as you undertake a circular walk of the reservoir perimeter. Black Redstarts are occasionally recorded in spring and summer, sometimes on the roofs of the factories on the industrial estates on the west side. The hawthorn hedges are worth checking for warblers on passage and for thrushes in winter, while large post-breeding feeding flocks of Goldfinches and Linnets can gather on seed heads in rougher areas of pasture.

Timing

With wildfowl being one of the key attractions, winter is clearly a prime time to visit. However, this reservoir is always worth checking in spring and autumn when migration brings a wider range of species and a better chance of something out of the ordinary, and even summer should not be ignored; wader migration seasons almost overlap in June, when other wanderers can include terns and even seaduck.

There are no special local considerations for watching wildfowl here other than the times at which access is possible (see below), though

numbers will be affected by water level and, on the south basin, disturbance from the sailing club at weekends. Bear in mind, however, that
the large circumference of the north basin alone, let alone both basins,
means that a minimum of two hours, preferably longer, will be required
for even the shortest circular walk.

Waders may pitch in at any time of day, but for gulls afternoon is best,
when birds come in from outlying areas to bathe and preen prior to roosting here or on William Girling Reservoir.

Access

The site is owned by Thames Water and access is by permit only; as this is
a raised reservoir, no part of the water is viewable from roads or footpaths
around the perimeter. Annual permits are available price £10 (£7.50 concessions) from the gatehouse at Walthamstow Reservoirs, Ferry Lane, E17
(0181 808 1527), this permit also covering the latter site. King George V is
open to permit-holders every day except 25–26 December from 7.00 am
until one hour after sunset. There are no day permits.

Access to the north basin is from the northwest corner via Enfield Lock,
though currently this gate is usually locked. Turn south off junction 25 of
the M25 onto the A10 (which eventually leads to the North Circular Road)
then almost immediately east onto the A105. Continue over the roundabout and after three-quarters of a mile (1.2 km) follow the road round to
the right; the next left turn into Ordnance Road takes you after half a mile
(0.8 km) to a car park near the site entrance. For the southern basin – and
for the longer route to the northern basin – keyholders can normally enter
either via the sailing club entrance in the southeast corner, along the
A110 Lea Valley Road near the crossroads with Sewardstone Road and
Kings Head Hill west of Chingford Mount, or from the locked car park in
the southwest corner, further west along the same road. During the Lea
Valley Bird Race, a local one-day event held each January, open public
access has been granted via either or both of these entrances.

By bus: number 121 from Turnpike Lane and Southgate underground
stations (both on the Piccadilly line) terminates at Enfield Lock, right on
the approach to the northwest entrance, while route 444 runs from
Turnpike Lane to Chingford station along Lea Valley Road. *By train:* the
closest overground station is Enfield Lock, with others at Ponders End and
Chingford Mount requiring a longer walk or bus ride for the sailing club
entrance; all are on lines running to Liverpool Street via Tottenham Hale
or Walthamstow, the latter two also being the best connections with the
underground (Victoria line).

Calendar

All year: Kestrel, Red-legged Partridge, Little Owl, Kingfisher, Grey
Wagtail.

Winter (November–March): Occasional diver and scarce grebe,
Cormorant, Teal, Shoveler, Goldeneye, Goosander, wildfowl and wader
oddities, gulls including occasional Mediterranean and 'white-winged'
species, chance of Rock or Water Pipit, Stonechat.

Spring (April–May): Ringed Plover, Ruff, Redshank, Greenshank,
Common Sandpiper and other waders, Little Gull, chance of Kittiwake,
Common and Black Terns, pipits, White and Yellow Wagtails, chats
(including Black Redstart) and other migrants.

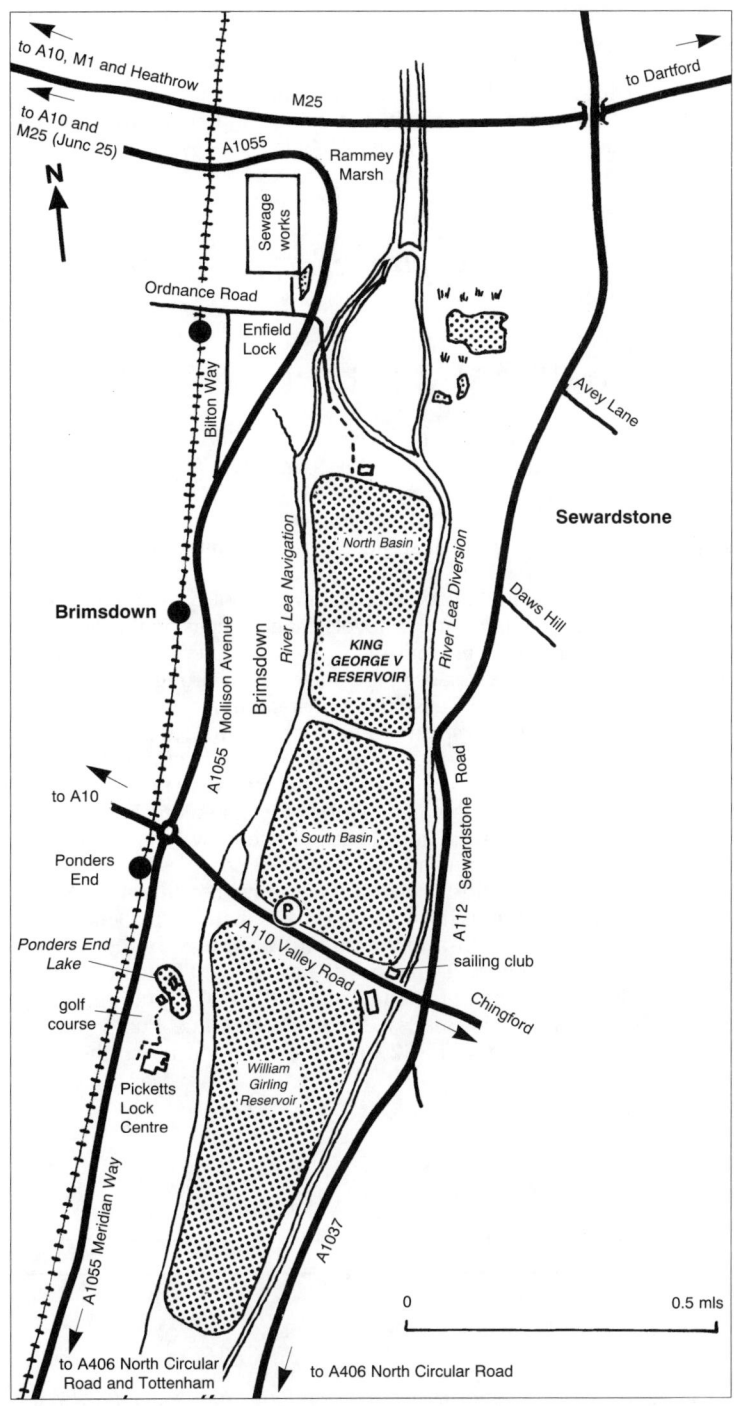

Summer (June–July): Shelduck, oddities including wildfowl, waders and terns, Black Redstart (scarce), common breeding birds.

Autumn (August–October): Teal, Shoveler, Ringed Plover, Ruff, Redshank, Greenshank, Common Sandpiper and other waders, terns including Black, pipits, Yellow Wagtail, chats.

OTHER SITES IN THE AREA

1A RAMMEY MARSH

OS ref: TQ 374996
Map p. 19

Any birder with time to spare after a visit to King George V Reservoir may well find it worthwhile calling in at this small Lea Valley site just across the road from the northwest entrance to the reservoir. At one time a sewage works with a number of sludge lagoons which proved attractive to waders, the destruction of some of the best habitat has somewhat reduced its appeal in recent years.

Wildfowl in winter include very small numbers of commoner dabbling species such as Mallard and Shoveler, and occasionally parties of Goosander wandering over from the Chingford Reservoirs. Waders can prove more interesting: passage in recent years has brought Curlew, Ruff, Wood Sandpiper, Spotted Redshank and small numbers of Greenshank and Little Ringed Plover. A speciality here is wintering Jack Snipe, though they can be difficult to locate; Green Sandpiper also occurs at this season. In good years for the species, Short-eared Owl may sometimes be encountered hunting in the area, perhaps over the rough grassland just east of the works. Passerine interest includes breeding Meadow Pipit, while Water Pipits are possible in autumn and winter and Grasshopper and even Marsh Warblers, Bearded Tit and Hawfinch have strayed to the area. Autumn gatherings of Pied Wagtails have reached more than 500 in October.

Rammey Marsh is about a mile (1.6 km) northwest of the reservoir; follow the same directions from the A10, turning right instead of left into Ordnance Road after the right-hand bend in the A105; turn immediately right again up a lane which leads to the works entrance. Public transport to Enfield Lock involves a 10–12 minute walk north along the A1055.

2 WILLIAM GIRLING RESERVOIR

OS ref: TQ 367945
Map p. 19

Habitat

This vast reservoir, an enormous one-basin construction larger still than both sections of King George V, lies immediately south of that water between the western fringe of Chingford and Edmonton. Essentially similar in appearance, its larger surface area, more steeply-shelving banks and 13-metre depth make it particularly important for roosting birds and a strategic refuge for those species suffering disturbance on other waters. Covering 139 hectares, it is large enough to hold nationally significant numbers of Tufted Duck and Shoveler at times and regionally important gatherings of Goldeneye, Goosander, Teal and Mallard. The main drawback is lack of access to the public, but, in the hope that this position may change, the site has been included here.

Species

William Girling Reservoir achieved ornithological fame long before its construction was completed. In 1947 four pairs of Little Ringed Plovers, a species which had colonised Britain in Hertfordshire just nine years earlier, were found nesting on its vast gravel bed. These birds may have been present in previous years and certainly continued breeding until it was filled in 1951, when the site assumed a new significance for both birds and birders.

Today William Girling Reservoir comprises the largest single body of water in the eastern half of London, and as such its potential for birds – in particular wildfowl and other diving species – is clearly enormous. This is the only regular wintering site in the London area for Black-necked Grebe, a species rarely recorded inland at this season in Britain, with birds appearing from September and remaining until the following March or early April; up to four or five may be present, though numbers have declined in recent years. Red-necked and Slavonian Grebes also make sporadic appearances in winter, and every year brings a wandering diver or two to this prime deep-water site.

Wildfowl can be particularly numerous here, though complex feeding and roosting strategies for the different species mean a constant turnover of birds and frequently a variable species list according to the time of day. Mallard, Teal and Shoveler are all present in good numbers outside the breeding season, often flying out at dusk to feed in the surrounding area, and many hundreds of Tufted Duck gather at peak times – especially in late summer after breeding. Goldeneye are regular in much smaller numbers – typically 20 or 30 – but the site is more important for its large gatherings of Goosander, up to 60 or so sometimes being present; these birds tend to use the site for roosting during the day and often feed elsewhere in early morning and late afternoon. Red-breasted Mergansers are occasionally found in winter, when other oddities such as Common Scoter, Scaup and Whooper Swan have also turned up.

Waders are regularly reported during migration times and occasionally in winter, though the high water level and lack of muddy fringes does not always lure migrants down. Among more likely shorebirds such as Oystercatcher, Ringed Plover, Redshank and Common Sandpiper (all typically in small numbers) have been some notable sightings of flocks passing straight over – including no fewer than 50 Bar-tailed Godwits together on one recent August day, and other unexpected goodies such as Grey Plover, Knot, Sanderling and Turnstone.

The gull roost here is even more spectacular than at King George V Reservoir across the road, with as many as 40,000–50,000 birds nightly at peak times in winter. Though 30,000 Black-headed Gulls dominate proceedings, counts of up to 15,000 Common Gulls (typically much lower) are noteworthy. As with all significant gull roosts, careful scrutiny has been repaid with the discovery of the very occasional Glaucous, Iceland or Mediterranean Gull arriving at dusk with the commoner species. Spring and especially autumn can also bring other gulls, chiefly small numbers of Little and the occasional wandering Kittiwake, but exceptional conditions such as the storm of 15/16 October 1987 may bring other surprises; after that event up to five Sabine's Gulls were the star attraction.

Terns can be noteworthy here, especially on passage when Arctic and Black may occur among larger numbers of Common. A White-winged Black Tern here briefly in September 1992 was exceptional, but Sandwich Terns have been noted in several recent autumns.

With virtually no vegetation around the steep banks, there is more limited scope for interesting passerines here compared to King George V. Skylarks, Meadow Pipits and Pied Wagtails are likely to comprise the bulk of interest at most times of year, though in spring and autumn Yellow Wagtails may be present in small numbers and Blue-headed Wagtail has occurred. Rock Pipits have occasionally been noted outside the breeding season, particularly in autumn, and chats could occur on passage.

Timing and access

Regrettably there is no public or permit access to this reservoir at the time of writing. Many London birders hope this position will change as, together with King George V Reservoir, this site comprises the most significant stretch of water for some considerable distance. With the works entrance to William Girling immediately opposite the Sailing Club gate to King George in Lea Valley Road, this would make an excellent combined itinerary.

Calendar

Winter (November–February): chance of a diver or scarce grebe, particularly Black-necked, Goldeneye, Goosander and other wildfowl, gulls.

Spring (March–May): Possibility of Black-necked Grebe (until early April), wildfowl numbers declining, occasional passage waders, Common and perhaps other terns, pipits and wagtails including occasional Blue-headed.

Summer (June–July): occasional wandering wildfowl, waders or terns.

Autumn (August–October): Black-necked Grebe, wildfowl numbers building up, passage waders, gulls and terns, perhaps small numbers of common landbird migrants.

OTHER SITES IN THE AREA

2A PONDER'S END LAKE

OS ref: TQ 362946
Map p. 19

Formerly home to the legendary sewage farm which hosted London's first Great Snipe in September 1959, this area just west of William Girling Reservoir today offers only a golf course lake in the grounds of the Lea Valley Leisure Centre at Pickett's Lock, a purpose-built complex on the site of the former works.

The birding potential at this venue is somewhat limited, but coverage in recent years has produced occasional notable finds including two of London's few Ring-billed Gulls, both in early 1993, Mediterranean and Glaucous Gulls, regular wintering Wigeon, Gadwall, Teal and Shoveler, and both Red-necked and Black-necked Grebes in addition to the local Great Cresteds and Littles. A small number of Tree Sparrows still breed in the area.

Directions for Ponder's End Lake are as for William Girling Reservoir, but continue west past the reservoir entrance to the roundabout and turn south along the A1055 Meridian Way; the Lea Valley Leisure Centre is on the left after a mile (1.6 km). On arrival follow signs for the hide along footpaths north of the centre. Bus W8 runs direct to Pickett's Lock from Enfield; overground trains from Liverpool Street stop at Ponders End station, just to the north of the site along the A1055.

3 WALTHAMSTOW RESERVOIRS

OS ref: TQ 353890

Habitat

The landscape at Walthamstow Reservoirs, another Lea Valley SSSI, differs distinctly from that of the larger Lea Valley waters to the north, with the smaller basins characterised by well-vegetated islands which provide ground cover for breeding waterbirds, and trees whose canopies are suitable for nesting and roosting Cormorants and Grey Herons. Rows of mature willows along the works roads and on the causeways, supported by scattered patches of undergrowth, provide additional habitat for passerines, while the short landscaped turf of the banks and verges often attracts feeding pipits, wagtails and occasionally finches, as well as providing grazing for the ubiquitous flocks of feral geese.

There are 10 basins in all: five smaller reservoirs in the main group along with the larger Warwick East and West Reservoirs, and three larger waters on the north side of the A106 Ferry Lane which divides the site. The River Lea runs north-south along the west side of the complex, in places fringed by dense hawthorns and scrub cover along its banks, and there is a network of man-made water courses which provide additional feeding for some species of wildfowl, Kingfisher and Grey Wagtail, and occasionally waders in hard weather.

Species

Although there is no shortage of water in this reservoir complex, Walthamstow seems to attract fewer divers and scarce grebes than King George V and William Girling to the north. Nevertheless, hardly a winter goes by without at least a Black-necked or Slavonian Grebe, if not a wandering diver, putting in an appearance. More obvious will be the wintering Great Crested Grebes, up to 50 or so (occasionally many more) being present outside the breeding season and perhaps a dozen pairs remaining throughout the summer. A few Little Grebes can also usually be located around the well-vegetated islands in the main group of reservoirs.

A dominant feature at Walthamstow is the large number of Cormorants in winter, with counts in recent years of up to 500 birds roosting at dusk in the tops of the taller trees; they make a spectacular sight in large V-formation groups as they fly up the Lea Valley from the Thames in the fading afternoon light. This species, which bred for the first time in London as recently as 1987, has established a fast-growing colony which currently numbers 136 nests; conversely, winter numbers here seem to be declining. Walthamstow is perhaps better known for its Grey Herons: the heronry of 116 occupied nests in 1994 is not only the largest in the London area but the second largest in Britain. The concrete banks are not an obvious lure for vagrant herons, but both Purple Heron and Little Egret have been recorded at least twice (including the latter once roosting in tree-tops with Grey Herons), and a Night Heron was found dead here in October 1980.

Wildfowl gather in considerable numbers between late summer and spring, with mixed rafts of ducks reaching 1,000–1,500 birds at peak times. Mallard is the dominant dabbler, with Teal and Shoveler the only other non-diving species likely to occur in three figures (this last species typically peaking on autumn passage); Gadwall are usually present in small groups but Wigeon are decidedly scarce. Tufted Ducks occur in nationally important numbers and can exceed 1,000, making this one of the top 10 sites for the species in the country, though Pochard generally remain in the low hundreds: a few pairs of the latter remain to breed. Among the bobbing rafts of diving ducks look out for the occasional Scaup in winter; Goldeneye also occur in small numbers at this time and Goosanders are regular, often roosting out on the larger water of Lockwood Reservoir during the day but sometimes feeding on the River Lea or one of its smaller channels, especially in the early morning. Green-winged Teal, Long-tailed and Ferruginous Ducks, Red-crested Pochard and both Common and Velvet Scoters are among the rarer visitors which have occurred, but Smew and Ruddy Duck are distinctly more likely. Wild swans and geese are irregular 'fly-overs', their numbers dwarfed by the huge numbers of feral relatives including Canada Geese (over 1,000 have been counted in late summer), numerous Greylags, a handful of Barnacles and several blue-phase Snow Geese, as well as up to three Ruddy Shelducks.

As in much of London, Kestrel and Sparrowhawk are the only locally breeding raptors, but Hobbies regularly hunt over the area from May to mid-autumn, often when large numbers of hirundines and Swifts are congregating on migration; the latter can be extremely numerous at peak times, and with Alpine Swift found here in June 1980 they should always be checked carefully. There is an outside chance of Osprey on passage, especially in spring, and though erratic in their appearances here (and never lingering) sightings further north in the Lea Valley indicate that birds pass through regularly. Peregrine has also occurred on several recent occasions outside the breeding season.

With so much water right on the Lea fly-way, Walthamstow is clearly attractive to migrating waders. Working against this, however, are the concrete rather than muddy margins to the basins; the problem is made worse in the fishing season by massed ranks of anglers taking up positions every few yards along the banks. Perhaps largely for this reason there have been no records of true wader rarities here and many of the more interesting records involving scarce species such as Avocet and the godwits are of overflying migrants. However, commoner species occurring in spring and autumn include Lapwing, Common Sandpiper, Redshank, Greenshank, the occasional Oystercatcher, and Ringed and especially Little Ringed Plovers. Winter is far less reliable for waders, but the fortunate observer may stumble across a Jack Snipe or two feeding along the muddy edge of a drainage channel – a habitat sometimes shared with Water Rail – or wandering parties of coastal shorebirds moving ahead of harsher conditions outside the area.

There is no gull roost at Walthamstow Reservoirs and numbers tend to be low here during the day, when birds are either out feeding on playing fields or rubbish tips, or 'loafing' on the adjacent filter beds (see Site 3C). However, the occasional Mediterranean has been reported in winter, and in passage periods, particularly after strong winds, there is a possibility of Little; such conditions also brought in Sabine's Gull in the late 1980s. Terns are likely on passage, notably Common which returns from late April and is often present until late September; numbers of local breeders are augmented by passage birds, and these may sometimes be accompanied by Arctic and occasionally Black. Sandwich and Little, as everywhere in London, are erratic visitors, and there are single records of Caspian and White-winged Black Terns from the 1960s and 1970s respectively. Other ocean-faring oddities to have occurred include Arctic Skua and a storm-driven Little Auk.

Long-eared Owls used to roost on the reservoirs most winters, but following disturbance they now seem to have deserted their former haunts. Perhaps more likely are day-flying Short-eared Owls which are occasionally found during the winter months, though records are sporadic at best. Kingfishers provide a welcome dash of colour along the various channels around the site and may be seen throughout the year in this section of the Lea Valley, while one recent October a Hoopoe provided even more exotic splendour here.

Swifts can number four figures in late May and July, and such is the availability of insect food in summer that feeding concentrations of several hundred are often visible at any time during their short breeding season. Similar concentrations of hirundines also occur during April–May and August–September, with House Martin usually the most numerous species.

Passage seasons see gatherings of Meadow Pipits and wagtails, with the latter including small flocks of Yellow and the occasional Blue-headed or White. Rock and Water Pipits have also turned up at this time or in winter, and both are worth keeping a look out for along the reservoir banks. Pied and Yellow Wagtails breed and Grey may also nest in the area. Occasional Black Redstarts are not infrequently reported on passage and the species is thought to have bred here in recent years. Other nesters include around 15 pairs of Sedge Warbler and a handful of Tree Sparrows, the latter just managing to hang on here in the older willows.

Passerine scarcities are otherwise unlikely, though there have been 'oddballs' including a lingering Woodlark and Lapland Buntings in spring and autumn. During the depths of winter when such species are unlikely, attention switches to the large roosts of Starlings and Woodpigeons which find the trees on the islands to their liking. On late winter afternoons thousands of birds can be watched flying in from nearby suburbs to feed before swarming like insects against the setting sky, as the Woodpigeons pile into the tree-tops and the Starlings mass together on overhead cables.

Timing

Winter offers a range of wildfowl and other interest, with a good option being an afternoon visit to sort through the rafts of wildfowl and watch the nesting Grey Herons (January–April) followed by a count of the roosting Cormorants. Spring and autumn provides the best chance of waders and may also offer terns and landbird migrants; though there are some breeding birds of interest, summer tends to be rather quiet and the birds predictable.

A visit at any time of day may prove productive, but weekends and bank holidays during the fishing season see peak angling activity which will frustrate the chances of would-be wader watchers. You should allow a half day to walk around this extensive site.

Access

Access to the reservoir complex is from entrances on the A503 Ferry Lane N17, by the Ferryboat Inn just east of Tottenham Hale; a gate on the north

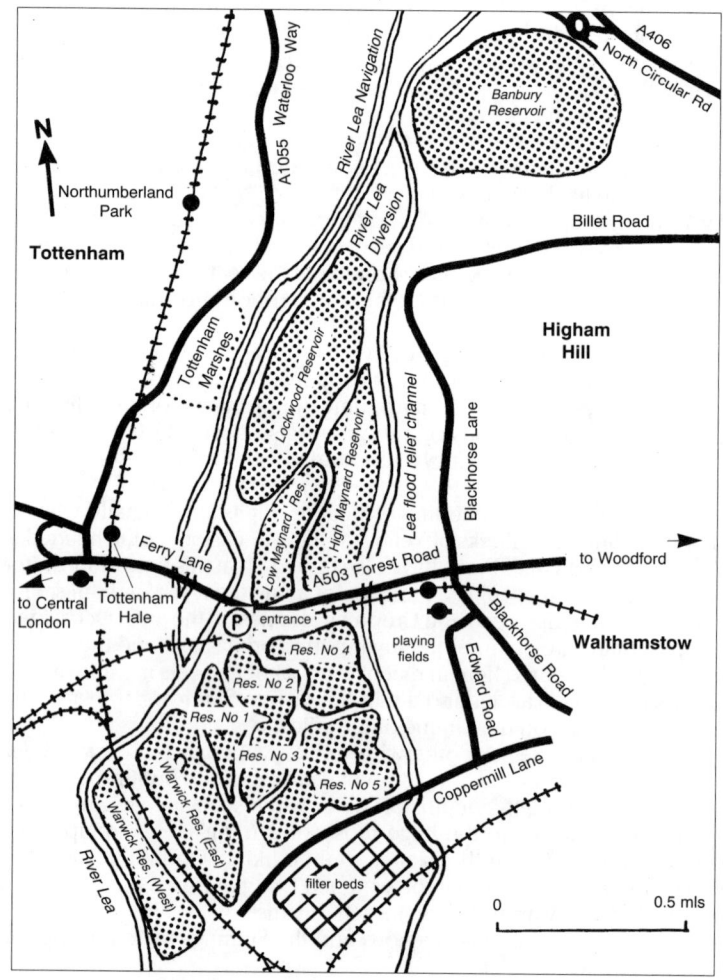

side of the road leads to Lockwood, Low Maynard and High Maynard Reservoirs, and the main entrance at the gatehouse on the south side accesses Reservoir numbers 1–5 and Warwick East and West Reservoirs. A permit must be obtained at the gatehouse, priced at £10.00 annually (£7.50 concessions) and including entry to King George V Reservoir, or £1.50 for a day ticket which covers this site only. Note that there is no access from the south side of the reservoirs onto Walthamstow Marsh or to the filter beds in Coppermill Lane.

Ferry Lane is easily reached by car from central London to the south-west via Camden Road, Seven Sisters Road and Tottenham Hale. From the east, leave the A406 North Circular Road at the Crooked Billet Roundabout south of Chingford (make sure you exit before the under-pass) and head west along Billet Road then south along Blackhorse Lane for about two miles (3.2 km); turn right (west) at Blackhorse Road station into Forest Road, and the gatehouse is half a mile (0.8 km) along on the left hand side.

By bus: numbers 41 (from Archway) and 123 and 230 (both from Wood Green) run to Tottenham Hale, the latter two continuing along Ferry Lane past the main entrance; number 158 stops at Blackhorse Road station. By underground: Tottenham Hale tube (Victoria line) is five min-utes' walk to the west along Ferry Lane, and Blackhorse Road on the same line 10 minutes to the east. By train: Tottenham Hale overground station is on the Cambridge line and well served by trains from Liverpool Street. A less frequent suburban service from Gospel Oak to Barking stops en route at Blackhorse Road station half-hourly from Monday–Saturday.

Calendar

All year: Great Crested Grebe, Cormorant, Grey Heron, Greylag and Canada Geese, Tufted Duck, Pochard, Kingfisher, Grey Wagtail.

Winter (November–February): Little Grebe, occasional scarce grebe, Gadwall, Teal, Shoveler, Goldeneye, Goosander, Ruddy Duck, occasion-al Smew, Water Rail, perhaps Jack Snipe.

Spring (March–May): Waders including Common Sandpiper, Redshank and Greenshank, Common Tern (from late April), perhaps other terns on passage, passerine migrants.

Summer (late May–July): Tufted Duck and odd summering wildfowl, occasional Hobby, Common Tern, Yellow Wagtail, Sedge Warbler, Tree Sparrow.

Autumn (August–October): Teal and Shoveler in increasing numbers, occasional Hobby (until September), overflying waders, terns, Yellow Wagtail and other passerine migrants.

OTHER SITES IN THE AREA

3A BANBURY RESERVOIR

OS ref: TQ 362915
Map p. 26

A deep-water basin offering much the same grass-clad concrete-banked surroundings as the other Lea Valley reservoirs, Banbury tends to attract similar species to the Walthamstow complex to the south and in fact is often treated as part of that group – though with its relatively small surface area used as a sailing club, the numbers and variety of birds present are generally significantly lower.

In winter the site has produced occasional surprises among the small flocks of Tufted Duck and other commoner species, with recent records including Slavonian Grebe. Goosanders are not infrequent in winter, and spring and autumn can bring parties of migrating gulls, terns and waders which sometimes include Little Gull and Black Tern. Along with wandering oddities such as Kittiwake there have been one or two real discoveries, most notably a Sabine's Gull in September 1989. Rarer still was the female Red-footed Falcon here in June 1992.

There is no public or permit access to Banbury Reservoir via the sailing club entrance, off the westbound carriageway of the A406 North Circular Road south of Chingford, but the site is viewable from the junction of Sinnott Road and Cogan Avenue E17, on the housing estate just north of Billet Road; a telescope is essential to view the reservoir from this vantage point. For full directions to the area, see under Walthamstow Reservoirs above.

3B TOTTENHAM MARSHES AND CEMETERY

OS ref: TQ 354910/
333911
Map p. 26

Lying west of Lockwood and Banbury Reservoirs, this tract of rough grassland, with precious little vegetation, attracts a much smaller range of species than Walthamstow Marsh to the south. Nevertheless, oddities such as Mediterranean Gull, Peregrine and Short-eared Owl have been reported here, and Long-eared Owl has occasionally wintered in the area. One or two pairs of Meadow Pipits breed (a rare event in the old county of Middlesex), Stonechats are regular in winter, and there have been occasional sightings of other interesting species including Black Redstart, Grasshopper Warbler and, bizarrely, even Hawfinch.

Access by car or public transport is as for Walthamstow Reservoirs via Tottenham Hale, but from there head north (not east) along Watermead Way (marked as 'north-south route' on old *London A–Z* maps) for half a mile (0.8 km) or so until you reach public footpath signs for the marshes.

About a mile (1.6 km) or so to the west, between White Hart Lane and the A10 Great Cambridge Road, the extensive area of green afforded by Tottenham Cemetery and Bruce Castle Park has attracted a good range of migrants in addition to a reasonable line-up of suburban breeding species. Regular coverage in spring and autumn has produced occasional Hobby, Ring Ouzel, Redstart, Pied Flycatcher and Wood Warbler.

Firecrest has occurred in several recent autumns and winters, and even Waxwing has been noted. There is a small lake which holds a pair of Pochard in summer.

The cemetery lies just north of the Roundway, off Lordship Lane N17. Buses serving the area include numbers 123, 144A, 217, 231, 243, and 444, and there are trains to White Hart Lane overground station from Liverpool Street. There is no convenient underground stop; the most direct route is the Victoria line to Seven Sisters, where you can change to the overground or catch a bus up the High Road to Bruce Grove and Lordship Lane.

3C WALTHAMSTOW FILTER BEDS

OS ref: TQ 355883
Map p. 26

Immediately south of the Walthamstow Reservoir complex is the Thames Water purification and treatment works in Coppermill Lane E17. The chief attraction of this site is as a 'loafing' spot for gulls outside the breeding season.

In winter large numbers of gulls congregate here during the day, using the settling tanks to bathe and the causeways for preening and sleeping. Birds depart north in the last hour before sunset to roost on the larger reservoirs, returning from dawn the following morning. The most numerous species is typically Black-headed Gull, with 1,000–2,000 frequently present in winter and early spring, though this is also one of the best daytime sites for Common Gulls in the London area: in February 1995 numbers peaked at a record 1,100, a figure surpassed elsewhere in the capital only at the bigger reservoir roosts. A regular returning Mediterranean Gull is often present from November to March, favouring the company of Common rather than Black-headed Gulls, and for the first time in winter 1994/95 there were multiple occurrences of this species with up to three adults present; in most recent years first-winter birds have also been recorded, making this perhaps the most reliable site for 'Meds' in the London area. Yellow-legged Gull has been found among the large numbers of Herring Gulls, and with Lesser Black-backs sometimes approaching three figures and small but regular numbers of Great Black-backs, this site deserves regular scrutiny in winter. The large white-winged gulls have yet to be recorded, however, perhaps reflecting their preference in this region for rubbish tips and the outer Thames.

Other avian interest includes the odd wildfowl of note, especially Goosander which have been known to alight on the settling tanks and the adjacent relief channel, and wandering waders including Little Ringed Plovers on the causeways and oddities such as Oystercatcher. There are good build-ups of hirundines and Swifts on passage, these gatherings sometimes attracting the attention of passing Hobbies in late spring and summer. Pied and Yellow Wagtails also gather here in spring and autumn, when mixed flocks of more than 50 of each species can be seen on the lawn of the Thames Water building; White Wagtail has also occurred. Other migrants including Black Redstart, Wheatear, Stonechat, Lesser Whitethroat, Reed Warbler and Turtle Dove have been known to drop in onto the football pitch or on the high bank on the east side of the beds.

To view the area, head west from central Walthamstow along Coppermill Lane E17; the filter beds are on the south side of the road after half a mile (0.8 km) or so. Buses 58, 158 and 230 stop at St James Street station, the nearest overground connection (on the Liverpool Street–Chingford line); 15 minutes' walk away along Coppermill Lane and Edward Road is the nearest tube station, Blackhorse Road (Victoria line). There is no direct access from Walthamstow Reservoirs onto Coppermill Lane.

4 WALTHAMSTOW MARSH   OS Ref: TQ 350878

Habitat

Despite its proximity to central London (less than 4.5 miles (7.2 km) from St Paul's Cathedral), this Site of Special Scientific Interest can on good days produce a range of birds almost reminiscent of an East Anglian fen. Sandwiched between South Tottenham to the west and Walthamstow to the east, and dissected through all points of the compass by railway lines, it nevertheless forms a valuable corridor between the reservoirs of the Lea Valley to the north and the lower Lea marshes and Thames to the south.

The habitat is dominated by an open landscape of semi-natural marshland which is home to a number of rare plant species. The site becomes damp usually only after heavy rain in winter when the Lea runs high and the water table rises to form small pools in the centre of the area. A small reedbed flanks the railway intersection known as The Triangle, but the most heavily vegetated area is the northern boundary adjacent to Warwick West Reservoir in the Walthamstow complex. Here, the Coppermill Stream is bordered by willows, hawthorns and brambles, and irises provide ground cover in the wetter areas. The stream runs into the Lea at Springfield Marina, to the south of which is the densest (but least productive) area of cover known as Horseshoe Thicket. At the opposite end of the marsh, sometimes known as Leyton Marsh, the landscape gives way to grassland, with a row of mature poplars screening off the riding school and ice rink to the south.

Species

The marshes are at their quietest in winter, when much of the vegetation in the open areas has died back to leave a rather uninteresting landscape. Nevertheless, with care some interesting species can usually be found, especially at the northern end of the marshes where the Coppermill stream forms a natural boundary with the reservoirs. This area tends to be the best at all times of the year.

In winter the stream is home to a few Mallard, Tufted Duck, Coot, Moorhen and perhaps a Little Grebe, while Grey Herons often flush from its banks at the merest hint of disturbance. The bigger clumps of irises usually hold a Water Rail at this time, though this species is hard to see in the dense cover unless a sharp frost forces it out into more open areas. If you have no joy here, look into the concrete-fenced enclosure, just north of the footbridge over the stream, or listen out for its noisy squealing call.

Kingfishers are often seen or heard along the stream from late summer through to spring, and up to three are sometimes present.

Out onto the marsh itself, a handful of Snipe and the occasional Jack Snipe in winter are likely to be the only waders logged during your visit. During migration times Common Sandpiper has been flushed from the stream but records of other species such as Lapwing, Redshank, Curlew and Oystercatcher all relate to 'fly-overs'. Common Terns are similarly mobile visitors but can sometimes be watched for prolonged periods fishing along the stream or plunging into the Lea at Springfield Marina from late April to September. As well as passage birds using the river as a flyway, local breeders from Walthamstow Reservoirs are often present and can be seen chasing each other in noisy parties.

Kestrels are a familiar sight hunting over the area, and at least one pair breeds nearby. Sparrowhawks have also colonised this sector of London, and are often visible soaring over the marsh or dashing through the trees around the stream in search of unwary passerines. Hobbies hunt over the area in passage periods when hirundines and Swifts are in greatest abundance, and Ospreys have twice been watched circling overhead in autumn before drifting off over the reservoirs.

Good numbers of Woodpigeons are augmented by a few Stock Doves, which often feed in small numbers on the playing fields or are seen flying over the marsh in the direction of Springfield Park, where they perhaps breed. Collared Doves have yet to penetrate this far into London and remain erratic visitors, as do Turtle Doves on passage. In contrast, the call of the Cuckoo is a familiar sound here in spring, with one or two birds often present from late April until the end of May.

Willow scrub in this area was formerly a winter roost site of Long-eared Owls, but following disturbance in the late 1980s – unfortunately often from over-enthusiastic birders – they have now left for quieter corners of the Lea Valley and there has only been one recent record. Short-eared Owls are also unpredictable here and are nowadays rarely reported, but intriguingly the balance may partly have been redressed by the colonisation of Little Owls, which are best looked for around the riding school.

The lack of true woodland in the area means that there are no resident woodpeckers, though Great Spotted are not infrequent visitors outside the breeding season. The open terrain of the southern half of the marsh is the best area for Skylarks, with birds present all year and perhaps two or three singing males holding territory in spring. Numbers increase in spring and particularly autumn, when overflying migrants are often visible and small parties may call in to feed on Leyton Marsh or the old in-filled aqueduct. Meadow Pipits share similar timings and habitat preferences, with sometimes 20 or so present at any one time, though this species does not breed here. Tree Pipits have also been noted on several recent occasions in spring and autumn, often when Yellow Wagtails are also on the move. In fact all three species of wagtail are often present here in spring and autumn, with Greys on the drainage channels, Yellows on the shorter turf and Pied almost anywhere; both of the latter have bred in recent years.

Only the southern area of the marsh provides suitable habitat for Wheatears, which rarely stop over on migration on the aqueduct or in the horse field. Whinchats are occasionally reported in spring and autumn but perhaps Stonechat is most likely, with the area around the railway lines sometimes holding three or four in winter. At this season a few Redwings are often present in the area, but Fieldfares mainly occur on spring and autumn migration. A male Ring Ouzel graced the football pitches by the railway line one recent April, and the end of this month brings the best chance of a singing Nightingale on passage: they are particularly partial to the dense cover of Horseshoe Thicket near Springfield Marina.

It is in spring that this area really comes alive. For any migrant heading north over the east side of London, the Lea marshes are the first expanse of green that offer any kind of shelter and food, and Walthamstow Marsh in particular, with its rich mixture of vegetation, draws down a good crop of passage visitors. Chiffchaffs are usually the first in during the middle of March, though one or two have taken to overwintering in recent years, followed by the occasional Blackcap by the end of the month. From early April Willow and Sedge Warblers arrive, and by the beginning of May the marshes are alive with the song of the latter species; up to 35 singing males have been counted, though most are migrants and fewer than half that number stay to breed. Reed Warblers also reappear in late April and stay to nest in suitable habitat. Together with smaller numbers of Whitethroats, Lesser Whitethroats and Blackcaps and the occasional migrant Garden Warbler, it is sometimes possible to record eight species of warbler – rarely even nine – in a short morning walk here. Regular coverage has also been repaid with several less common species, including Wood Warbler in Springfield Park, an overwintering Dartford Warbler, a singing male *tristis* Chiffchaff one November, several 'reeling' spring Grasshopper Warblers and, astonishingly, London's second-ever Subalpine Warbler, a well-watched male in song on 15 May 1994.

The return passage of warblers begins as early as late July, with the mix of vegetation clearly just right to sustain a good turnover of birds until mid-September. The hawthorns, brambles and elders along the northern boundary of the marsh are literally jumping with Reed, Sedge and Willow Warblers, Blackcaps and Whitethroats, with smaller numbers of Lesser Whitethroats and, later in the season, Chiffchaffs. Systematic counting

Grasshopper Warbler

here has revealed more than 60 individuals of eight species, with Garden the scarcest; this is likely to be a gross underestimate, with many more Reed and Sedge preferring the reedy cover of the marsh proper. Among the bigger arrivals of migrants may also be the occasional Spotted Flycatcher or, exceptionally, even a Pied.

After the excitement of autumn has died down, the marsh becomes relatively quiet and the scrub rather devoid of birds. Bearded Tit has been found in late autumn and winter, when occasional roaming tit flocks may contain a few Long-tailed Tits or a Goldcrest, and both Bullfinch and Siskin are possible at this time of year; the latter is usually found in the stand of alders on the east side of the railway by the stream, often in company with Goldfinches. Flocks of Linnets are most conspicuous in autumn, but a few are always present in winter when resident Reed Buntings are also most obvious in the leafless marsh vegetation. Tree Sparrows bred here until the early 1990s and still occasionally turn up in autumn or winter, particularly in the area around the railway line between the reservoirs just north of the marsh, or in the willows at Springfield Marina, their last known breeding site.

Timing
Spring and autumn see the widest variety of species on the marsh and the chance of a real 'goodie' on migration, so a full tour of the site in these seasons will be most rewarding. There are good populations of breeding birds in summer including six species of warbler, while in contrast winter is the quietest season in the local ornithological calendar.

As soon after dawn as possible is generally the best time to visit the marsh, particularly in spring and autumn when passerine migrants (especially warblers) are at their most active; visits from mid-morning onwards can produce far fewer birds in terms of numbers and species. Allow three hours to cover the area.

Disturbance by dog walkers, joggers, horseriders and even canoeists along the stream can be a real problem. Late in the day sees a reduction in human activity, but is also likely to produce fewer birds. Unfortunately, the site is often used as a dump by fly-tippers and by 'joy-riders' burning out stolen cars. The area should be avoided after dark.

Access
Follow the same route as for Walthamstow Filter Beds (site 3B) but continue down Coppermill Lane until the road disappears under the railway line by the raised playing fields. Park here and walk under the railway to the northeast section of the marsh, generally the best area to bird. Walthamstow Marsh can also be reached via Tottenham from the west; turn east off the A107 Clapton Common down Spring Hill along the northern flank of Springfield Park to the Lea, from which two footbridges lead over to the marsh. On the southern side, access is via the car park of the Lea Valley Ice Centre on the A104 Lea Bridge Road.

By bus: route 253 runs along Clapton Common, with numbers 22A and 55 serving nearby Clapton, and numbers 38, 48, 56 and 333 stopping along Lea Bridge Road at the southern end of the marsh. *By train:* Clapton station is on the Liverpool Street–Chingford Line. From the station, turn left down Gunton Road to North Millfields recreation ground: walk diagonally across the open grassy area, checking the gull flock as you go (autumn–spring), to Lea Bridge by the Prince of Wales pub. There is no local underground station.

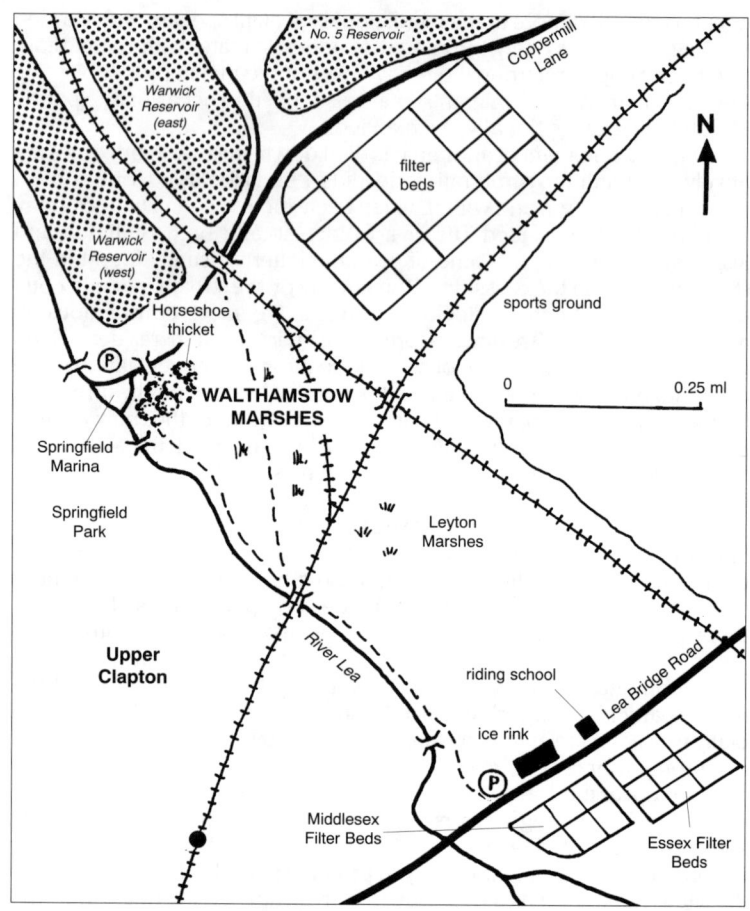

Calendar

All year: Sparrowhawk, Kestrel, Stock Dove, Little Owl, Skylark, Pied Wagtail, Linnet, Reed Bunting.

Winter (December–February): Little Grebe, Water Rail, Jack Snipe (rare), Snipe, Kingfisher, Grey Wagtail, Stonechat, Redwing, chance of Chiffchaff, Long-tailed Tit, Goldcrest, occasional Siskin.

Spring (March–May): Hobby (from May), Common Tern, Cuckoo, Meadow Pipit (March and early April), occasional Tree Pipit, Yellow Wagtail, Nightingale, warblers including Grasshopper and Garden (from mid-April).

Summer (June–July): Occasional Hobby, Common Tern, Skylark, Reed and Sedge Warblers, Whitethroat, Lesser Whitethroat, Blackcap, Willow Warbler.

Autumn (August–November): Hobby, Kingfisher, Meadow and Tree Pipits, chats, Redwing, Fieldfare, warblers, Spotted Flycatcher, Goldcrest, occasional Tree Sparrow.

OTHER SITES IN THE AREA

4A MIDDLESEX AND ESSEX FILTER BEDS

OS ref: TQ 359865/363868
Map p. 34

Situated immediately to the south of Walthamstow/Leyton Marsh on the opposite side of Lea Bridge Road, these two former waterworks lie just metres apart but have rather distinct avifaunas – partly owing to the different rates at which natural vegetation has become established since they fell into disuse and subsequent management of the sites as nature reserves.

Middlesex Filter Beds, separated from Hackney to the west by the Lea Navigation Channel, is a small walled nature reserve whose sunken beds are variously wooded or flooded with landscaped gravel margins, aquatic vegetation and pond sculptures. Wintering species include small numbers of Chiffchaffs and one or two Water Rails, while up to 34 Blackbirds have been counted roosting together here. Among 30 species of birds recorded breeding are Sparrowhawk, up to 24 pairs of Reed Warbler and a very special resident – Tree Sparrow. Several pairs remaining at this ultra-urban site is something of an achievement given the dire national standing of the species. Migrants and occasional visitors have included Turtle Dove, Pied and especially Spotted Flycatchers, Brambling, Siskin, Arctic Tern, Marsh Harrier, Mediterranean Gull and the incredible sight one October of a Guillemot flying upriver and then circling the filter beds before moving off!

Hobbies are often seen overhead in the summer and early autumn and also over the Essex Filter Beds, a stone's throw to the east. The more open and extensive habitat here offers greater appeal than Middlesex Filter Beds to waders, mainly on passage although several species have bred. The latter category includes both Ringed and Little Ringed Plovers and Lapwing, and in one recent year Snipe oversummered.

Little Ringed Plovers

Regular species outside the breeding season include anything up to 50 Snipe and the occasional Jack Snipe and Green Sandpiper in winter, while Black-tailed Godwit, Ruff, Greenshank and Wood Sandpiper have all dropped in on passage. Wintering wildfowl are present in good numbers, with up to 200 Mallard, 50–100 Teal, and small gatherings of Gadwall, Shoveler and Wigeon. Passerines include regular wintering Stonechat and occasional migrants of note such as Wheatear, Whinchat and Ring Ouzel, and there has been one recent record of Marsh Harrier.

Middlesex Filter Beds are open to the public at weekends from 10.00 am to 4.00 pm; the entrance is a short walk south along the towpath from the car park behind the Prince of Wales pub in Lea Bridge Road E5. There is no public access at present to the Essex Filter Beds, although Lea Valley Park plans announced in the 1980s suggested the possibility of establishing an interpretative centre here and linking these two neighbouring sites with a footbridge. In the hope that this development is pursued, the entrance to the site would seem likely to remain on the south side of Lea Bridge Road opposite the riding school, from where the few current keyholders gain access.

By bus: numbers 38, 48, 56 and 333 stop by the filter beds in Lea Bridge Road, while numbers 22A and 55 serve nearby Clapton. *By train:* Clapton station is on the Liverpool Street–Chingford Line. From the station, turn left down Gunton Road to North Millfields recreation ground: walk diagonally across the open grassy area, checking the winter gull flock as you go, to Lea Bridge by the Prince of Wales pub. There is no local underground station.

4B HACKNEY MARSHES   OS ref: TQ 370860

Formerly a vast area of marshland extending from Hackney south towards the Thames, wholesale drainage and landscaping means that the chief claim to fame of the area today is as one of the largest complexes of football pitches in the world. However, this massive acreage of short green turf flanking the River Lea between Hackney and Leyton is an important feeding area for gulls in winter.

Birds seem to use this site en route from the reservoir roosts at William Girling and King George V to the Thames, where they spend much of the day. The first two hours after dawn are best, with few birds present at other times. In early morning the football pitches can be teeming with more than a thousand birds of all five commoner species, with, perhaps surprisingly, Herring being the most dominant – groups totalling several hundred often include good numbers of wintering Scandinavian *argentatus* birds alongside the British *argenteus* race, a useful opportunity for comparison. The relatively high proportion of large to small gulls here may increase the chances of stumbling across a wandering Glaucous or Iceland, though Mediterranean has certainly been found here and is perhaps the most likely rarer species to occur.

There are few other species of note in the area, though in late autumn and winter Redwings sometimes occur in small flocks on the football pitches and in summer Reed Warblers can be heard singing in bankside vegetation along the Lea. The river is tidal here but rarely offers anything except Tufted Duck, Coot and Moorhen, the occasional fishing Common

Tern in summer and regular Grey Herons feeding on the exposed mud or wading in the shallows.

The best area for viewing the gull flocks is from the north side of the A106 Eastway/Ruckholt Road, the dual carriageway extension of the A102(M) link to the Blackwall Tunnel. Park in the sports pavilion car park immediately west of the new Spitalfields market off the eastbound carriageway. Buses 308 and W15 stop at this point, or you can take the underground to Leyton (Central line), from where it is an eight-minute walk west along Ruckholt Road. The closest overground station is Hackney Wick: from here it is a 10-minute walk left along Post Lane, Carpenter's Road and Waterden Road to the Eastway junction near the sports pavilion.

4C VICTORIA PARK   OS ref: TQ 360837

Perhaps one of the most unlikely birding sites in the capital, this is really one to repay regular local coverage rather than a special visit. Much of the park is the uninteresting formal landscape beloved by city-dwellers rather than birds, though there are more secluded corners, particularly in the western section, with denser stands of cover that can attract migrants. Both Firecrest and Pied Flycatcher were found here by one diligent observer in autumn 1994, and the following spring Redstart and a fine male Pied Flycatcher graced the park on the same day. Hobbies have been seen several times in summer passing over the area, and there is an ornamental lake which is home to common wildfowl including Canada Goose, Mallard and Tufted Duck and, in winter, small numbers of Shoveler and Pochard.

The canal towpath which runs along the south side of the park can be worthy of investigation, especially in winter when Grey Wagtail and Kingfisher can sometimes be seen. In summer, Common Terns occasionally fish along the stretch just a little further to the east, by Hackney Wick station. In the freeze-up of February 1991 a Black-throated Diver visited this waterway very briefly, but the most bizarre local record must surely be London's only Black-headed Bunting, a male (considered to be wild) at nearby Bromley-by-Bow in August 1986.

Victoria Park lies half a mile (0.8 km) southwest of Hackney Marshes, immediately west of the A102(M) at Hackney Wick. There are numerous public access points, and Grove Road E3 cuts the park in two just east of the lake. By public transport, take buses 8, 52, 277 or 333 (summer only); the nearest overground station is Cambridge Heath (connecting to Liverpool Street) some 15 minutes' walk to the west. By underground, take the Central line to Bethnal Green and walk east along Roman Road for about three-quarters of a mile (1.2 km), then turn left up Grove Road to the park.

EAST LONDON

5 EPPING FOREST OS ref: TQ 420985

Habitat

Epping Forest is the most extensive area of woodland within the M25, and as such is important for a number of breeding species, some of which are difficult to find elsewhere in the region. It is hard to comprehend, therefore, that little more than 300 years ago it was 10 times the size of its present-day 6000 acres (2400 ha), unfragmented by roads and not subjected to over-use by weekending hordes from the capital.

The forest stretches for some 11 miles (17.6 km) from Epping in a crescent-shaped belt southwest to Wanstead Flats, along a clay and gravel ridge between the Lea and Roding Valleys, though with much of the southern section broken down into isolated tracts among the residential areas of Woodford, Snaresbrook and Wanstead, the forest 'proper' effectively ends after around 5.5 miles (8.8 km), where it meets Woodford Golf Course between Chingford Green and Woodford Wells.

A large area of the forest still comprises mature broadleaved woodland, with beech, oak, hornbeam and birch the dominant species, but there are extensive areas with little or no understorey. In places the tree cover gives way to open 'plains' with scrubby vegetation and scattered young trees favoured by Tree Pipits in summer and other open-country species on passage, but coniferous tracts are relatively scarce. Rides dissect the area in many places, facilitating access to the most interesting birding sites. A number of ponds provide habitat for a small range of waterbirds, especially in the southern areas around Chingford, Whipps Cross and Wanstead, where the habitat is decidedly more open and in places used for livestock grazing.

Species

Like all woodlands Epping Forest is at its quietest in winter, with most interest for birdwatchers concentrated around the ponds.

Perhaps the most productive of these is Connaught Water, a one-time gravel pit situated on the edge of the forest between Chingford and Loughton. Here, the variety of wintering waterfowl includes all the expected common species such as Mallard, small numbers of Gadwall, Shoveler, Wigeon, Tufted Duck, Pochard, a few Great Crested and Little Grebes, Moorhen and numerous Coot. An interesting development in recent years has been the presence of a few feeding parties of Goosanders visiting from the Chingford Reservoirs. The guaranteed wildfowl speciality in the forest, however, is the 'exotic' Mandarin, a feral species established in Britain mainly at wooded waters near the capital. This is as good a place as any

39

to see it, with up to 30 or so sometimes present at peak times in winter and a handful of pairs staying to breed in recent years in the summer – particularly at Connaught Water. In summer, however, they can be much more difficult to see, frequenting the wooded islands or swimming on the water concealed by overhanging vegetation. If you have no joy at Connaught Water, try the small wooded ponds just west of the A104 main road to Epping which runs through the middle of the forest.

Aside from a few Shoveler on the bigger ponds (including a regular winter flock on the Hollow Pond, Whipps Cross), occasional winter visits by Goldeneye and other commoner wildfowl and summer and autumn sorties by Common Terns to Wanstead Park, waterbirds of any description are few and far between. One exception to this rule was the Black Stork seen flying over on 7 July 1991, a far cry from the Grey Herons and Cormorants that more typically complete the scene.

Kestrel and Sparrowhawk breed, and Hobby has become a much more familiar sight in summer. Owls are also relatively well represented, with Tawny resident in the woods and a few Littles around the forest fringe and on adjacent farmland (particularly on the Copped Hall estate and Cobbins Brook on the north side of the M25). Barn Owl is occasionally seen in the area. Equally nocturnal are the four or five pairs of Woodcock that breed here and can be seen or heard 'squeaking' from dusk onwards as roding birds mark out their breeding areas over the tree-tops; they can be looked for anywhere, and may also be encountered in winter when they can sometimes be seen in daytime. Stock Doves also nest and Cuckoos can be heard in spring and summer throughout the north of the area.

Epping has good populations of all three woodpeckers – Green, Great Spotted and Lesser Spotted. The former are most frequently encountered in the clearings and plains, Great Spotted in the north of the forest (though they have been described as locally common elsewhere) and Lesser Spotted are best searched for in any area with old oaks and other suitable drumming or nesting trees. Wrynecks were a feature of the forest before the species' decline in Britain wiped it out from the Southeast; they probably last bred at Loughton in 1949, and have since only been represented by very occasional wandering migrants.

Perhaps strangely, the Epping Forest area has established a reputation for the most unlikely of migrants. The rarest by far was Britain's first Naumann's Thrush, the central Siberian race of Dusky Thrush which itself has only occurred on eight previous occasions. This crowd-pulling vagrant remained from January to March 1990 on the Chingford edge of the forest where, amazingly, its finder scored again with a well-watched Olive-backed Pipit in October 1992. A short distance to the southeast, Buckhurst Hill has been visited by a Barred Warbler in 1986 and Yellow-browed Warblers in both 1990 and 1991. Rarer still, however, was a Short-toed Treecreeper back on 26 May 1975 – then only the fifth British occurrence (and the only accepted 'sight' record) and still the only one in London. In the same year the capital's fourth Red-rumped Swallow graced Wanstead Park, at the southern end of the forest, for a day in June.

Putting such memories to one side, day-visitors should instead hope for more expected migrant landbirds in spring and autumn. At such times a few pairs of the declining Tree Pipit are in evidence on grassy slopes with scattered trees and bushes, from where they can launch into conspicuous song flight; Chingford Plain is one of the most accessible areas for this species but birds are usually also present in suitable habitat elsewhere in the forest. Whinchats are also possible in the more open areas and Redstarts could occur anywhere on passage in suitable habitat, though at best only one pair still breeds – the result of a long local decline first documented at the turn of the century. In contrast, Nightingales manage to maintain a more obvious presence, with the denser undergrowth in the Connaught Water area holding up to eight singing males in recent seasons. Ring Ouzel is also a possibility on migration, perhaps best searched for on Chingford Plain, and from October to March the local thrush contingent is boosted by good numbers of Fieldfares and Redwings, especially around the forest fringes. A study of winter populations in Epping Forest in 1971-72 found that the thrush family then made up over 12 per cent of all birds present, with Blackbird especially numerous. Together with Woodpigeon, Greenfinch and Blue and Great Tits, these species accounted for over half the total of birds wintering in the forest.

Nightingale

This picture changes completely in spring and summer when the woodland bird community is at its densest. Blackcap, Willow Warbler and Chiffchaff are most numerous, while smaller numbers of Garden Warbler, Whitethroat and Lesser Whitethroat are present, the latter in more open and scrubby areas such as Chingford Plain where reeling Grasshopper Warblers may occur on passage; Wood Warblers no longer breed but are occasionally found on spring migration. Spotted Flycatchers chase aerial prey from late May to September and the few breeding pairs of Goldcrests are most likely in the areas with conifers; this latter species may be found in less specialised habitat in the forest in winter.

Particular attention should be paid to the tits, for as well as Great, Blue, Coal and Long-tailed this is one of the very few sites around the capital capable of producing both Marsh and Willow; the latter, however, has declined across the London area and is now believed to number just a single breeding pair here. In contrast Marsh Tits are more widespread, and Connaught Water is again a good area for this species. Nuthatch and Treecreeper are resident throughout the forest.

A surprise find on the forest fringe at Woodford Golf Course in July 1994 was a fine male Red-backed Shrike, proving that the unexpected can turn up at any time and any place, and Golden Oriole has proved an equally unlikely past visitor. More staple fare comes in the form of corvids, this London/Essex border country marking the closest breeding sites of Rook and Jackdaw to the northeast of the capital. The former species in particular tends to avoid the urban fringe in deference to the more adaptable Carrion Crow, and away from the token rookery in Epping High Street (just five nests) is most often seen here around the hard shoulder of the M25 or probing the soft earth of fields close to the forest edge.

The woodland line-up is completed by a full contingent of finches, with all the capital's breeding species found here. Chaffinches are widespread and particularly conspicuous in winter, when flocks sometimes numbering hundreds (exceptionally thousands) feed on beechmast on the forest floor. The High Beech area is one of the most consistent sites for these gatherings, often drawing in small numbers of Bramblings as well; this species should also be looked for in the Copped Hall area on the north side of the M25. Hawfinches are much harder to pin down, though at least a couple of pairs breed and there must be a chance of bumping into this chunky but secretive finch in any suitable habitat in the northern half of the forest: the woods around Chingford Plain and Connaught Water may provide your best chance of a glimpse of this scarcity in the canopy or passing overhead as it utters its distinctive *zik* call. In 'irruption' years Epping Forest has held parties of Crossbills, with notable recent records including a group of 31 in June 1991; at such times any group of conifers would be worth checking. Siskin and Redpoll are possible in winter, most likely in favoured alder and birch habitat respectively, but the latter no longer seems to breed. Similarly, Tree Sparrows formerly nested but, following the national decline which has affected most sites for the species in the capital, they can no longer be expected even in this extensive wooded area.

Timing

Late April–June offers the best chance for the biggest variety of woodland species, particularly if you want to catch up with specialists such as Nightingale and Tree Pipit; these species are much less likely to be located by song after this time. A little earlier in the season will perhaps produce more drumming woodpeckers which may be easier to locate in tree-tops with less leaf cover, while autumn brings the chance of unusual migrants in the area, and in winter roaming tit flocks and the highest numbers of Mandarins are among the attractions.

In places, especially in the southern sector, the forest is subject to heavy use from dog walkers, horseriding and day-trippers; the ponds can be heavily affected by boating activities (model and full size!). Avoid anything but early morning visits on weekends during the summer; weekdays are a lot quieter at all times of the year. In such a large area you can clearly spend a whole day birding, but if time is of the essence then two hours or so in the forest around Connaught Water and on Chingford Plain will be your best bet.

Access

There is open access to most parts of the forest with numerous well-signed car parks and picnic areas from which you can explore. The area

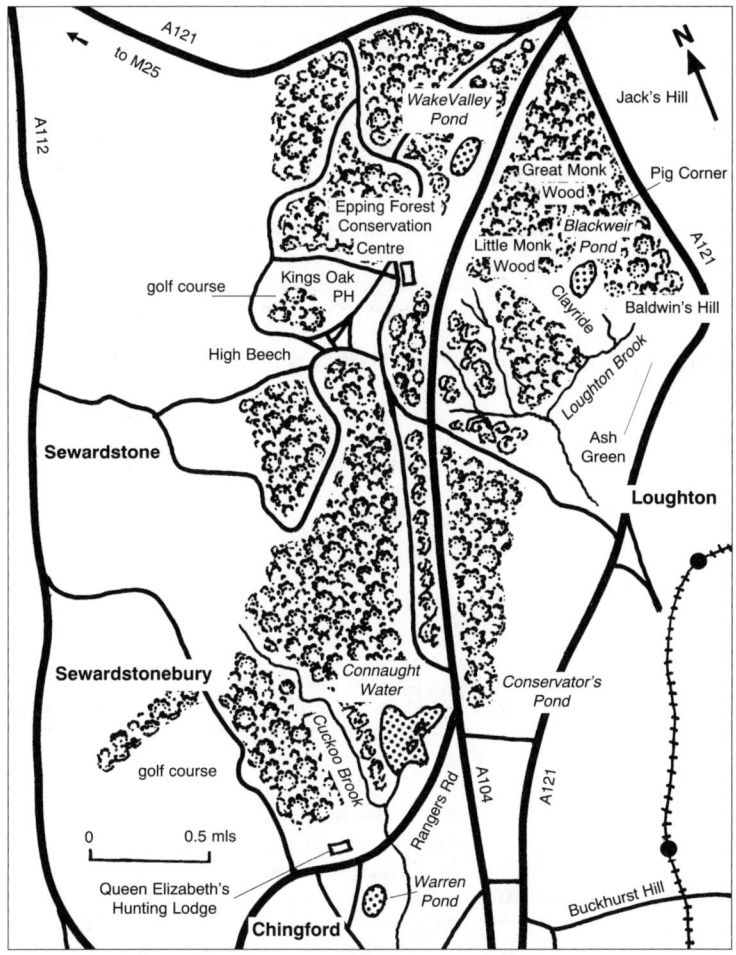

around Connaught Water and Chingford Plain offers perhaps the best range of interesting species, though if in the area High Beech to the north is always worth checking. If time is short, avoid areas where there is clearly no undergrowth. Some of the best forest edge habitat can be found around Woodford Golf Course.

By car: from the north, leave the M25 at Junction 26 and head southeast on the A121 towards Theydon Bois and Loughton. At the roundabout, turn right (south) onto the main A104 Epping New Road into the heart of the forest. From the south, turn off the A406 North Circular Road just west of the M11 approach at South Woodford, and head north on the A104 into the main areas of the forest.

By bus: to the forest proper, numbers 20 and 167 run to Loughton and Debden on the east side and 97, 212, 379 and 444 run to Chingford, while the 502 (Harlow–Romford) runs through the forest between Epping and Debden via the Wake Arms roundabout. Other routes also serve the north of the forest, and there are numerous services to the Woodford, Snaresbrook and Wanstead areas. *By underground:* the Ongar branch of the Central line stops at Buckhurst Hill, Loughton and Theydon Bois to the east of the forest. *By train:* Chingford station (trains from Liverpool Street via Walthamstow) is a short walk west from Chingford Plain and Connaught Water.

Calendar

All year: Mandarin, Sparrowhawk, Kestrel, Woodcock, Stock Dove, Little, Tawny and Barn Owls, Green, Great Spotted and Lesser Spotted Woodpeckers, Goldcrest, Willow (rare) and Marsh Tits, Hawfinch.

Winter (November–March): Great Crested Grebe, Gadwall, Shoveler, occasional Goosander, Fieldfare, Redwing, Brambling, Siskin, Redpoll.

Spring (April–May): Cuckoo, Tree Pipit, Nightingale, warblers including occasional Wood, migrants.

Summer (June–August): Occasional Hobby, Tree Pipit, Nightingale, Redstart, common breeding warblers, Spotted Flycatcher.

Autumn (September–October): Migrants including chats, warblers and thrushes in the more open areas.

6 FAIRLOP WATERS OS ref: TQ 458459

Habitat

This country park lies on the dividing line between the suburban spread of the London Borough of Redbridge and the open Essex countryside. This gives it, and the surrounding farmland, a slightly different avifauna to superficially similar habitats at sites such as Dagenham Chase and Barking which are otherwise enclosed by development of one kind or another. This in part explains the presence of farmland species such as Corn Bunting and, in winter, Golden Plover.

The landscape at Fairlop is essentially flat open country, dominated by the main lake in the centre of the area and an ugly 'leisure' complex and golf range around the main car park, neither of which does anything for the scenic view or for the reputation of Essex Man as a trend-setter in taste and decor. Leaving such prejudices and the buildings behind, visiting birders soon become ensconced in a more appealing landscape of rough grass with scrubby cover, marshy corners and scattered trees – ideal terrain for a number of interesting breeding birds and regular visitors for which Fairlop has established a reasonable reputation.

There is a strong emphasis here on public amenities, with a much-used golf course and driving range, a riding school and an active water sports centre which would seem to militate against productive birding. However, the area is large enough to withstand crowds of day-tripping city-dwellers and dog walkers, and in fact the obvious focus of the leisure development in the centre of the area may help to preserve other sections of the country park from over-use. Such is the birding potential of this site that by 1995 a total of 165 species had been recorded, and between 110–115 are logged annually by the tiny but dedicated core of local observers.

Species

The attraction of the lakes at Fairlop has been proved by the regular appearance of interesting waterbirds. While the site may not be able to match the pulling power of the larger reservoirs in the Lea Valley to the west, recent records of Great Northern Diver, Black-necked and Slavonian Grebes, Shag, Scaup, Long-tailed Duck and Common Scoter – the latter including a flock of 39 in October 1991 – demonstrate its potential with regular coverage. A good deal of bird activity is focused on the main lake in the centre of the site, dominated by the large numbers of Canada Geese and gull flocks, but the two smaller lakes in the south of the area are the best for variety and numbers of birds (especially in winter) and are worth checking for regular Great Crested and Little Grebes, Tufted Duck, Pochard, Teal and other species. Wigeon have reached the impressive total of 570 at this site, though deep-water species such as Goldeneye tend to be hard-weather visitors.

Other than the ubiquitous Kestrel and Sparrowhawk, raptors are most likely to comprise migrant Hobbies in autumn. There have, however, been two records of Hen Harrier, and in January 1995 the site recorded its first Merlin. The rural aspect to Fairlop's position means it is the best corner of the London area for Red-legged Partridge, with up to six pairs around the fields between here and Hainault, and Pheasant is resident in the area. Water Rail is a possibility during winter, when wheeling flocks of Lapwing and Golden Plover are a very visible feature: numbers of both species can reach 2,000 in a good winter, making this the best site in the London area for the latter species. If they are not visible from the area

Lapwings and Golden Plovers

around the main lake or in the sky, check the farmland to the east of the site as far as Marks Gate Road; they occasionally also get onto fields south-east of here, on the southern side of the A12 Eastern Avenue. There are some fears that this area may decline in importance for the species if plans for gravel extraction on local farmland are enacted. Also notewor-thy in winter is the presence of small numbers of Jack Snipe, though as always with this species birds can be difficult to locate as they feed in the wetter areas of long grass or in damp hollows. Snipe are more likely to be encountered and have even been noted in suitable habitat in May, rais-ing hopes of breeding, while Little Ringed Plovers are confirmed nesters in the area. Other waders are more expected during passage periods, with wanderers in recent years including Oystercatcher, Avocet, Bar-tailed Godwit, Curlew, Whimbrel, Spotted Redshank and Ruff among the more regular species; the latter category includes Common Sandpiper at both passage seasons and Green Sandpiper in autumn.

Gulls can be numerous here but rarely outstanding, with Black-headed the dominant species in winter when good numbers are attracted by vis-itors feeding the geese. Spring migration brings more interest in the form of tern passage through the London area, and in some years, especially in late April and May, Fairlop may receive some of the benefit. Common is the most likely species, but flocks of up to 35 Arctic and 11 Black Terns have been noted at this time and Sandwich and Little have both also been recorded. Much more unexpected was the Razorbill found here in December 1988.

Stock Doves are regularly seen in the area though do not breed on the site itself, and Turtle Dove and Cuckoo are annual on passage. Little Owl breeds in the area and the open terrain has attracted occasional passing Short-eared Owls, while there have been a handful of records each of Barn and Long-eared. The presence of scattered trees makes this site par-ticularly conducive to Green Woodpeckers, and both Great Spotted and Lesser Spotted have also been noted.

In late autumn watch out for the flashing blue of passing Kingfishers, and in both passage seasons for the good numbers of Swallows and mar-tins that can gather here. Skylarks are resident and a few pairs of Meadow Pipits and Yellow Wagtails breed, their numbers being swelled by migrants on passage when flocks of the latter may number as many as 20 in spring and 40 in autumn. Both White Wagtail and the Scandinavian race of Rock Pipit have occurred on spring migration, while rarer still were the two Richard's Pipits found here in September 1987 and May 1992 – excellent inland finds of this rare Siberian migrant.

Chats may also be in evidence during passage times, particularly after winds with an easterly element. Wheatears are best looked for in spring and Whinchats in autumn, though exceptionally 41 of the former were count-ed here on 24 August 1986. Scarce London migrants making occasional appearances include Black Redstart and Ring Ouzel, while a Dartford Warbler was found here in October 1994, a rare British occurrence north of the Thames. More typically, the visitor can expect to find commoner war-blers in evidence on migration and in summer including breeding Reed Warbler and Whitethroat, and perhaps also Lesser Whitethroat and Willow Warbler; the area around the lagoon is best for these species. Goldcrests are regular in winter, and Bearded Tit has occurred in late autumn.

Other species here include the commoner corvids and finches typical of this type of habitat, along with Yellowhammer and one other note-worthy species. This area is a stronghold for Corn Bunting, with up to 12 breeding pairs being a noteworthy concentration of this nationally declining species; outside the breeding season up to 50 have been seen together. Also noteworthy was the Lapland Bunting recorded here on two dates in December 1990, demonstrating the site's potential for turning up surprises at all times of the year.

Timing

There is more than enough birding potential here to make Fairlop Waters worth a visit in its own right. Aside from the resident Yellowhammers and Corn Buntings, breeding birds are not outstanding for this part of London, so spring and autumn for migrants and oddities and winter for wildfowl and the Golden Plover flock will prove the most rewarding seasons. Visit early to avoid water sports activity and weekend crowds, or on quieter weekdays.

Access

To reach Fairlop Waters take the A406 North Circular Road and A1400 Southend Road/Woodford Avenue east from north London or the A12 Eastern Avenue west from Essex and the east to the Gants Hill roundabout, heading northeast along the A123 Cranbrook Road for a mile (1.6 km) or

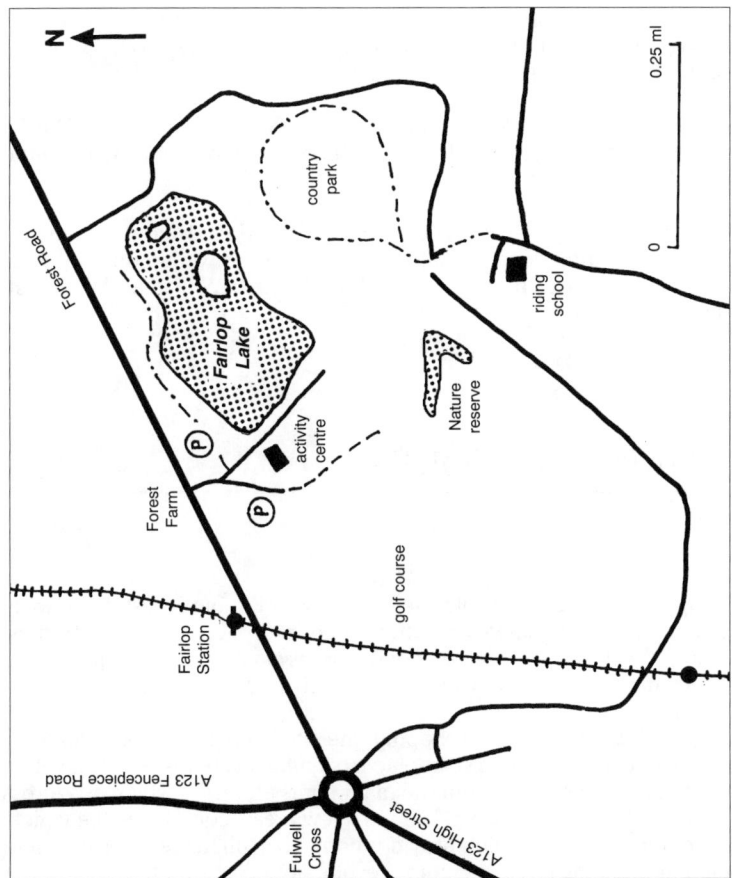

so until it becomes High Street at Barkingside. After another third of a mile (0.5 km), turn right at the roundabout onto Forest Road and right again after three-quarters of a mile (1.2 km) into the country park car park. To explore the farmland, continue east along Forest Road and check the fields from vantage points along here and Hainault Road, Billet Road and Whalebone Lane North to the east.

By bus: numbers 247, 275, 362 and 462 all serve Barkingside or Barkingside station, just southwest of Fairlop. *By underground:* Fairlop station (Central line) is half a mile (0.8 km) west of the main entrance to the country park on Forest Road. There is no convenient overground station.

Calendar

All year: Great Crested Grebe, Sparrowhawk, Kestrel, Red-legged Partridge, Stock Dove, Little Owl, Green Woodpecker, Skylark, Meadow Pipit, Linnet, Yellowhammer, Reed Bunting, Corn Bunting.

Winter (November–February): very occasional diver or scarce grebe, Wigeon, Teal, Shoveler, Tufted Duck, Pochard, wildfowl oddities, occasional Water Rail, Golden Plover, Lapwing, Jack Snipe, Snipe, perhaps Short-eared Owl, Goldcrest.

Spring (March–May): Little Ringed Plover, Common Sandpiper and other passage waders, Common and other terns, Turtle Dove, Cuckoo, hirundines, Wheatear, migrant warblers.

Summer (June–early August): Little Ringed Plover, Swift, House Martin, Yellow Wagtail, Reed Warbler, Whitethroat, perhaps Lesser Whitethroat and Willow Warbler.

Autumn (mid-August–October): Hobby, Little Ringed Plover, Common and Green Sandpipers and other passage waders, Common and other terns, Turtle Dove, hirundines, Yellow Wagtail, Wheatear, Whinchat, migrant warblers.

7 HAINAULT FOREST   OS ref: TQ 476932

Habitat

Competing for attention with the much larger Epping Forest to the west, Hainault Forest in many ways offers better prospects for visiting birders. Though a substantial piece of woodland, its smaller size and richness of habitat makes it easier to work productively and all of the best areas can be explored in a morning's birding on foot.

As in the denser parts of Epping, the site is characterised mainly by beech, oak, hornbeam and, in places, significant stands of birch, with a good understorey away from the main paths and rides which criss-cross the area. Conifers are also present in a few areas, completing the variety of woodland habitat which provides home to a full range of resident and migrant breeding birds, including several notable species.

There is a lake in the centre of the forest, the surrounding area of which is short-mown turf or rougher grass with scattered scrub. To the southeast the forest is bordered by a golf course, to the west by Hainault itself and on other margins by farmland.

Species

The lake in the centre of forest holds a few resident commoner waterbirds and in winter may attract the occasional Water Rail. Ruddy Ducks have been noted displaying in spring, although the exotic Mandarin, which has established itself on the ponds of nearby Epping Forest, has yet to settle here. Aside from good numbers of gulls (including several hundred Common) at this season, there is the chance of an overflying wader on passage and Red-legged Partridges on the surrounding farmland; however, it is really the forest proper in spring and summer that merits attention.

An eye to the sky should give you Sparrowhawk and Kestrel, and perhaps even the chance of a Hobby from May to August. The dense woodland holds breeding Stock Dove, Cuckoo and Little and Tawny Owls, the latter being particularly well represented with around eight pairs. Woodpeckers can also be found in some numbers, with censuses of breeding pairs recently revealing 16 of Great Spotted, 12 of Green and six of Lesser Spotted – giving the visitor an excellent chance of seeing all three species in a morning's birding.

A few pairs of Swallow breed and all three hirundines are sometimes noted in numbers on passage. Scrutiny of migrants can always prove worthwhile, as demonstrated in May 1992 when London's seventh Red-rumped Swallow was found here. Meadow and Tree Pipits retain a token breeding presence, but the latter may take some finding in so much suitable habitat and is easier to find on Chingford Plain in Epping Forest. Much the same is true for Nightingale, which is only an infrequent migrant at Hainault. Redstart and even Ring Ouzel have appeared on passage and Grasshopper Warblers are sometimes heard reeling in spring and early summer, though they do not breed. The more regular warblers include good numbers of Whitethroat, Blackcap, Willow Warbler and Chiffchaff, and the 'sixpence on a plate' song of Wood Warbler should be listened for in spring: a pair sometimes stays on to breed. Goldcrests also maintain a tiny breeding presence here and even Firecrest has been heard singing in the breeding season.

Census work has also revealed good numbers of commoner birds at Hainault, with around 80 pairs of Blue Tit and 60 of Great Tit. Coal and Long-tailed are also widespread and Marsh Tit is nowhere commoner in the London area; on the debit side, however, Willow Tit has recently become extinct as a breeding bird, with just the occasional individual putting in appearances outside the breeding season. Unusually, Treecreeper is significantly commoner here than Nuthatch.

Hole-nesting Jackdaws and Starlings provide a noisy backdrop in spring to the presence of less conspicuous forest birds. In several years these have included Golden Oriole, a difficult species to see at the best of times but all the more so here in the dense forest canopy.

As well as commoner finches such as Chaffinch, Greenfinch and Goldfinch, Redpoll breeds in very small numbers but is commoner in winter, when Siskins may also be present. Bullfinches are common and the total of four breeding pairs of Hawfinch in 1994 demonstrates this site's potential compared to the larger Epping Forest. In 'irruption' years any pines in the area are worth checking for Crossbills from midsummer, though as almost everywhere in the London area this species' appearances are always unpredictable. Rarer still was London's fourth Common Rosefinch reported here in September 1994. A few pairs of Yellowhammer are still present, though the species has undergone a 70 per cent decline here in the last 20 years.

Timing

Although resident species include numerous attractions, like any expanse of woodland winter can be a very quiet time to visit. Your time looking for the regulars will be better spent in early spring, especially because leaf cover is still limited and the three woodpeckers will be at their most active. Throughout spring and early summer the forest is alive with birdsong, and a full morning, starting with the dawn chorus, can easily be spent at this large site.

If you have time to play with, combining a two–three hour stint here soon after dawn with a mid-morning visit to Fairlop just to the southwest will make a very productive spring itinerary.

Access

Hainault Forest can be reached from the M25 by turning south towards London onto the M11 at junction 27 and leaving that motorway shortly after at junction 5. Turn south onto the A1168, then left at the T-junction along the A113 towards Abridge, and soon after first right down Pudding Lane for about 2 miles (3.2 km) to Chigwell Row. At the main crossroads here turn left to reach Lambourne End after another 1.5 miles (2.4 km) to access the forest from the north side; park in the car park opposite the pub and follow the footpath into the country park itself. This is one of the best areas of forest, so explore as many footpaths as time permits, and allow even longer if you wish to work your way through to the lake in the southwest corner.

Alternatively, from the crossroads at Chigwell Row continue southeast along the A1112 Romford Road, turning left (northeast) after almost a mile (1.6 km) up Fox Burrow Road to the car park near the lake. From here you can work the southern area more easily, although the best parts of the forest itself are further to walk to. The A1112 south of the forest becomes Whalebone Lane North and runs south to join the A12 just west of Romford.

By bus: numbers 247, 362 and 511 stop in Romford Road by the southwest corner of the forest. *By underground:* from Hainault station (Central line) catch a 247 bus east up New North Road to Romford Road. There are no convenient overground stations.

Calendar

All year: Sparrowhawk, Kestrel, Red-legged Partridge on adjacent farmland, Stock Dove, Little Owl, Tawny Owl, Green Woodpecker, Great Spotted Woodpecker, Lesser Spotted Woodpecker, Meadow Pipit, Goldcrest, Marsh Tit, Nuthatch, Treecreeper, Redpoll, Hawfinch, Yellowhammer.

Winter (November–March): Occasional Water Rail at the lake, gull flocks on the grassland, Fieldfare, Redwing, Siskin.

Spring (April–May): Chance of Hobby (from May), Cuckoo, hirundines, Tree Pipit (from late April), occasional Grasshopper Warbler, Whitethroat, Blackcap, Willow Warbler, Chiffchaff, good chance of Wood Warbler.

Summer (June–August): Occasional Hobby, Cuckoo, Swallow, Tree Pipit,

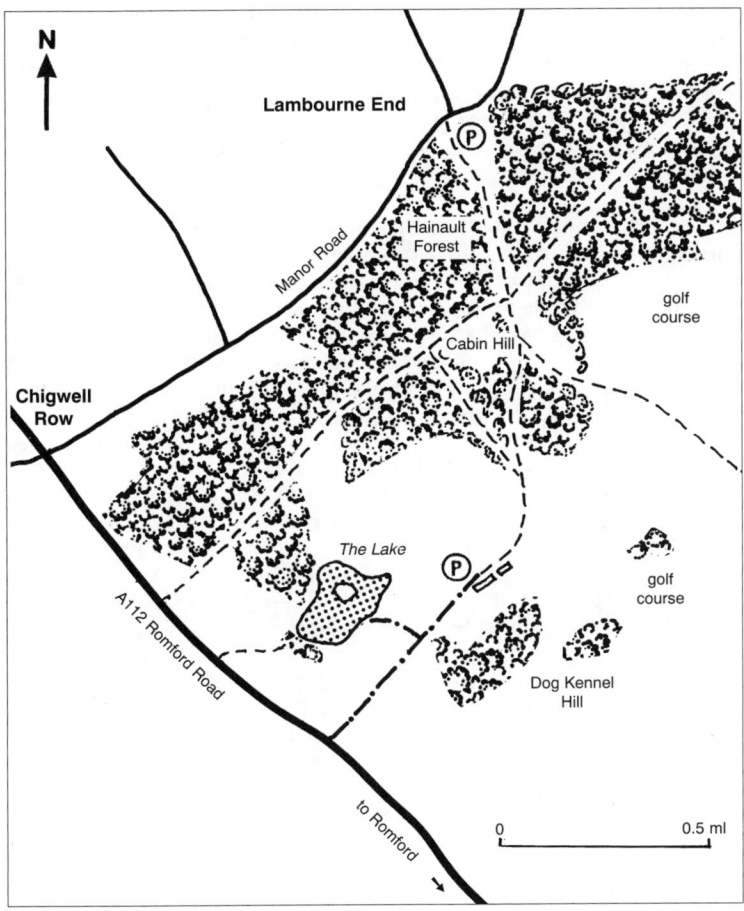

Whitethroat, Blackcap, Willow Warbler, Chiffchaff, Wood Warbler (most years).

Autumn (September–October): Hirundines, common migrants, Fieldfare and Redwing (from mid-October).

8   DAGNAM PARK   OS ref: TQ 550933

Habitat
Formerly one of the most reliable sites to find roosting Hawfinches in winter, Dagnam Park also has other strings to its ornithological bow. Lying in the easternmost corner of the London area to the north of Harold Hill, its rural location gives it an avifauna rather untypical of much of the urban fringe.

Areas of open closely-mown and rough grassland, the latter decidedly coarse in places with scattered young tree growth, are fringed by belts of mature deciduous woodland. Together these comprise attractive habitat to breeding birds which include one or two 'specialists' such as Turtle Dove and Tree Pipit, in addition to the elusive Hawfinch. There is no wetland habitat except for several small ponds which hold a few breeding waterbirds. This site has an excellent record for turning up unusual migrants.

Species

The combination of wooded surroundings and ponds explains the presence of Mandarin Duck here. This hole-nesting species has expanded considerably from its Surrey base in the past two decades and, having colonised Epping Forest, has made Dagnam Park its most easterly outpost in the London area. The only other recent waterbirds of note relate to reports of wandering Egyptian Goose and Mediterranean Gull, two other species which have occurred with increasing regularity in the region.

Instead it is the more notable woodland and open country species which put Dagnam Park on the London birding map. Resident Stock and Collared Doves are joined in summer by Turtle Dove and Cuckoo, while Green, Great Spotted and Lesser Spotted Woodpeckers can all be found in the area. Little Owl no longer breeds but may still occur on nearby farmland. Ground-nesters such as Skylark and Yellow Wagtail would probably find the habitat here more to their liking for breeding were it not for the effects of disturbance, caused partly by unauthorised trail-biking; as a result both species retain only a minimal presence in summer.

The rough grassland is attractive to species such as Whinchat, Wheatear and Redstart in spring and autumn, and migrant Ring Ouzel is a distinct possibility here. Warblers breeding in good numbers include Whitethroat, Blackcap, Willow Warbler and Chiffchaff, and the variety is boosted during migration when they are occasionally joined by less common migrants such as Grasshopper and Wood Warblers and Pied Flycatcher. Firecrest has also been recorded, with individuals making prolonged stays in two consecutive recent winters.

Any British site that can maintain a population of Hawfinches, albeit a small one in this instance, is clearly of at least local importance. Although the species has not been proved to breed here in the last few years and is very hard to locate in summer, the winter roost gatherings of up 15 or so individuals have been noteworthy. However, recent habitat 'management' work has unfortunately reduced the numbers using the area regularly. Other seed-eaters are also much in evidence in winter, when flocks of Greenfinches and Chaffinches can reach three figures, and Yellowhammer is also resident.

For reasons probably as much to do with observer diligence as with geographical location, Dagnam Park has a varied and interesting list of unexpected migrants. The course of the Ingrebourne River along the eastern edge of the park may help to serve as a minor fly-way, and is perhaps also the reason why overflying waders, including scarcer species such as Grey Plover and Spotted Redshank, have been recorded here. Spring and autumn have both brought dividends in recent years, ranging from regionally rare wanderers such as Marsh Harrier, Arctic Skua, Crossbill and Lapland Bunting to national scarcities like Waxwing and Richard's Pipit. Whether casual visits also succeed in producing such noteworthy species remains to be seen, but as is often the case past records are a good indicator of future potential.

Hawfinches

Timing

For the best chance of seeing Hawfinches a winter visit is essential. This species is by no means guaranteed here but numbers are usually high enough to give you a reasonable chance of locating them in the last two or three hours of the day, as they come in to roost. There is not much else in the way of avian excitement at this time, so a spring or autumn trip to maximise on migration potential will give you the greatest rewards. Remember that there is still a chance of Hawfinch in summer, and even if you are unlucky a range of other breeding birds on an early morning visit should provide enough interest. If you can, avoid weekend daytimes when most disturbance occurs.

Access

Dagnam Park lies just west of the M25 at its intersection with the A12 at junction 28. The most direct access is from the A12 about one mile (1.6 km) west from this junction (though only from the eastbound/north carriageway); follow the road north for a short distance through the housing estate before turning right at the school to the main park entrance. If you are unfamiliar with the area, remember that the nearest town to Dagnam Park is Harold Hill, and not frequently-confused Dagenham some distance to the southwest.

By bus: numbers 296 and 374 run to Dagnam Park Square from Ilford and Romford respectively. *By train:* at just over two miles (3.2 km) away the overground station at Harold Wood is the nearest. Walk north to the A12, then east towards the M25 before following directions as above. There is no local underground station.

Calendar

All year: Mandarin Duck, Red-legged Partridge, Pheasant, Stock Dove, Collared Dove, woodpeckers, chance of Little Owl on adjacent farmland, Skylark, Jackdaw, Yellowhammer.

Winter (November–February): Fieldfare, Redwing, outside chance of Firecrest, roosting Hawfinches.

Spring (March–May): Redstart, Whinchat, Wheatear, chance of Ring Ouzel, departing winter thrushes, migrant warblers including occasional Grasshopper and Wood, Brambling, possibility of oddities.

Summer (June–early August): Turtle Dove, Cuckoo, Tree Pipit, Yellow Wagtail, outside chance of Hawfinch.

Autumn (mid-August–October): Redstart, Whinchat, Wheatear, chance of Ring Ouzel, Redwing, Fieldfare, migrant warblers and perhaps Pied Flycatcher, possibility of oddities.

9 DAGENHAM CHASE   OS ref: TQ 514858

Habitat

In the otherwise unprepossessing east London landscape of dense residential developments, factories and industrial estates, the green oasis of Dagenham Chase stands out like a sore thumb. Nestling in the Dagenham Corridor between Romford to the north, the famous Ford works at Dagenham to the southeast and Becontree to the west, the Chase comprises some 150 hectares of pasture, wetland, scrub and, in places, a few small stands of trees.

As recently as the turn of the century much of the surrounding area was still undeveloped farmland, and the Chase seems to have escaped urbanisation since then by virtue of its Green Belt status. Gravel extraction for local building began in the 1920s and continued until the 1970s, creating a series of pits which now serve as fishing lakes and as habitat for small numbers of wildfowl. Much of the rest of the area is pasture grazed by horses, which helps to maintain its open rural character, but in recent years the site has been extensively landscaped – most notably in the newly-designated Eastbrook End Country Park, an 84-hectare area which forms the western boundary of the site. Perhaps the most attractive habitat falls within the Chase Nature Reserve, a 65-hectare stretch of pasture and scrub along the Rom valley which incorporates the excellent wetland known as the Slack; just to the northeast is The Willows, the most wooded habitat in the area and a good spot for migrant passerines.

Just over a third of the site is a nature reserve managed by the London Wildlife Trust (its largest reserve) on behalf of the London Borough of Barking and Dagenham, which owns all of the Chase bar 14 hectares east of the River Rom, marking the boundary with the London Borough of Havering. The combined efforts of a full-time warden, the Dagenham Bird Group and numerous visitors to this prime east London site had bolstered the area list to a very impressive 177 species by January 1995, of which around 130 are recorded annually; perhaps 40–50 might be expected in a full morning's visit.

Species

A visit at any time of the year should aim to take in the lakes and the Slack, which between them usually produce a good range of species. Up to four pairs of Great Crested Grebes are resident and Little Grebe is present for much of the year, with one or two pairs breeding occasionally. Small numbers of Cormorant are usually visible outside the breeding season and Grey Herons can often be seen stalking the shallows of the lakes or the Slack. Rare visitors have included Shag and Bittern.

Mute Swan and Canada Geese breed but other geese, even Greylags, are scarce here; wanderers have included Egyptian and even a Brent Goose, seen grazing on flooded playing fields. Shelduck are usually irregular visitors, although a pair bred in 1994, but dabbling duck are well represented in autumn and winter with good numbers of Mallard, Shoveler and Teal, and occasionally a handful of Wigeon and Gadwall. Only Mallard breeds, although all except Wigeon may remain in very small numbers in spring and summer, when there is the added possibility of Garganey. Tufted Duck nests but, along with Pochard, is more common in winter; species such as Ruddy Duck, Goldeneye, Goosander and Smew, on the other hand, remain distinctly scarce here.

Dagenham Chase has amassed an interesting list of raptors in recent years. Wandering Red Kite, Marsh and Hen Harriers and Common Buzzard have all been recorded, though none has lingered. Aside from resident Sparrowhawk and Kestrel, Hobbies are regular over the area in spring and autumn, with sometimes two or three on the wing together, but much more sporadic in midsummer. Merlins have put in erratic winter appearances, but Peregrine is rarer still and is not recorded annually.

Both partridges and Pheasant occur in the area but are infrequently reported. Water Rails are regular in winter, especially around the Slack, and up to four have been counted: sporadic summer records have indicated breeding, though as yet this has not been confirmed. Waders also find the area attractive, with winter gatherings of up to 2,000 or so Lapwing and occasionally a few Golden Plover on Eastbrook School playing field, and perhaps 30 or 40 Snipe (in some years many more) on the Slack; Lapwing also breeds and Snipe has probably done so, a rare event nowadays in the London area. A few Jack Snipe may be present in winter, although their unobtrusive nature means they are infrequently reported. The rarest British representative of this family, a Great Snipe, was found here in early June 1989, while other oddities have included a Stone Curlew flying north one April and Temminck's and Little Stints, Knot, Avocet, Sanderling, Spotted Redshank and both species of godwit. There have been occasional passage appearances of Oystercatcher, Ringed and Grey Plovers, Curlew Sandpiper, Dunlin, Curlew and Whimbrel, but more likely are Little Ringed Plovers from April to August (scarcer midsummer), Ruff, Greenshank and Green, Wood and Common Sandpipers in either spring or autumn. Redshank is also regular and has bred.

In winter most of the gulls in the area concentrate on the playing fields at Eastbrook School, with perhaps 2,000 or so Black-headeds making this the dominant species. Common, Herring and Lesser Black-backed can also be numerous and there are usually a few Great Black-backs as well. Smaller numbers of gulls also occur on the Slack, with Mediterranean the most likely scarcer species in winter; at other times of year Yellow-legged and Little Gulls and Kittiwake have also occurred. Look out for Common Terns in summer, and even Black Terns which very occasionally grace the lakes on passage. Proving the variety of birds that can turn up at this excellent wetland, Arctic and Sandwich Terns and even Arctic Skua have also been recorded.

A few Stock and Turtle Doves are reported annually, and Cuckoo breeds. Long-eared Owls have used the Chase as a winter roost site for the last 14 years, and in good seasons may reach almost double figures though they can be very difficult to locate. Short-eared Owls also make occasional winter forays to the area, though typically in much smaller numbers outside influx years.

Kingfishers are occasionally seen in the area, particularly along the river, although they don't breed within the Chase itself. All three woodpeckers are also reported intermittently though again do not seem to nest regularly; Great and Lesser Spotted are most likely to be found in The Willows. The open areas hold a few pairs of Skylarks and Meadow Pipits, and in spring and autumn gatherings of hirundines can number in the hundreds. Yellow and Pied Wagtails also occur on passage, the former especially on the damper pasture and the latter in winter as well, when one or two Grey Wagtails are also present; this species nests nearby and is occasionally seen in summer.

The rough pasture and scrubby cover, particularly around Crowfoot Marsh to the south of the Slack and undisturbed areas of the country park, prove attractive to chats on migration, and Redstart, Whinchat, Stonechat and Wheatear are all recorded annually. Ring Ouzels are scarce throughout the London area but this is one of the better places to search for passage birds, April and September perhaps being the best months. Fieldfares and Redwings boost the local thrush population from autumn through to early spring, and occasionally involve some large influxes.

In summer, waterside vegetation resounds to the song of Reed and Sedge Warblers, the former outnumbering the latter by about eight to one. Good numbers of Whitethroats breed and a few Lesser Whitethroats can be heard rattling away in hedgerows during the summer; most remarkable, however, is the occurrence of this species in two recent consecutive winters. Blackcap and Willow Warbler also breed but the lack of suitable woodland means Garden Warbler and Chiffchaff (both former breeders) are restricted to passage periods, the latter also occurring in winter when Goldcrest are regular and even Firecrest might be found. Spotted Flycatcher is a passage migrant here and Pied has been recorded on autumn migration; again, The Willows may provide the best chance of this species.

Like other reedbed sites in the region Dagenham Chase occasionally benefits from late autumn 'irruptions' of Bearded Tits, and there is always a chance of this species appearing in stands of *Phragmites* or reedmace in October and November. The 'true' tits are restricted to just Long-tailed, Great and Blue, and both Nuthatch and Treecreeper are rarities in this largely unwooded landscape. Even some of the birds of the nearby Essex countryside are absent as regular visitors, and species such as Rook, Jackdaw and Tree Sparrow are irregular at best. Other oddities which have put in recent appearances are Golden Oriole in two successive years, an immature Red-backed Shrike in autumn 1991 and a Great Grey Shrike in November of the same year.

The commoner finches are joined in winter by the occasional Redpoll and perhaps Brambling and Corn Bunting, and as well as resident Reed Buntings a small flock of Yellowhammers is regular at this time of year, often in the area around the riding school. In February 1992 they helped to make ornithological history by teaming up with a male Pine Bunting, the first occurrence of this major national rarity in London.

Timing

Dagenham Chase is worth a visit at any time of year, although midsummer sees the least activity on the Slack and may therefore provide the lowest trip total. Winter sees good numbers of wildfowl and gulls, and spring and autumn the best range of waders and other migrants – plus the proven possibility of a rarity or regional scarcity.

Like most sites early morning pays dividends, with weekends the time of most disturbance – particularly around the overcrowded angling lakes. In winter don't ignore late afternoon visiting, which brings the chance of hunting owls, and perhaps even a raptor, over the more open areas.

Access

Dagenham Chase lies due south of Romford. From the M25, turn off at junction 28 (from the north) or junction 29 (from the south and east) and continue west to the Gallows Corner roundabout on the A12. From here continue southwest along the A118 through Gidea Park to Romford town centre, from where Dagenham Road runs south from the hospital to the Chase. Turn left off Dagenham Road a quarter of a mile (0.4 km) south of a second hospital, at Rush Green, into Chase Road and park at the main car park.

From the west, take the A406 North Circular Road and then at Gants Hill the A12 towards Romford, turning off right (south) onto the A1112

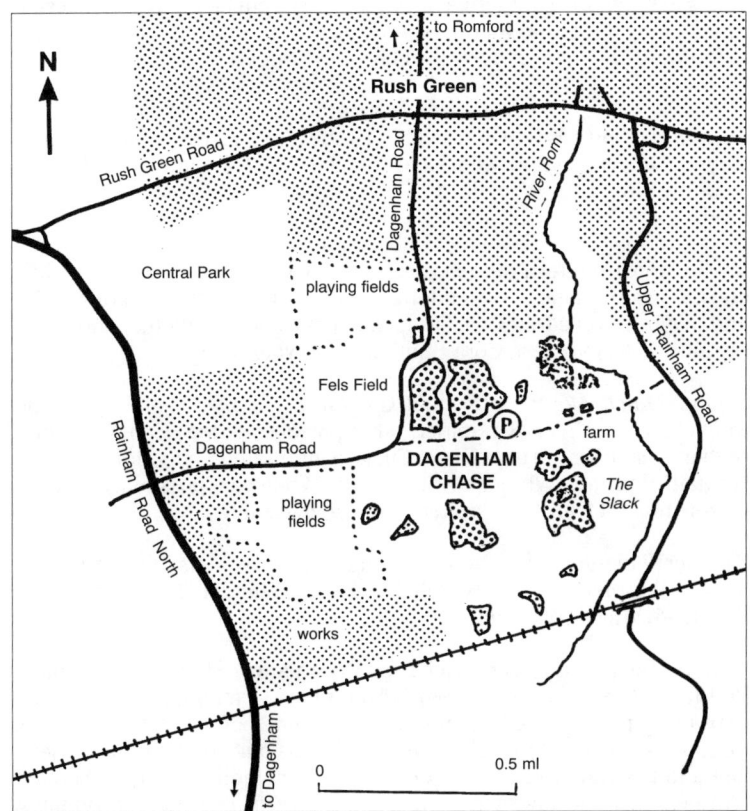

Whalebone Lane North. Follow this south over the crossroads, bearing left into the Broadway at the next main intersection and then right at the roundabout onto Rainham Road North (still the A1112). After two-thirds of a mile (1 km) turn left into Dagenham Road and continue east for another half a mile (0.8 km) past the playing fields (check the gulls in winter) to reach the Chase from the west side at the Farmhouse Tavern. It is worth noting that the A1112 west of the Chase becomes Rainham Road South and continues south via Ballards Road to connect with the A13, the most direct route to central London.

Much of the area has open public access, though the cemetery, riding stables, paddocks and the private fishing lake are off limits to visitors. Public footpaths access the site from Dagenham Road, Upper Rainham Road, Foxlands Lane and Chase Road, and there is a good network of paths within the Chase itself. The London Wildlife Trust office is currently situated in a portacabin on the east side of Dagenham Road, just north of White Hart Lakes.

By bus: number 174 from Harold Hill (and Romford) to Dagenham runs along Dagenham Road on the west side of the Chase (alight at the request stop by the Farmhouse Tavern), and the 252 stops in Upper Rainham Road on the east side. *By underground:* from Dagenham East (District line), turn left into Rainham Road South, right along Foxlands Crescent and then second right into Winstead Gardens, from where a left turn into Foxlands Lane takes you along the north side of the Rhône-Poulenc Rorer works to reach the southern end of the Chase (check the works lakes en route – they have held Shag). *By train:* the nearest overground station is at Romford (regular services from Liverpool Street).

Calendar

All year: Great Crested Grebe, Little Grebe, Grey Heron, Sparrowhawk, Kestrel, Lapwing, Snipe, Kingfisher, Great Spotted Woodpecker, Skylark, Meadow Pipit, Grey Wagtail.

Winter (November–February): Cormorant, Teal, Shoveler, Gadwall, Merlin (rare), Water Rail, occasional Golden Plover, Jack Snipe (difficult), outside chance of Mediterranean Gull in gull flocks, Long-eared and maybe Short-eared Owl, Stonechat, occasional Chiffchaff and possibly Firecrest, Goldcrest, Corn Bunting, Yellowhammer.

Spring (March–May): Occasional Garganey, Hobby (from May), Little Ringed Plover, Green Sandpiper, other passage waders, Common Tern, perhaps Black Tern, Turtle Dove, Cuckoo, hirundines, occasional Yellow Wagtail, Redstart, Whinchat, Stonechat, Wheatear, possibility of Ring Ouzel, migrant warblers, Spotted Flycatcher, oddities.

Summer (June–July): Hobby, occasional passage waders, Common Tern, Sedge Warbler, Reed Warbler, Lesser Whitethroat, Whitethroat, Blackcap, Willow Warbler.

Autumn (August–October): Occasional Garganey, Hobby, Ruff, Snipe, Redshank, Green Sandpiper, Wood Sandpiper, Common Sandpiper, perhaps other passage waders, hirundines, Common Tern, Yellow Wagtail, Redstart, Whinchat, Stonechat, Wheatear, possibility of Ring Ouzel, Fieldfare and Redwing (from October), migrants including warblers, Spotted and perhaps Pied Flycatcher, outside chance of Bearded Tit, oddities.

Habitat

Situated just north of Rainham and east of the outermost London suburbs of Dagenham and Hornchurch, Berwick Ponds benefit from both their strategic position in the Ingrebourne Valley and their true rural location – this is the first unenclosed area of farmland due east of London. There are two main stretches of water, extending in long fingers east and west from Berwick Pond Road. The larger of the two, on the west side of the road, has an extensive reedbed and a small wood at the far end (marked on some maps as Abbey Wood). Beyond the wood the Ingrebourne River runs southwest towards the Thames, providing a natural boundary with South Hornchurch to the west. In places the river valley can be very damp, often with enough standing water to attract migrating waders in spring and autumn and wildfowl in winter.

Otherwise the surrounding landscape is rather typical of agricultural Essex, with fields mainly given over to a variety of crops but with livestock paddocks, hedgerows and pollarded oaks in the immediate area providing habitat for a number of species otherwise relatively scarce in the London area.

Species

The prime attraction at this site is the reedbed, but the immediate environs of the ponds are worth taking in on any visit for their interesting variety of farmland species.

Wildfowl are noteworthy here at all times of the year. Most significant in winter are the concentrations of Teal (sometimes in hundreds) and rafts of diving duck, though summer should not be ignored: Teal, Gadwall and Shoveler all breed, as does Pochard in important numbers (around 10 pairs), Ruddy Duck has become increasingly regular and Garganey may make sporadic appearances, especially in late summer. A few pairs of Little and Great Crested Grebes are also resident, and in recent years Common Tern has established a toehold breeding presence.

Kingfishers are often a colourful feature on waterside perches along the river or at the ponds, and Water Rails can sometimes be seen feeding furtively around the reedy margins in winter; this site is also the most reliable in the London area for the species in summer, with up to four pairs in the breeding season. There are also large numbers of Moorhens, with over 100 sometimes present in winter and often feeding in groups out on the muddier livestock paddocks.

The reedbeds are occasionally home to an elusive species which is rather erratic in its appearances in the region. Bearded Tits are prone to irruptions in autumn and sometimes can be found here in October and November, a few occasionally remaining for the winter months.

Waders to be expected in winter include gatherings of Golden Plover and Lapwing in the area, the latter sometimes in substantial flocks, good numbers of Snipe (over 100 have been recorded) and the occasional Jack Snipe. In summer, there are a few breeding pairs of Redshank and Ringed Plover has nested, though not regularly. On passage Greenshank and Common and Green Sandpipers are likely in spring and from July to

Bearded Tits

September; other species occurring in recent years include Curlew, Oystercatcher, Ruff, Wood Sandpiper and Spotted Redshank.

The site's proximity to Rainham Marshes may account for the occasional sighting of Merlin here, with birds appearing intermittently in the area most winters; they have used the site regularly on occasion and have perhaps even roosted here. Hen Harriers were formerly almost regular, birds hunting the areas around the ponds and the Ingrebourne valley during the day and returning to Rainham at dusk to roost, but this habit seems to have been a short-lived phenomenon. Aside from Kestrel, Sparrowhawk and increasingly regular Hobby in summer, other predators are most likely to include resident Little and the odd Short-eared Owl in winter. In the latter season Long-eared Owls have occasionally also been found roosting in the area.

Migrating parties of Sand Martin, House Martins and Swallows hawk insects en masse over the ponds on their way through in spring and autumn; numbers can reach several hundred, with Sand Martins peaking perhaps into three figures in April, followed by Swallows and House Martins. Both Pied and Grey Wagtails are frequently encountered around the ponds, the former sometimes in large numbers in winter, and Yellow Wagtails arrive in April, with a few pairs remaining to breed in summer. Meadow Pipits and Skylarks also nest, the latter forming large flocks on neighbouring farmland outside the breeding season. There is a good variety of commoner warblers in summer, including substantial populations of Reed and Sedge in the reedbeds and along the river valley, and Grasshopper Warbler, an elusive breeding bird in London, has also held territory here. More intermittent in their appearances are occasional passage White Wagtails and Rock and Water Pipits around the muddy edges of the ponds or chats and the occasional Redstart and Ring Ouzel in the scrub and rougher grassy areas.

The rural nature of the area makes it especially notable for breeding populations of certain farmland species otherwise scarce in the capital. Alongside the ubiquitous Reed Buntings, up to 10 pairs of both Yellowhammer and Corn Bunting breed in the area: try looking around the paddocks for the former and in the pollarded oaks along the road to the north of the ponds for the latter. A few pairs of Tree Sparrow hang on in this area and can be looked for in hedges on the farmland to the north and east, and Grey Partridge can also be found in the surrounding fields, though they are best looked for before the crops grow high in midsummer. This is a good area to hear the 'purring' of Turtle Doves in summer, and Cuckoos are likely from the end of April through to July.

Timing

There is a sufficient diversity of habitats and species to make this area worth a visit at almost any time of year. Winter will produce the biggest numbers of wildfowl and common waders such as Lapwing and Snipe, the best chance of seeing Water Rail, and flocking passerines on the farmland. Spring and autumn offer the opportunity of finding something a little out of the ordinary among migrant waders, wagtails or other passerines, but even summer can be productive with breeding Corn Bunting, Tree Sparrow, Turtle Dove and other species. A two or three-hour stint will give you enough time to cover the area fully.

Fringed by a housing estate on the south side and Hornchurch Country Park to the northwest, Berwick Ponds often suffers from disturbance during the day. The ponds are particularly popular with anglers during the fishing season.

Access

Berwick Ponds can be reached via the A13 from central London (leave the City east on Commercial Road), the A406 North Circular Road (turn east onto the A13 at the intersection south of Barking) and the M25 (head west from Junction 31). From the A13 three-quarters of a mile (1.2 km) east of the A125 roundabout, turn left (east) onto Upminster Road and continue through the residential area for half a mile (0.8 km). Reaching open farmland, continue for another quarter of a mile (0.4 km) before turning left (north) onto Berwick Pond Road. The ponds are another half mile (0.8 km) along on either side of the road after the S-bend.

Do not be tempted to stop on the road to view the eastern pond; there is a small car park on the left on the north side of the ponds, from where you can walk back down the road to view. A footpath tracks the north side of the larger western pond (where the main reedbed is located) from the car park to the wood at the far end. To get to the river valley, follow this path round to the right (north) before the western end of the pond, and continue as far up to view as you wish.

By bus: routes 165 and 287 run from Romford and Barking respectively along Upminster Road North, just south of Berwick Ponds. *By train:* it is about a 1.5-mile (2.4 km) walk from Rainham station northeast along Upminster Road and Berwick Pond Road to the ponds. There is no local underground service.

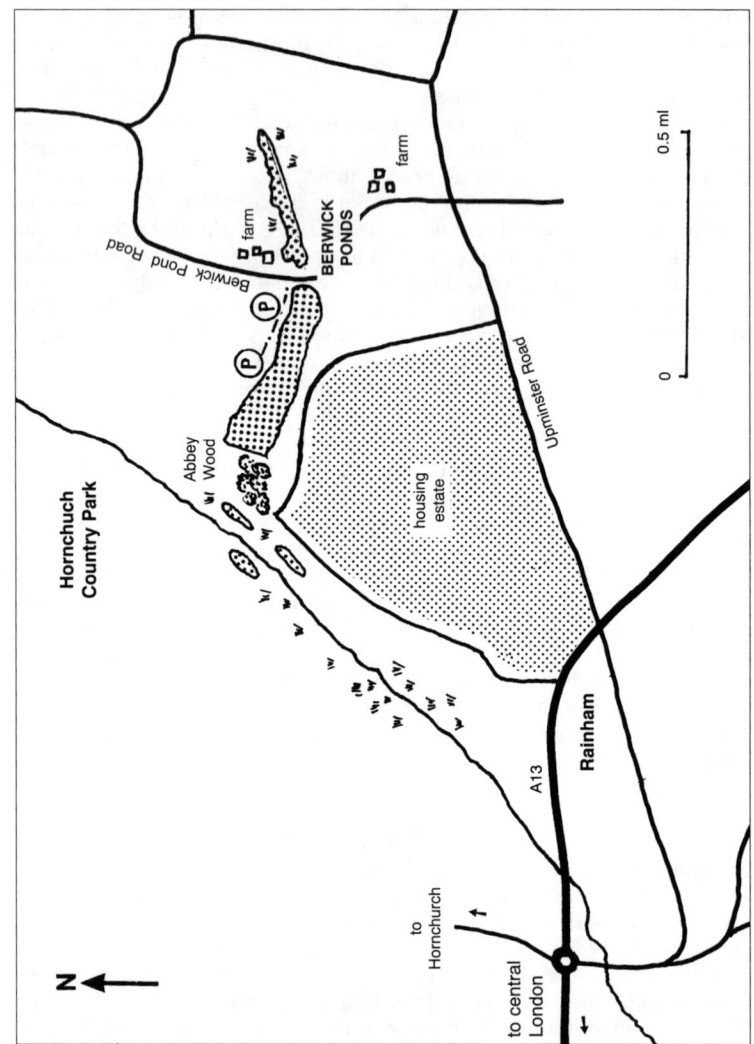

Calendar

All year: Gadwall, Teal, Shoveler, Pochard, Tufted Duck, Grey Partridge, Water Rail, Little Owl, Kingfisher, Skylark, Pied Wagtail, Tree Sparrow, Yellowhammer, Reed Bunting, Corn Bunting.

Winter (November–March): Good numbers of Teal and other wildfowl, occasional Merlin, Golden Plover, Lapwing, Snipe, Jack Snipe, outside chance of Bearded Tit.

Spring (April–May): Passage waders, hirundines, Yellow and occasional White Wagtail, migrant passerines perhaps including Redstart or Ring Ouzel, warblers including Grasshopper.

Summer (June–July): Occasional Garganey (from late July), Hobby, start of return wader passage, Common Tern, Turtle Dove, Cuckoo, Yellow Wagtail, warblers including Reed, Sedge and perhaps Grasshopper.

Autumn (August–October): Passage waders, hirundines, occasional Rock or Water Pipit, chance of Bearded Tit (from October).

OTHER SITES IN THE AREA

10A BELHUS WOODS COUNTRY PARK OS ref: TQ 565825

This Essex County Council site is a mixture of woodland and flooded pits which makes a worthwhile additional stop if you are visiting Rainham or Berwick Ponds. Great Crested and Little Grebes breed along with Mallard, Tufted Duck and other common waterfowl, and one or two pairs of Gadwall are usually present in summer; outside the breeding season numbers of this species can approach three figures. Waders are usually represented by common species such as Lapwing and Snipe, but Ringed Plover has held territory here and passage visitors have included unlikely species such as Bar-tailed Godwit. Common Terns are regular in summer and have attempted breeding. The woods hold a good range of species typical of the London area including all three woodpeckers, a variety of warblers and Marsh Tit as well as the commoner species, while the more open areas around the pits have breeding Meadow Pipit and Yellow Wagtail and good numbers of Fieldfare in winter. Rarer visitors have included Common Buzzard, Grasshopper and Wood Warblers, Black Tern and Great Grey Shrike.

Belhus Woods CP lies about 1.5 miles (2.4 km) southeast of Berwick Ponds. From there, leave the car park south on Berwick Pond Road, and turn left (east) into Upminster Road. Follow this road for a mile (1.6 km) or so, ignoring a left turn in the process, until you reach the next junction at a main road. Turn right here towards Aveley, and the entrance is on the left past the sand pit after about another three-quarters of a mile (1.2 km). Bus number 373 from Romford stops outside the country park; there are no convenient train services in the immediate area.

Call in at the visitor centre (there is a café and other facilities) to obtain a map of the area and find out if any interesting birds have been seen. The ranger service organises a number of events, including birdwatching walks and activities for children (for details telephone 01708 865628).

THE LOWER THAMES

11 RAINHAM MARSHES OS ref: TQ 525800

Habitat

Against a riverside backdrop of container storage depots, derelict factories, car breakers' yards and the mother of all rubbish tips, the term 'marshes' in Rainham's case at first seems to be an offence under the Trades Descriptions Act. The fact that it is something of an eyesore is no doubt the reason why the area has so often come under the scrutiny of developers. Having been proposed for a variety of schemes including a Disneyland-style theme park and the Channel Tunnel rail link, part of the area has now finally succumbed to the new A13 route linking east London with the M25.

This view is a short-sighted one on the part of the planners as Rainham's open landscape of rough grassland, marshes, reedbeds and pools, combined with the saltings and foreshore of the Thames, make it one of the most important bird sites in the capital. This remains the case, although the nature of the habitat has changed in recent years. The end of pumping from the Thames signalled a major reduction in the amount of water and wet mud at the site, and there are now very few pools of any importance for birds. The result is greatly reduced numbers and variety of wetland birds, especially wildfowl and waders, and the vagrant-filled days of the 1970s and early 1980s now seem long past.

However, in spite of the new road under construction across the northern part of the area, which should leave at least most of the marshes intact, and notwithstanding the serious disturbance caused by trail-bikers, falconers and every other manner of public intrusion, the habitat at Rainham should continue to provide refuge for marshland birds. An extensive part of the site is used as shooting ranges by the Ministry of Defence, though this seems to affect the birds little and probably actually helps to protect this area from other disturbance and habitat degradation.

Rainham's significance has been recognised through the designation of much of the area as a Site of Special Scientific Interest, and with a bird list of 210 species the site should continue to feature on the itineraries of any birdwatcher visiting London.

Species

Rainham's varied birdlife at all times of the year leaves few gaps in the systematic order, and even divers and grebes are well represented on the site list. Although Little Grebe is the most regular representative of this group on the marshes, the Thames attracts other species. Great Crested is present every winter, and both Red-necked and Slavonian have occurred in hard weather. Divers are similarly likely only after atypical conditions on the coast, but both Black-throated and Red-throated have turned up, with a remarkable influx of up to 12 of the latter recorded in early 1986, along with up to eight Guillemots at the same time.

The position of Rainham so far downriver – where salt water from the estuary meets fresh water from the river – also means it has a longer list than most London sites of coastal species, including storm-driven seabirds. In recent years these have included Fulmar, Manx Shearwater and Leach's Storm-petrel. One or two Shags are seen most winters among the large numbers of Cormorants, a few of which remain throughout the summer. Grey Herons also frequent the foreshore or gather in small numbers on the lagoons, and what must appear to be an attractive and extensive wetland site from the air has also lured down vagrant Purple Herons on three occasions and Spoonbill several times over the years.

Rainham is particularly important for its wildfowl, and in winter large numbers of various species gather on the marsh and along the Thames. Flights of Teal number several hundred at this time, if not a thousand or more, and up to 200 Shelduck and Mallard are often present. A small flock of Wigeon is regular in the Aveley saltings area, while up to 50 or so each of Gadwall and Shoveler tend to favour the Thames and the lagoons respectively. One or two pairs of these species and Teal are often present (though not always breeding) in summer, as are a few pairs each of Shelduck and Mallard. Aside from regular groups of Pochard and Tufted Duck, the marshes tend to attract a few Pintail in winter (this site formerly held important numbers) and one or two Garganey in spring and autumn, the latter also having bred. The most likely other ducks are Red-breasted Merganser and Goldeneye on the Thames or perhaps even a Scaup or Common Scoter in hard weather. Geese other than the ubiquitous Canada are similarly unpredictable, although parties of Brents are occasionally noted moving along the river; in severe conditions this species can occur in some numbers, as demonstrated by the flock of 550 on the Thames in February 1991, the largest ever in London. The river sometimes holds another wildfowl surprise in the form of Ruddy Shelduck, with occasional individuals – generally presumed to be either escapes or feral birds (hybrids have also been seen) – found among the Shelduck flocks most years.

The extensive open tracts of grassland and reedbeds make this site one of the best for raptors in the London area. Marsh Harrier is nowhere more likely than here, and the occasional hunting Hen Harrier is also recorded most winters although is no longer guaranteed. Sparrowhawks are regular and Short-eared Owls quarter the area in winter, good years bringing up to 10 or so birds to feed on the local short-tailed field vole population; as many as 17 have been counted in peak years. Falcons are represented chiefly by the ubiquitous Kestrel, with hovering birds continually dotting the horizon throughout the year, but both Peregrine and Merlin are prone to sporadic winter appearances and spring and summer skies should not be ignored for the occasional hunting Hobby. Particularly noteworthy here have been London's first Lesser Kestrel from 31 July to 3 August 1974, and Red-footed Falcons in May and June 1990 and June 1991. Other wandering raptors have included Montagu's Harrier, Osprey and Rough-legged Buzzard.

Less exciting but still noteworthy are Rainham's Grey Partridges, with this species having undergone a decline in the London area (as in much of the country) which now seems to have halted. Around seven pairs breed, and are most commonly encountered in the area around the rubbish tip or

Short-eared Owl and Oystercatchers

along the footpath to the river east of the Tilda Rice factory. Pheasants are more widespread.

Two of London's seven Cranes have turned up here, in July 1957 and May 1982, adding to the site's hot-spot reputation acquired largely through its shorebirds. The combination of tidal foreshore, pools and damp grassland makes this site attractive to waders, and Rainham's list must be the envy of many coastal sites: it is perhaps surpassed in the London area only by Staines Reservoir. However, the site has degenerated significantly for waders in recent years and many of the scarcer species no longer occur with any regularity. There are small but locally important breeding populations of Oystercatcher, Ringed Plover, Lapwing and Redshank, and numbers of all these species are swollen in passage periods and winter by birds from further north. Dunlin can reach several thousand here at peak winter times, when perhaps 200 or more Ringed Plover can also be found on the foreshore. Several hundred Redshank are present in winter and during migration, when Greenshank are also regular, though typically peaking just into double figures. Curlew and Whimbrel occur singly or in small parties in spring and autumn, either moving straight through or pausing to feed on the exposed mud of the Thames before continuing their journey. The pools have attracted passage Spotted Redshank, Ruff, Little Stint and Curlew, Wood, Common and Green Sandpipers, with small numbers of the last two also present in winter. At this time Snipe numbers can reach three figures and one or two Jack Snipe may also be present. This is a better place than most in London to encounter traditionally coastal shorebirds such as Grey Plover, Bar-tailed Godwit, Knot, Sanderling and Turnstone, but though all are recorded most years they can be unpredictable in their appearances. Far rarer are the American species which swell Rainham's track record for vagrants: these include London's only Western Sandpiper (and one of only six national records) in July 1973, a Baird's Sandpiper in September 1977, a Buff-breasted Sandpiper in July 1986 and a Solitary Sandpiper in September 1974.

The combined attractions of the Thames foreshore and the large rubbish tip make this site an instant lure to gulls, particularly for numbers of the larger species. Among the hordes of Black-headed and Common Gulls and mixed flocks of Herring, Lesser and Great Black-backs may lurk the occasional Glaucous or Iceland, though they can be hard to detect among the thousands of commoner gulls present. Rainham provides one of the best chances for these two white-winged species in London, and is also the prime site for Yellow-legged Gulls in the capital; this southern European form of Herring Gull, now widely regarded as a separate species, occasionally reaches three figures at this site, with June to October being the best time. Mediterranean Gulls are also occasionally found, and sharp-eyed birders have twice identified Ring-billed Gull here – still a true rarity in southeast England. Little Gulls may turn up occasionally on passage and Kittiwake has occurred along the Thames frontage.

Terns also use the river as a fly-way at migration times, though the recent demise of West Thurrock Power Station a short way downstream and its food-rich outflow that used to draw these birds up the estuary could have a long-term impact on numbers here. As everywhere in London Common Tern is the most likely species to be encountered, but Arctic and sometimes Black Terns occasionally move through in small numbers and even Sandwich and Little are a possibility.

The grazing marsh and rubbish tip attract sizeable flocks of Stock Doves in winter, and Turtle Doves breed in summer and are regular on passage. Cuckoo also nests and Kingfisher may be expected throughout the year. Large numbers of hirundines occur in spring and autumn, with the latter season producing the biggest gatherings: up to 3,000 Sand Martins can be watched hawking insects along with similar numbers of House Martins and several hundred Swallows, and a few pairs of both the last two species also nest. Far commoner in the breeding season are Skylarks and Meadow Pipits, with more than 100 pairs of each holding territory on the marshes and firing ranges and never being out of earshot in spring and summer. A few pairs of Yellow Wagtail also breed, but this species is more numerous in spring and autumn when one or two Blue-headeds may also be present. From late autumn until early spring Rock and Water Pipits are one of its main attractions, and more than 20 of both species have been counted: they sometimes favour the lagoons, but more often the foreshore (especially around the derelict concrete barges east of the Tilda Rice factory) and the saltings.

Also regular are Black Redstarts, with at least one pair sometimes breeding in the industrial area at the western end of the marshes. Stonechats nest in numbers – an estimate in 1990 put the figure of around 25 pairs as 90 per cent of the species' combined population in London and Essex – though more recently perhaps only 12 or so pairs breed, with varying numbers (sometimes few or none) in winter. Whinchat and Wheatear are confined to passage periods though both can be numerous in this rough grassland habitat, and Ring Ouzel occasionally appears on spring migration. Rainham's penchant for exciting finds has not been restricted to waders: a passing Hoopoe was found here one April, while rare passerines have included Red-throated Pipits in May 1982 and September 1993, a singing male white-spotted Bluethroat in April 1994 and an Aquatic Warbler in August 1981.

Warblers are chiefly represented by large numbers of Sedge and especially Reed, with up to 200 pairs of the latter breeding. Whitethroat is also numerous, but the few other breeding warblers and occasional Spotted Flycatcher are restricted mainly to the Mar Dyke at the Purfleet (easternmost) end of the area. Grasshopper Warbler occasionally reels from rank vegetation in spring and summer and Bearded Tit, formerly regular in good numbers in winter, can occur in small numbers from late autumn, though appearances of both these species are nowadays somewhat unpredictable.

When checking the gull flock on the rubbish tip, scrutiny of the assembled corvids should also reveal Rooks and Jackdaws among the numerous local Carrion Crows and Magpies. The sea aster on the lagoons and other vegetation holds large numbers of Linnets and Goldfinches in late summer and autumn, with many hundreds often present. Among other commoner finches and the occasional party of Bramblings in winter, the presence of a few Twite, usually around the edge of the lagoons or near the tip, makes this site particularly special as the only regular haunt of the species in London. Lapland Buntings have also been more regular here than anywhere else in the capital, occurring annually in recent years, and wandering Snow Buntings, though now very rare, have dropped in during several recent winters. Reed Buntings breed across the area in good numbers and form large flocks in winter, when Tree Sparrows might also be found and there can be sizeable gatherings of Yellowhammers and Corn Buntings. A hard-weather concentration of at least 600 of the latter in January 1987 was especially noteworthy.

Timing

A visit to Rainham at any time of year can prove productive, with passage waders more or less constantly present from March to October (fewer in midsummer) and larger numbers in winter of several species along with numerous wildfowl. The latter season also offers the best chance of raptors and even on quiet days the vast numbers of gulls on the tip will keep patient observers occupied for hours. Outside the summer months the Thames is likely to be one of the main focuses for your visit, so check tide times in advance and aim to be along the foreshore within two hours of high tide.

Rainham is heavily abused by the activities of trail-bikers, who can prove very frustrating if you are trying to birdwatch in the area. Machines are frequently ridden across the grassland at weekends, disturbing birds and reducing your chances of a good trip list. Falconers have also been a problem here, with unauthorised hunting of wildfowl creating a serious problem on occasions and forcing ducks to keep on the move over the lagoons and marshes. Subject to tide times, the earlier the better should be the motto for your visit, and avoid weekends if you can. Importantly, do not leave any valuables unattended in your car.

Access

Rainham Marshes is reached via the A13 from central London (leave the City heading east on Commercial Road), the A406 North Circular Road (turn east onto the A13 at the intersection south of Barking) or from the M25 onto the A13 westbound (leave the motorway at Junction 31). Turn

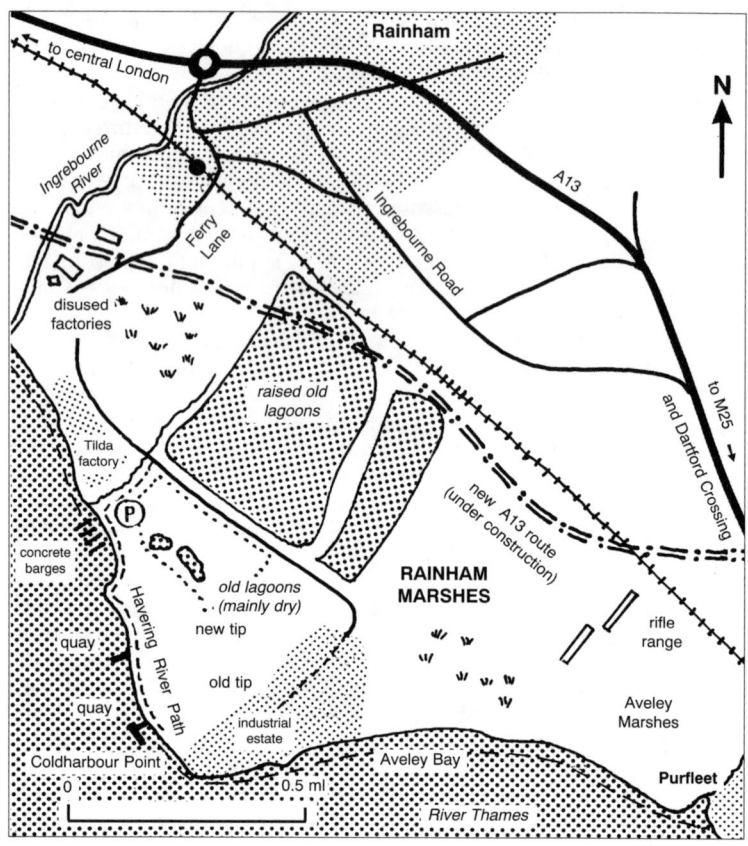

off the A13 south onto the B1335 into Rainham, and turn right after the station into Ferry Lane. Crossing the railway, the road skirts a container depot on the right and overlooks the marshes on the left; bear left along the edge of the marsh, slowing down to check for Black Redstarts (March to October) on the derelict factories on the right. A little further past the last factory (a working Tilda Rice site), park in the lay-by at the beginning of the first raised lagoons and walk southwest along the channel to view the river. The area around the derelict barges is the best for Water Pipits and can also produce waders.

From here, if time permits, you can follow the Havering River Path east along the shore of the Thames and over the dredging pipeline to scan the gulls and other species on the tip. There is a constant procession of gulls between the tip and the river where they bathe or gather on the barges. It is worth continuing this walk along to Coldharbour Point to scan the river for movements of terns and other species. Crossing back over the pipeline, either retrace your steps to return to the road via the barges or cross over the brow of the low hill which otherwise shields the lagoons from view. These are worth checking at all times of year.

Once back at the road, there are several footpaths leading up to the raised lagoons on the north side of the road from this point eastwards, all of which can be worth exploring; the further you venture from the road, the less disturbance (and hopefully more birds) there should be. Further along past the other end of the lagoons, park before the road bears right into a ramshackle industrial area and take the footpath east along the south side of the firing ranges to view the river, saltings and freshmarsh at Aveley Bay. En route pay constant attention to the ranges for hunting raptors and various other species. Check the ditches, small pools and scrub on your way out over the old, now vegetated, dump to the seawall, from where wildfowl, waders and gulls can be viewed. If the visibility is good scan across to the south side of the Thames to check the foreshore at Crayford Ness or the Darent river mouth.

By bus: numbers 165 and 287 run to Rainham from Romford and Barking respectively. *By train:* to Rainham overground station (from Liverpool Street/Fenchurch Street) via Barking. *By underground:* travel as far as Barking (District line), where you should change to the overground or bus number 287.

Calendar

All year: Shelduck, Gadwall, Teal, Mallard, Shoveler, Tufted Duck, Kestrel, Grey Partridge, Pheasant, Oystercatcher, Ringed Plover, Lapwing, Redshank, Stock Dove, Barn Owl, Kingfisher, Skylark, Meadow Pipit, Stonechat, Jackdaw, Rook, Reed Bunting, Corn Bunting.

Winter (November–February): Perhaps scarce grebe, diver or Shag on the Thames, outside chance of Brent Goose, Wigeon, other wildfowl including occasional Pintail, raptors including Sparrowhawk and possibly Hen Harrier, Peregrine or Merlin, chance of Grey Plover, Dunlin, Ruff, Snipe and occasional Jack Snipe, Green and Common Sandpipers, gulls including Mediterranean and an outside chance of Glaucous or Iceland, Short-eared Owl, Water and Rock Pipits, Fieldfare, Redwing, chance of Bearded Tit, Tree Sparrow, Brambling, small numbers of Twite most years, Lapland Bunting (rare), Yellowhammer.

Spring (March-May): Possibility of Garganey, Ringed and Little Ringed Plovers, Grey Plover, Dunlin, Ruff, chance of Bar-tailed Godwit, Curlew, Whimbrel and Spotted Redshank, Greenshank, Green and Common Sandpipers, possibility of other coastal species such as Turnstone, Sanderling or Knot, Little Gull, Common, occasionally Arctic, Black and perhaps other terns, hirundines, Rock Pipit (until end March), Water Pipit (occasionally until early April), Yellow Wagtail, Black Redstart, Whinchat, Wheatear, chance of Ring Ouzel, migrant warblers including occasional Grasshopper.

Summer (June–July): Occasional hunting Hobby, Ringed and Little Ringed Plovers, Yellow-legged Gull (from July), Yellow Wagtail, Black Redstart (most years), Sedge, Reed and occasionally Grasshopper Warblers, Whitethroat, Lesser Whitethroat.

Autumn (August–October): Possibility of Garganey, Ringed and Little Ringed Plovers, passage waders including Little Stint, Wood and Curlew Sandpipers, Yellow-legged Gull (especially August), perhaps Little Gull, Common, Arctic, Black and occasionally other terns, large numbers of hirundines (mainly late August–early September), Yellow Wagtail (until September), Whinchat, Wheatear, occasional Bearded Tit (from October).

Habitat

Overshadowed by the avian attractions of Rainham to the east and bordered by an equally unprepossessing landscape of industrial development, container storage, electricity infrastructure and housing estates, the marshes (now largely rough grazing) and foreshore at Barking face an uphill task in attracting visiting birders.

This is a pity, as the combination of muddy foreshore, patches of scrub and extensive rough grassland, in places very damp (there is significant standing surface water in winter), provides enough variety of habitat to produce an interesting range of passage, wintering and, in a few instances, breeding birds.

The grassland extends from not far south of the A13 right up to the river wall, though new housing development has begun to despoil the northern area. In places the dimpled landscape gives away its recent past as a dumping site, but grass and a few low bushes have now covered the rubble to form a terrain very attractive to Skylarks, Meadow Pipits, chats and Linnets. The northern area of grassland is more prone to flooding in winter, though despite some reedy dykes and muddy ditches few birds seem to favour this area. Instead, attention is best paid to the drier southern section near the tarmac footpath and the river wall, and the small area of hawthorns (for migrants) at the eastern end of the footpath.

The foreshore of Barking Bay offers extensive mud at low tide which attracts good numbers of wildfowl, waders and gulls. To the west, similar habitat can be found at the mouth of Barking Creek (actually the mouth of the River Roding). There is also a small nature reserve of woodland and scrub managed by the London Wildlife Trust just north and west of the electricity substation between the marshes and creek, though this too has been earmarked for development.

Species

Most ornithological interest in winter is confined to the Thames frontage, when wildfowl, waders, gulls and other species can be present in large numbers. Cormorants can be watched fishing out in the middle of the river or in small numbers perched on boats or waterside constructions, often sitting motionless with wings held open. Shelduck occur in good numbers, with sometimes more than 100 present in late autumn or winter, and in recent years a pair has bred. Teal is the other dominant duck in winter, with anything up to several hundred lining the foreshore or gathering around the mouth of Barking Creek. Mallard are common along the river frontage here, and a few Tufted Ducks may be found at the mouth of the creek, often feeding around the North Sewage Outfall just upstream. Sadly, Pintail are no longer regular. Other species of note are most likely after hard weather; these have included Common Scoter, Red-breasted Merganser and even Smew, while Red-necked and Slavonian Grebes have also been noted in such conditions. An April record of Garganey on the foreshore here is similarly exceptional.

Waders find the exposed mud of Barking Bay much to their liking, and in winter impressive flocks of Redshank and Dunlin may be present. The latter is dominant with counts often into three figures, whereas Redshanks typically peak at around 50. Lapwings prefer to gather on the mud at Creekmouth, where several hundred may be found packed tightly together among the gulls and other waders outside the breeding season; in summer a few remain on the marshes and may breed. Common Sandpipers favour the creek in spring and autumn and Ringed Plover and Oystercatcher are not unexpected in winter and on passage, when there is the chance of something more unusual – like the small summer-plumaged party of Bar-tailed Godwit, Knot, Turnstone and Sanderling which called in here late one May afternoon.

Good numbers of gulls gather on the foreshore here and at Creekmouth, though a scan across the river to Crossness may often reveal frustratingly larger numbers on the south side. All five commoner species are present in winter, though in late summer there is also a possibility of Yellow-legged Gull here with such large numbers just a short distance downstream at Rainham. October 1987 and its infamous 'hurricane' brought a heavy passage of Little Gulls west along the Thames here, peaking at 30 birds, but this must have been overshadowed by the spectacle of no fewer than 13 Sabine's Gulls gathering on the river. Less well known is Barking's claim to fame as host of the first British Mediterranean Gull back in 1868.

Terns are both less numerous and regular than at Rainham on passage, though Common, Arctic and even Black have been noted in autumn, typically feeding offshore or moving west upriver: 200 of this last species which did this during the major movement in southeast England of 6 September 1992 must have made a spectacular sight. The Woolwich Ferry crossing just upriver can also provide views of terns mid-river.

Landbird interest is overshadowed by the attractions of the river, but the extensive area of grassland does have its advantages. Grey Partridges can still be found here, though they require some searching, and coveys of as many as 16 birds have been found in recent autumns. The short, rough turf is ideal for Skylarks; singing birds are never out of earshot here in the breeding season or on mild winter days, and at the latter time of year small parties seem particularly conspicuous. Meadow Pipits and especially Linnets occur in even bigger flocks outside the breeding season; both species breed. A Water Pipit was found among a party of Meadows near the foreshore in February 1995, and it is possible that this species and Rock Pipit are more regular than records suggest along the river here.

In spring and autumn Yellow Wagtails may be expected, and the site can also attract Wheatears and Whinchats in some numbers; the latter species may occasionally breed. Stonechat has also been recorded throughout the year, though is perhaps most likely in winter when Fieldfare and possibly Redwing may be present in small numbers. The derelict factories west of the grassland look ideal for Black Redstarts, which have bred at nearby Beckton. There has, however, been a dearth of records of Ring Ouzels on passage in what would seem to be very suitable habitat. Most of the commoner warblers may be expected on passage, though the lack of cover other than a few reedy channels and rudimentary scrub means breeding numbers on the marshes are small. They instead prefer the LWT reserve area around the power station, where Whitethroats can be especially numerous. In summer 1996 a pair of Marsh Warblers raised young in the area – the first confirmed breeding record in London for some years, while autumn of the same year brought a rare Barred Warbler.

The line-up is otherwise completed by raucous scavenging parties of Carrion Crows and Magpies and hunting Kestrels, though Merlin and Peregrine have also been logged over the marshes. Occasional parties of Stock Doves, which presumably flight in to feed from outside this treeless area, are present in winter at least; as you leave the site, look out for Collared Doves on the roofs of the factories or houses on the adjoining estates.

Timing

A visit in passage periods will bring the greatest range of species and the most likely chance of something unusual, be it waders on the river or chats and other migrants in the grassy scrub. Winter has more impressive numbers of wildfowl and waders but less variety, while in summer the visitor can expect little except commoner breeding species.

Weekends are subject to most disturbance from other users of the site, so early mornings and weekdays are likely to be quietest. However, this may not be much of a choice as you really need to combine a visit with a rising tide; check the tide times and aim to arrive about two hours before high tide. Allow a minimum of one-two hours for a visit to the marshes, and at least another half an hour if you want to take in Creekmouth as well. Bear in mind also that the south-facing view of the foreshore from the riverbank at Barking means you can be looking straight into the sun.

Access

Turn off the A13 two miles (3.2 km) west of Dagenham south onto Renwick Road (three light grey and red tower blocks on the north side of the A13 provide a good landmark for the unfamiliar visitor). After almost a mile (1.6 km) Renwick Road bears to the right at Barking National Grid substation and becomes River Road. Park in the lay-by opposite the power station entrance and cross the red metal stile to walk east to explore the grassland area and scrub or south to the foreshore. For the LWT reserve area, cross the road and head west over the green stile along the south side of the substation; there is another entrance further north along Renwick Road.

Having worked this area to your satisfaction, from the lay-by continue west along River Road round to just past the Crooked Billet public house. Here a public footpath on the left will take you to the river wall overlooking the mouth of Barking Creek. It is easy to miss the gate, so look out for the 'National Rivers Authority emergency vehicle entrance' sign. Take care when looking over the river wall, as birds on the creek flush easily.

Thames Water's Beckton Creek Trail runs along the west side of Barking Creek, and there is a hide within the Thames Water site overlooking the river. Unfortunately it's not possible to cross the creek from the east side to get to this area: the only access is via the Thames Water site entrance in Jenkins Lane (weekday office hours only), off the A13 just east of its intersection with the A406 North Circular Road. There is a logbook in the hide giving details of recent sightings. There are car parking facilities, including a special car park for the disabled.

By bus: during peak hours from Monday to Friday number 387 runs beyond Barking town centre to Creekmouth and continues along River Road and Renwick Road for the marshes, while route 369 stops slightly further north on the Thames View Estate. *By underground:* from Barking station (District line) one of the above bus routes is necessary to reach the Thames birding areas. *By train:* overground services run to Barking from central London and from north London on the suburban Gospel Oak line.

Calendar

All year: Shelduck, Grey Partridge, Lapwing, Skylark, Meadow Pipit, Linnet.

Winter (November–March): Cormorant, Teal and other wildfowl, Redshank, Dunlin, gulls, Stock Dove, Grey Wagtail (along the creek), winter thrushes.

Spring (April–May): Passage waders, Yellow Wagtail, Whinchat, Wheatear, commoner warblers and other migrants.

Summer (June–July): Occasional Whinchat and Stonechat, Reed Warbler, Sedge Warbler, Whitethroat, Lesser Whitethroat, Willow Warbler.

Autumn (August–October): Wildfowl numbers start building, passage waders, terns, Whinchat, Wheatear and other migrants.

OTHER SITES IN THE AREA

12A DOCKLANDS   OS ref: TQ 3680–4480

Stretching from the west side of Barking Creek for five miles (8 km) along the Thames towards the City, the Docklands area features a contrasting landscape of skyscrapers and business parks, industrial zones, a small airport, deep water docks and a 'city farm' at Mudchute on the Isle of Dogs – at first sight not the mix of sites and habitats that would prove attractive to many species. The area is liberally broken up by tracts of wasteland and rubble ignored by developers, and it is in selected corners of this urban rocky habitat that one of London's true specialities may occasionally still be found: the Black Redstart.

Between Beckton in the east and Wapping in the west, right on the fringe of the City by Tower Bridge, a handful of Black Redstarts still appear each year. On quiet spring mornings (Sundays are best, when there is least disturbance from traffic, construction work and the public) listen out for this delightful visitor singing its short and simple rattling song from suitable perches near waste ground, preferably with a little vegetation in the vicinity. Unfortunately numbers are tiny and even then not all are breeding birds, with unmated males moving on to leave just one or two pairs in most years. Reliable areas have included Beckton, Silvertown, Leamouth, Limehouse Basin and Wapping, but birds sometimes shift location from one year to the next – probably due to site development and the rapid growth of vegetation such as buddleia on waste ground.

There have been few other avian attractions here since the highly productive Surrey Docks site on the south side of the river at Rotherhithe was redeveloped in the late 1970s, but this stretch of the Thames is worth checking for gulls (including regular Yellow-legged) outside the breeding season and perhaps the occasional tern on passage. Common Terns regularly occur as far upriver as Limehouse Basin (TQ 392808) where they have shown interest in newly-created breeding habitat in one of the old dock basins near Leamouth, and Shelduck may be present in summer, though other interesting wildfowl are scarce except perhaps during cold spells. Groups of Great Crested Grebes are sometimes noted on the deeper basins of the Royal Victoria and Royal Albert Docks. Parties of Linnets forage among some of the more weedy areas and Grey Wagtails are sometimes noted around basins and watercourses: both species may breed in the area.

The general area is well signposted south of the A13 east of the City, but use an *A–Z London Street Atlas* to find your way through to vantage points which overlook the river. For Black Redstarts, simply try working any suitable-looking habitat in spring.

By bus: this large area is well served by bus routes, including numbers D11 and 277 to Leamouth, 173, 262 and 276 to the Beckton area, D1, D5, D6, D8 and D9 to the Isle of Dogs, and P14 which runs from Rotherhithe on the south side of the river through Limehouse to the Isle of Dogs. *By docklands light railway:* this service connects with and replaces the underground system in this area, with stations close to the river including Island Gardens at the southernmost point of the Isle of Dogs. Other overground services stop at Canning Town (just northeast of Leamouth) and Custom House (near Royal Victoria Dock).

13 GREENWICH AREA
OS ref: TQ 390775

Habitats, species and access

Abutting the southern shore of the Thames opposite the Isle of Dogs is the popular tourist spot of Greenwich, famous for its Royal Observatory, National Maritime Museum and the *Cutty Sark*. Less well known is the Royal Park which houses the first two of these crowd-pulling attractions. Few, if any, birders currently cover this area systematically and very little is known of its present-day avifauna, though within the last 25 years interesting sightings from the area were still appearing in the *Bird Life of the Royal Parks* annual report (now no longer published). Records then included breeding Tufted Duck, Pochard, Tawny and Little Owls, Lesser Spotted Woodpecker, Nuthatch, Treecreeper, Jackdaw and Tree Sparrow and passage Wigeon, Water Rail, Oystercatcher, Woodcock, Common Tern, Turtle Dove, Cuckoo, Wheatear, Stonechat, Whinchat, Redstart and Crossbill, with Redwing, Fieldfare, Siskin and Brambling in winter. Clearly the status of some of these species will have changed, and the site without doubt deserves some renewed attention: the area known as The Wilderness, in the southeast corner of the park, offers the most cover and arguably the least disturbance.

Reports from the river frontage at Greenwich are rare indeed and this area is clearly poorly covered, but occasional movements of Common Terns and the relative proximity of Barking and Thamesmead downstream suggest that regular observations may produce more records of note.

The southern end of Greenwich Park adjoins the high ground of Blackheath, a wide open area of grass but with very little else in the way of habitat. The only likely ornithological interest here is the gathering of gulls in winter which has included Mediterranean, though early morning visits in spring and autumn have produced the odd Wheatear and other infrequent migrants. Hobbies have been seen on several occasions in summer. Greenwich lies just north of the main London–Kent A2 road immediately west of the A102(M) Blackwall Tunnel southern approach. The park can be accessed from various points, with the entrances to the best birding area of The Wilderness being in Charlton Way SE3 and Maze Hill SE3, just north of the A2 Shooters Hill at Blackheath.

By bus: numbers 89 (from Bexley and Lewisham) and 108 (from Stratford and Poplar on the north side of the Thames) stop closest to the Shooters Hill end of the park, and various other routes serve the centre of Greenwich closer to the river. By train: services from central London stop at Greenwich and Blackheath stations. There is no local underground service.

14 THAMESMEAD

OS ref: TQ 474811

Habitat

Glance through the London Bird Reports of 25 years ago or more and you will be hard put to find the name Thamesmead anywhere. Instead, frequent references to impressive wildfowl and wader counts along the Thames between Woolwich in the west and Erith in the east, especially at sites such as Woolwich Bay, Plumstead Marshes and Crossness, provide a better clue to the ornithological history of this area. Although years of abuse of the inner Thames resulted in heavily polluted waters with little wildlife for many years, the programme to clean it up in the 1960s brought spectacular results with huge flocks of wildfowl becoming a feature of the area by the turn of the decade.

Sadly, this success was not consolidated and the drainage and infilling of Woolwich Bay, which still lies undeveloped to this day, was one of several projects which blighted the area's ornithological importance. The construction of vast 'new town' housing estates across what was once the marshland home to breeding waders further degraded this important habitat, and even as recently as 1973 an extensive reedbed with a huge Reed Warbler colony was destroyed to make way for a wildlife-unfriendly boating lake.

Today, despite the widespread development of much of the area, what is now collectively known as Thamesmead retains at least some of its attraction for birds. The Thames frontage, especially the tidal mud at Crossness, remains important for reasonable numbers of wintering wildfowl, waders and gulls, while some remnant grazing marsh at Erith continues to prove attractive to species such as Meadow Pipit and Stonechat. In amongst the dual carriageways and housing developments, artificial lakes provide habitat for a few commoner waterbirds including Great Crested and Little Grebes, while the patches of scrub and woodland, in some places quite extensive, are home to a variety of commoner breeding species.

The area attracts little attention from birders outside the immediate area, which is surprising given that more than 170 species have been logged here in recent times.

Species

The Thames is unsurprisingly the single biggest avian attraction in the area, especially in winter when the foreshore can be teeming with thousands of birds. The river also acts as a fly-way and suitable weather (any wind with an easterly component) often produces shorebirds, terns and Little Gull in spring and especially autumn.

The dominant wildfowl are Shelduck and Teal, which may number more than 100 each, and very occasionally even as many 200 may be present; though these numbers are impressive for the London area, they are a far cry from the early 1970s when these species peaked at 1,600 and 1,720 respectively. In those days large numbers of Pintail, Mallard, Pochard and Tufted Duck were also recorded, but now only the latter three species are regular and in much reduced numbers. Mallard can be found throughout the area, while Tufted Duck commute between the river and lakes, mainly Thamesmere West where other duck can include Wigeon, Shoveler, Gadwall, Goldeneye and Scaup, especially in cold weather. Red-breasted Merganser and Common Scoter have occurred on the Thames itself. As with wildfowl everywhere, hard weather tends to swell numbers and increase the prospect of finding something unusual.

Between them the river and lakes attract a fair selection of other waterbirds, with Cormorants particularly conspicuous in winter and Grey Heron, Mute Swan and Canada and Greylag Geese resident in the area. A handful of pairs of Great Crested and Little Grebes breed, but with visits by the rarer grebes and divers almost unknown here the most likely other waterfowl are the ubiquitous Moorhen and Coot, the latter being particularly numerous in winter when one or two Water Rails may also frequent the margins of Thamesmere West and East lakes.

Outside the summer months the Thames foreshore is productive for waders. Dunlin is the most numerous species, with perhaps 100–200 present from late autumn through to spring and numbers increasing in colder weather. Look out for small groups of 'stop-starting' Ringed Plover running amongst them on the mud, and bigger gatherings of Lapwing and Redshank. Ruff and Common Sandpiper are the most likely other waders in winter along the river, with one or two of each reported every year here, while a few Snipe and Green Sandpiper occur in Halfway Reach Bay. Small concentrations of Jack Snipe are regular in winter but the best area for this species is unfortunately on private land. Passage seasons bring other shorebirds and the chance of more interesting species dropping in: Greenshank is regular and Grey Plover, Curlew, Whimbrel and Bar-tailed Godwit occasional. Little Ringed Plovers may occur from late March but no longer breed due to habitat redevelopment. A pair of Oystercatchers is usually present in the summer at Crossness. Other species are rare stragglers, but have included Avocet, Black-tailed Godwit, Temminck's Stint and Curlew Sandpiper as well as wandering coastal species such as Knot, Sanderling and Turnstone. Remarkably, a Wood Sandpiper wintered at Thamesmere West in early 1990.

Large numbers of Black-headed Gulls gather on the muddy foreshore in winter, along with Common, Herring and both black-backs in smaller numbers. Records of Mediterranean Gull have increased recently but Yellow-legged is relatively scarce this far upriver. Little Gull occurs most years on passage, though a remarkable 50 birds were watched moving upriver after the severe weather of October 1987. The only regular tern is Common, one pair of which bred for the first time in 1994 (at Thamesmere West); this species can also be seen over the Thames in spring and especially autumn, when up to 60 birds have been counted, and Arctic, Little, Sandwich and Black have also been found at this time. Any other activity on the river is likely to be confined to storm-driven seabirds, with Gannet, Leach's Storm-petrel, Shag, Arctic Skua and even Puffin all making unexpected appearances here.

Herring, Yellow-legged and Lesser Black-backed Gulls

Having made the river your first port of call and then checked the lakes, it is well worth spending at least some time birding the scrub or working the grazing marsh at Belvedere and Erith. Pheasant is resident in small numbers and in summer the local Stock and Collared Doves are joined by Turtle Dove and Cuckoo, both of which breed here. Owls of any description are erratic and most likely to include rare appearances of wandering Barn and Short-eared; visiting birders should instead expect to see predators in the form of resident Kestrel and Sparrowhawk. Hobbies have made sporadic autumn sorties over the marshes, while even rarer fly-bys have been performed by Peregrine, Osprey and Red Kite.

The community of breeding passerines on the grazing marshes and wasteland includes Skylark, Meadow Pipit and until recently Yellow Wagtail, though the latter is now confined to passage migrant status. Rock and Water Pipits are found in winter or on migration in late autumn and early spring, when Wheatear, Whinchat (especially autumn, best looked for at Erith Marshes) and the very occasional Ring Ouzel also occur. Stonechats have bred intermittently but are most likely in winter, and Black Redstarts have also nested at industrial sites in the area.

The line-up of breeding warblers is headed by Whitethroat and Willow Warbler, with a few pairs of Reed and Sedge in suitable waterside habitat and smaller numbers of Lesser Whitethroat and Blackcap in the scrub. Chiffchaff has bred and is occasionally found in winter, though the most noteworthy representative of this family to occur at this time of year was the male Dartford Warbler which frequented scrub at Crossness for three months in 1989–90. Other rare wanderers in recent years have included Firecrest, Pied Flycatcher, Nightingale, Bearded Tit and Woodlark.

The more wooded areas hold little except commoner breeding species such as Great, Blue and Long-tailed Tits and Great Spotted Woodpecker, but waste ground, marshes and other open habitat can prove attractive to finches. Linnets and Goldfinches often feed in large numbers on seed-heads in autumn and winter, and both Greenfinch and Chaffinch are common. Siskin, Redpoll and even Brambling are a possibility in winter, but the only buntings likely here are the resident Reeds. Corn Bunting and Yellowhammer both formerly bred but are now erratic winter visitors; far rarer still are Snow and Lapland Buntings, comprising one and two late autumn records respectively.

Timing

For the most impressive numbers of wildfowl, waders and gulls, time your visit for the late autumn and winter months: remember to check the Thames tide times before setting out. Two to three hours within high tide should leave enough mud exposed to make feeding conditions on this shore of the river at their most attractive, but there is a fair degree of commuting by birds between here and Barking on the north bank; make sure you take a telescope. Spring, especially May, and autumn, notably August–September, are good times to stroll along Riverside Walk or visit Crossness for passage shorebirds, terns and gulls; in the right weather conditions (easterly or southeasterly winds) passage times can also produce commoner passerine migrants such as Yellow Wagtail, chats and warblers.

Notwithstanding the birds, the main advantage of checking the Thames foreshore from this side of the river is that the light is better; if viewing the mud at Crossness, any glare from the sun will be behind you for much of the day. Disturbance is not so great a problem here as it is at many Thames-side sites, but the lakes in the residential areas can be very popular, especially during summer and at weekends. However, the Thamesmeres are free of all activities except fishing, and Thamesmere West is always worth at least a quick look.

Access

To reach the area from central London, take the A2 as far as Deptford, then follow signs for Greenwich and Woolwich. Leave Woolwich east-wards on the A206, turning left just before Plumstead onto the A2016 along Pettman Crescent and then onto Western Way. The area immediately left (west) of the road here is Thamesmead West.

Continue on the A2016 eastwards to Thamesmead, turning left at the main roundabout onto the A2041 Central Way to Thamesmead Central. Riverside Walk is accessible from Central Way: walk north 150 metres east of the east car park at the Safeway supermarket in the town centre. Once at the riverside, walk west to view Thamesmere East and West and the river itself. Back at Central Way, continue onwards northeast to Thamesmead North. Leave Central Way at the roundabout at its junction with Carlyle Road onto Crossway, following this road through one roundabout and turning left at a second onto Summerton Way. Go straight over the mini-roundabout, through an iron gateway marked 'RGC' and head towards the golf club, bearing left just before the club house onto the river bank at

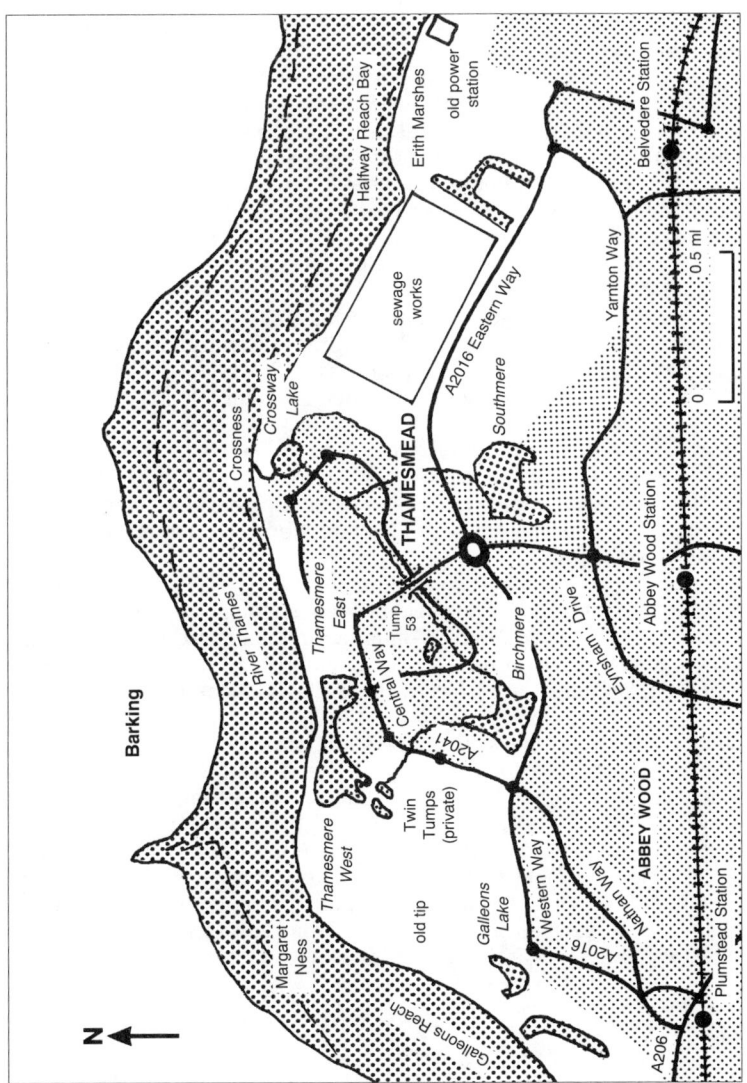

Crossness. Check the foreshore thoroughly between here and the sewage works to the east; there is no public access to the latter site, though some of it can be checked from the bank.

Leave the Crossness area back along Summerton Way, turning left at the first proper roundabout onto Crossway, and left again onto Carlyle Road to get back onto the A2016, which is here known as Eastern Way. This dual carriageway takes you east along the southern edge of the sewage works to Thamesmead East; Erith Marshes lie on the south and northeast sides of the A2016 and can be explored to a limited extent from the track marked on maps as Crossness footpath (south side) or from the public footpath leading west from Norman Road (northeast side). Various other roads, most leading to or between industrial sites, can be accessed from roundabouts at the eastern end of the A2016; some of these roads give reasonable views over the grazing marshes.

This is a deceptively large area and your Ordnance Survey map and *A–Z London Street Atlas* will prove particularly useful if you want to make your outing more than just a brief visit. Three to four hours can easily be spent birding productively here at the right times of year.

By bus: a good number of buses serve the area, including routes 178, 244, 272, 401, 472 and X53. Several of these connect with the nearest train stations at Plumstead, Abbey Wood and Belvedere, all of which lie some distance to the south of the best birding areas.

Calendar

All year: Great Crested Grebe, Little Grebe, Cormorant, Grey Heron, Shelduck, Sparrowhawk, Kestrel, Pheasant, Stock Dove, Great Spotted Woodpecker, Skylark, Meadow Pipit, Reed Bunting.

Winter (November–February): Little Grebe, Gadwall, Teal, Shoveler, Tufted Duck, Pochard, occasional Water Rail, Ringed Plover, Lapwing, Dunlin, Ruff, Snipe, Green and Common Sandpipers, Grey Wagtail, Rock and/or Water Pipits, Stonechat, Fieldfare, Redwing, perhaps Chiffchaff, Siskin, Redpoll.

Spring (March–May): Little Grebe, Oystercatcher, Ringed Plover, Lapwing, Dunlin, Greenshank, Common Sandpiper, wader oddities, Little Gull, Common Tern, Turtle Dove, Cuckoo, hirundines, Rock and/or Water Pipits (March only), Yellow Wagtail, Wheatear, migrant warblers.

Summer (June–July): Oystercatcher, Turtle Dove, Cuckoo, Swift, Swallow, House Martin, occasional Stonechat, Reed Warbler, Sedge Warbler, Blackcap, Whitethroat, Lesser Whitethroat, Willow Warbler.

Autumn (August–October): Occasional Hobby, Oystercatcher, Ringed Plover, Lapwing, Dunlin, Ruff, Greenshank, Common Sandpiper, wader oddities, Little Gull, Common and perhaps other terns, hirundines, chance of Rock and/or Water Pipits (from late October), Whinchat, Wheatear, migrant warblers and oddities.

15 DARTFORD MARSHES   OS ref: TQ 544774

Habitat

On the south side of the Thames opposite Purfleet and immediately west of the M25 at the Dartford suspension bridge, an obvious landmark for visitors to the area, this stretch of open country marks the end of continuous urban spread from southeast London and the start of the Kent countryside.

Although parts of the area still become waterlogged in winter, and some of the birds are reminiscent of the avifauna of the North Kent Marshes farther east along the Thames estuary, the area is essentially farmland with scattered stands of trees and scrub. Ploughed fields and rough pasture are interspersed with hedgerows, occasional reedy dykes and patches of hawthorns, and there is a pig farm which proves attractive to large numbers of feeding gulls, corvids and other species. The Darent river, which flows into the Thames at Dartford, marks the western boundary of the site and forms a natural division from Crayford Marshes to the west.

Despite the quite extensive areas of arable land, the destructive impact of a variety of developments on this area has been significant. In the centre of the marshes lies Joyce Green Hospital, the leafy grounds of which offer some of the most verdant habitat in the area, while the eastern boundary is dominated by the huge superstructure of Littlebrook Power Station. The latter is fringed on the west side by a series of enclosed reedy settling pools at the Long Reach Sewage Works, and to the south by two much larger gravel pits which attract wildfowl and other species in winter. A disused fireworks factory and war-time concrete munitions bunkers, several complexes of farm buildings, a clay pigeon shoot, motorcycle scrambling track and radio-controlled model aircraft site illustrate the many other human pressures on this site, which has further been blighted by the construction of the dual carriageway A206 Dartford by-pass to the south of the hospital, linking into the M25 river crossing. Nevertheless, the marshes still manage to remain a strategically important habitat for an interesting range of species.

Species

With so much of the marshland now drained, the focus for wildfowl, waders and other waterbirds is concentrated largely on the Thames foreshore and the gravel pit at Littlebrook. Geese of any species are infrequent here, but Dartford must be one of the few sites in the London area where in winter Brent is as likely as Canada or Greylag. Shelduck can be expected along the Thames throughout the year, with one or two pairs occasionally breeding but higher numbers in winter when parties of Teal, Gadwall and Wigeon might also be found around the mouth of the Darent. In contrast, Shoveler and Mallard are more frequent at Littlebrook GP, with the latter species also breeding in small numbers in some of the ditches. Diving duck are also most likely on the gravel pits and typically comprise small numbers of Tufted Duck and Pochard, though the occasional Goldeneye and even Scaup, Smew, Red-breasted Merganser and Goosander have been noted. Other species such as wandering divers and grebes are unlikely with only a handful of records in recent years, either on the pits or the Thames.

Outside the summer months, when waders are restricted to a few pairs of Lapwing, Ringed Plover, Redshank and, rarely, Oystercatcher, shorebirds can occur in some numbers along the Thames foreshore. In winter the dominant species is Dunlin, with counts into the thousands not unknown, followed by upwards of 100 Redshank. Perhaps 50 or so Ringed Plovers are often joined by a few Grey Plovers and Oystercatchers, while flocks of Lapwings may be present either along the foreshore or out on the fields. In March 1985 one such flock was found to contain a summer-plumaged adult Sociable Plover, a most unexpected find of this major British rarity. Other rare waders here have included Pectoral Sandpiper, Avocet and Grey Phalarope, but more likely are occasional wandering coastal species on spring or autumn migration such as Sanderling, Turnstone, Knot and Bar-tailed Godwit. Greenshank are regular in spring and autumn as are Ruff and the occasional Curlew in winter, when there has been a handful of records of Spotted Redshank. Common Sandpipers are also numerous on passage, either on the foreshore or along the Darent when low tide exposes suitable mud for feeding, and Green Sandpipers are periodically flushed from drainage ditches on the marshes outside the midsummer months. Since most of the freshmarsh was drained and developed, however, there have been far fewer significant gatherings of Snipe and Jack Snipe: despite the record count of 1,000 of the former species here in January 1987, numbers now rarely make double figures, and sightings of Jack Snipe are today decidedly sporadic.

Gulls are represented by varying numbers of the five commoner species, with Yellow-legged perhaps the next most likely to be encountered, typically in late summer and autumn either along the Thames or at Littlebrook GP which birds sometimes use as a bathing site. Mediterranean Gulls have become increasingly regular in very small numbers here since the mid-1980s, and in winter 1994/95 up to seven different birds were observed among the gull flocks feeding at the pig farm. Glaucous Gull remains a very scarce visitor but Little Gulls are occasionally seen in small numbers, mainly in autumn, at the power station outflow. After the storms in October 1987 up to 15 were present here, along with a juvenile Sabine's Gull.

Little Gulls and Black Terns

The attractive feeding conditions the outflow creates also draw regular gatherings of terns; Common is typically the most numerous but both Arctic and Black are regular, with numbers of all three higher in autumn. Look out for other species wandering upriver from the estuary: these have included Sandwich and Little and once even a White-winged Black, though the Bridled Tern watched a short distance downriver at West Thurrock and Swanscombe on 2 June 1991 just failed to cross under the Dartford bridge and make it onto the site list.

In contrast, skuas rarely enter the Thames this far upstream, and there have been just a few records of Arctics, three of Pomarine and two of Great. The best chance is perhaps after severe weather in autumn, when the river has also been paid brief visits by both Leach's and European Storm-petrels.

There are plenty of other species to recommend the marshes away from the attractions of the river. This is one of the few sites in the London area where Hen Harriers have appeared regularly, and though very rare in recent years there is still a chance of either this species or a marauding Merlin or Peregrine in winter; in recent years this latter falcon has taken to roosting on Littlebrook Power Station. Sparrowhawk and Kestrel are resident in the area and Hobbies are occasionally seen on passage; other raptors are rare but have included Marsh Harrier in at least three recent years and Montagu's Harrier twice. Predators are also represented by Long-eared and Short-eared Owls, both of which are recorded annually; this last species is the most likely to be encountered, with up to three individuals present most winters. Barn and Little Owls bred in the area until relatively recently but are now apparently absent, while Tawny Owl is a scarce visitor encountered chiefly in the grounds of the hospital.

The arable land contains good numbers of Pheasants and a few Grey Partridges. In winter several hundred Woodpigeons and impressive numbers of Stock Doves (over 100 have been seen together) are possible in mixed flocks on the farmland or around the food-rich slurry of the pig farm. Collared Doves are also numerous and in summer a few breeding pairs of Turtle Doves are present in the more wooded areas, which might also produce a 'Great Spot', the only locally resident woodpecker.

Out on the fields there are good numbers of breeding Skylarks which form large flocks in the winter months. Gatherings into three figures are not unusual, and exceptionally 1,000 have been present in one flock. Look out for smaller numbers of resident Meadow Pipits, and perhaps even a Rock Pipit or two along the muddier edges of the Thames and Darent in winter. However, Water Pipit remains very rare here despite the regular occurrence of small flocks in winter across the river at Rainham. Aside from a few pairs of Pieds around the sewage works, wagtails are largely a feature of spring and autumn, when both Pied and Yellow move through in small numbers throughout the area; look out for the occasional Blue-headed or White Wagtail among them, especially in spring.

Equally obvious on migration are chats which find the open habitat here ideal. Wheatears are regular from March to early May and from August to October, sometimes in distinct falls of up to 20 birds and at least twice including individuals of the larger, brighter Greenland race *leucorhoa* in spring. At least one pair of Stonechats still nests and the species can be seen throughout the year here, especially around the rough ground behind the Thames river wall. Whinchats no longer breed but can be very numerous on passage, the rougher areas of pasture and weedy fields providing perfect habitat in autumn when as many as 10 or more may be present for extended periods. The power station hosts nesting Black Redstart. Ring Ouzels have been noted on several occasions in late April, but more likely are passage and wintering flocks of Redwings and Fieldfares.

In spring and summer the reedy ditches and marshy vegetation contain breeding Sedge and, especially, Reed Warblers. Whitethroat, Lesser Whitethroat and Blackcap are all common and one or two pairs of Garden Warblers are present around Littlebrook most years. Willow Warblers can be found in suitable habitat in summer and a few pairs of Chiffchaffs are usually present in the more wooded areas, with a few birds sometimes being noted in winter. Wood Warbler, Firecrest, Redstart and Pied Flycatcher are scarce passage migrants, and following a decline which has affected many other sites in the capital, Spotted Flycatcher is now also restricted to the status of migrant.

The few small reedbeds in the area have played host to parties of Bearded Tits on several occasions in late autumn and winter, though their appearances are far from predictable. The 'true' tits are better represented, with Blue, Great and Long-tailed breeding and Coal Tit occasionally being recorded.

The area has always proved attractive to corvids, with extensive rubbish dumping, landfill and pig-farming activities providing numerous scavenging opportunities. Magpies have increased significantly in the area and, according to a recent paper on Dartford's birds, counts of up to 60 are now not exceptional. Carrion Crows are also very common, and with smaller numbers of Rooks and Jackdaws often present, especially around the piggery, this is one of the few London sites that might give you four species of crow in one binocular view.

Finches gather in even greater numbers in autumn and winter, when Linnets, Greenfinches and Goldfinches can be found in single-species or mixed flocks throughout the area, often feeding busily on seed-heads or rising and falling in twittering groups over the marshes. Resident Chaffinches are joined by Continental birds and perhaps even a few Bramblings in winter, when they may flock in ploughed fields in loose association with Skylarks and Reed Buntings. One or two Lapland Buntings have been discovered at this time, though more typical are small parties of Corn Buntings and a few Yellowhammers; several pairs of both still breed in the area.

The ornithological attractions of this site are underlined, as always, by the possibility of finding something a little out of the ordinary, and over the years Dartford Marshes has accrued a longer list of rare visitors than most other hot-spots in the capital – in no small part due to the dedicated regular coverage of the area by a handful of local observers. A site list of around 190 species in recent times offers more than enough inspiration in the form of Purple Heron, Puffin, Hoopoe, Wryneck, Richard's Pipit and Woodchat and Great Grey Shrikes among the line-up of more regular species.

Timing

The range of resident, passage and wintering species is enough to make a visit at any time of year productive, though with much of the emphasis on waders, wildfowl and migrants the months of August to May are likely to be best. Make sure you check the tide times before your visit, and aim to arrive at the river wall about two hours before high tide.

If at all possible avoid visiting the area at weekends, when most disturbance takes place. The combination of shooting, scrambling and plane-flying means that, although you can easily find quieter corners of the area to work, birds are likely to have been disturbed and will either be flighty or may have even left the area. All these activities have been known to take place on weekdays too and throughout the year, so even with the best of planning there is no easy answer to avoiding disturbance here.

Access

From the north, take the M25 south over the Dartford Crossing above the Thames and exit immediately left after the toll booths (£1 for cars). Follow signs for Erith, turning left at the first roundabout and straight over the second onto the A206 University Way. Turn off right (north) at the first roundabout along this road towards Long Reach Works. There are several lay-bys along this road where you can park and from where you should be able to access the west side of Littlebrook GP. From here continue north towards the Thames, after a third of a mile (0.5 km) reaching the works; turn right in front of the site entrance down a rough (but reasonable) track to the

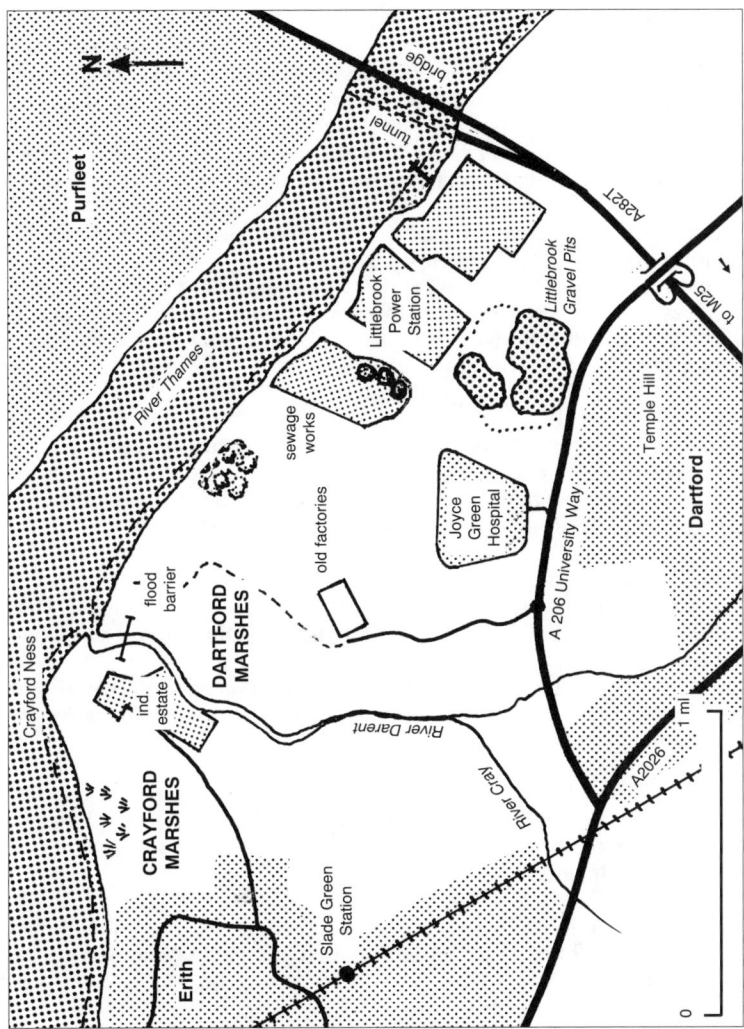

back of the power station, checking the ditches, marshy pools and scrub as you go. Park at the end of this track and look over the river wall to check the foreshore and, especially in spring and autumn, the power station out-flow 'patch' on the Thames.

There is no vehicular access from the Littlebrook side to the rest of the marsh, so return to the A206 and turn right (west), leaving the by-pass again to follow signs for Joyce Green Hospital. Turn left in front of the hos-pital and continue along this road, checking the fields and hedgerows as you go. After about three-quarters of a mile (1.2 km), past the scrambling track and just beyond the entrance to the disued fireworks factory on the right, park up and check the area around the pig farm for gulls and other species. Then proceed down this track for another mile (1.6 km) or so until you reach the river wall, checking fields along the way for finches and buntings in winter and migrants in spring and autumn. Park by the river wall, scan the foreshore and walk left towards the mouth of the Darent, ensuring that you do not flush any roosting waders and wildfowl. This track can become extremely muddy, if not impassable, in wet conditions, in which case drive as far down it as possible, park and do the rest of the area on foot.

If you are travelling to Dartford Marshes from central London, follow signs for A2/M2 Dover which will eventually bring you onto the A2 Rochester Way. Turn off onto the A2018 at Dartford Heath towards Dartford, and from the north side of the one-way system in the town centre follow signs for Joyce Green Hospital.

By bus: numbers 476 and 477 run to Joyce Green Hospital; many other services serve the Dartford area. *By train:* Dartford station (frequent services from London Bridge) is about a mile (1.6 km) walk from Joyce Green Hospital via the Temple Hill estate.

Calendar

Resident: Shelduck, Mallard, Sparrowhawk, Kestrel, Pheasant, Grey Partridge, Oystercatcher, Ringed Plover, Lapwing, Redshank, Stock Dove, Great Spotted Woodpecker, Skylark, Meadow Pipit, Stonechat, Long-tailed Tit, Linnet, Reed and Corn Buntings, Yellowhammer.

Winter (November–February): Wigeon, Gadwall, Teal, Shoveler, reasonable chance of Peregrine and possibly other scarce raptors such as Hen Harrier or Merlin, occasional Water Rail, large Dunlin flocks on the foreshore and other waders including regular Grey Plover and Ruff, good numbers of gulls including occasional Mediterranean, Long-eared and Short-eared Owls, Rock Pipit, Fieldfare, Redwing, Chiffchaff, Jackdaw, occasional Bramblings in the finch flocks.

Spring (March–mid-May): Hobby, Common Sandpiper, Greenshank and other waders on the foreshore, Common Tern, Cuckoo, Yellow Wagtail, Wheatear, Whinchat, outside chance of Ring Ouzel, migrant warblers, Spotted Flycatcher.

Summer (late May–July): Turtle Dove, Reed and Sedge Warblers, Whitethroat, Lesser Whitethroat, Garden Warbler, Blackcap, Willow Warbler, Chiffchaff.

Autumn (August–October): Hobby, Common Sandpiper, Greenshank and other passage waders, Yellow-legged and Little Gulls, Common, Arctic and Black Terns (power station outflow), Yellow Wagtail, Wheatear, Whinchat, outside chance of Bearded Tit (from October).

OTHER SITES IN THE AREA

15A CRAYFORD MARSHES

OS ref: TQ 532775
Map p. 87

To the west of Dartford Marshes on the other side of the River Darent, Crayford Marshes is a similar landscape of arable land and rough pasture divided by reedy dykes and occasional hedgerows and taller trees. Its boundaries are demarcated by the River Cray to the south, which flows into the Darent about a mile (1.6 km) upstream from the flood barrier, and the urban fringes of Slade Green, Crayford and Erith to the west. The marshes jut out into the Thames at Crayford Ness, which faces the saltings of Aveley and Rainham across the water. The similarity of habitat between the marshes at Crayford and neighbouring Dartford means that there is little difference in the birds, although the numbers and variety are limited by the smaller size and highly developed nature of this area.

The foreshore here can prove as productive as at Dartford, with the falling tide revealing the remains of fossilised trees among which good numbers of waders find rich pickings. As well as commoner species such as Dunlin, Ringed Plover and Redshank, watch out for less numerous migrants including Grey Plover, Greenshank and Common Sandpiper and oddities such as Knot, Turnstone, Curlew, Whimbrel, Curlew Sandpiper and Little Stint during passage times. The Crayford bank of the Darent is often a better place to view roosting waders, which usually congregate on rising tides on mud on the east side of the river mouth; in the afternoon the light is also better from this side. Other waterbirds are as expected at Dartford, with good numbers of gulls including the occasional Yellow-legged in late summer and early autumn and Mediterranean in winter. Cormorant, Grey Heron and Shelduck are in evidence anywhere along this stretch of the Thames, though other wildfowl are decidedly scarcer.

Out on the grazing marshes and arable land a few pairs of Lapwing, Ringed Plover and Redshank attempt to breed most years. The passerine community here includes Skylark, Meadow Pipit, Linnet and Reed Bunting, but Corn Buntings also breed in small numbers and even Whinchat has lingered recently in late spring, though has not yet recolonised the area. Wheatear occurs on passage, while Stonechat has certainly bred in recent times and is not uncommon in winter. In spring and autumn migrating parties of Yellow Wagtails often linger in the area, and this species has oversummered here at least twice in recent years. Warblers include the commoner *Sylvia* species in the scrub and good numbers of Reed Warblers along the ditches, while in winter Rock Pipit is a possibility on the river mud.

Rarer occurrences have included Leach's Storm-petrel, Brent Goose, Avocet, Black Tern, Ring Ouzel, Grasshopper Warbler and Snow Bunting, while among the more unusual older records are a Woodlark in 1952, the last Cirl Bunting in the area in 1953 and three Fulmars together in September 1954, followed a week later by London's first Red-breasted Flycatcher, a male near the mouth of the Darent.

Accessibility is more of a problem than at Dartford, with much of the arable land not viewable from roads or public footpaths. By road the area can be reached along the same route as for Dartford Marshes, but from the M25 continue west along the A206 University Way until you reach Slade Green, just north of Crayford. Continue on to Erith and enter the area via Erith Manorway. The Thames can also be viewed at Erith itself from the embankment at Corinthian Manorway, a cul-de-sac off the A2016 where Lower Road meets West Street.

By bus: the 89 and B13 from Lewisham and Eltham respectively stop at Slade Green, from where follow directions as above. *By train:* services run to Slade Green station from London Bridge.

15B DARTFORD HEATH   OS ref: TQ 516733

Divided by the A2 and a network of other roads to the southwest of Dartford, this broken-up tract of heath and woodland today has less appeal for birders than its ornithological heritage deserves. This is the site that gave its name to the Dartford Warbler, the first specimens of which were shot near here on 10 April 1773; this species has long since vanished from the area, however, and the last birds on breeding territory in Kent were seen in 1891.

Comprising largely deciduous woodland with numerous stands of birch and, in more open areas, gorse and other scrub, the area still retains a good range of commoner species synonymous with this diminishing type of habitat. Sparrowhawks and Kestrels are resident and Hobbies are not infrequent in the area during the summer months. Great Spotted Woodpecker breeds, and there is a good range of the commoner warblers, tits and finches. Stands of birch and alder should be checked for Siskin and Redpoll in winter, as should the more open areas for the declining Yellowhammer which still retains a toehold here. As always, do not ignore the sky: records of note include White Stork.

Directions are as for Dartford Marshes via the A2 Rochester Way (see above); the heath straddles this main road to the south of Dartford. Parking is straightforward and there is open access to most parts of the site. Buses serving the area include routes B15, 475, 476, 477, 478 and 492, this last being the best connection to train services at Dartford station.

SOUTHEAST LONDON

16 FOOT'S CRAY MEADOWS OS ref: TQ 480715

Habitat

Although overshadowed by the better-known Darent Valley a short distance to the east, the course of the Cray also offers several productive birding sites. The river runs northeast from Orpington to Dartford before joining the Darent near Slade Green and flowing into the Thames. In doing so it forms a natural boundary between the outer suburbs of southeast London and the Kentish countryside northwest of the North Downs, and its green margins at Foot's Cray must appear attractive to many migrants passing over the suburban fringe to the west.

Foot's Cray Meadows comprise a large expanse of open riverside parkland, meadows and playing fields with scattered trees, restricted areas of woodland and very limited scrub cover on either side of the River Cray. The most significant belt of trees is North Cray Wood on the western side just north of the main car park, running east towards the river, though there are several other smaller wooded areas and stands of vegetation, all of which provide cover for breeding and feeding passerines in this essentially open amenity area. Four bridges join the east and west banks of the river, the course of which has well-vegetated banks in many places dominated by willows. There are also several islands in the river which provide disturbance-free roost sites for wildfowl and other species.

The whole area is managed by the ranger service of the London Borough of Bexley, which maintains a noticeboard at the main car park providing occasional information on birds and natural history in the area. For more information contact the ranger service on 0181 309 6638.

Species

At first glance this site appears so open and well-used by the public that the first-time visiting birder may not appreciate its ornithological attractions. Impromptu conventions of dog walkers seem to be the most obvious signs of animal life, but closer inspection of favoured areas, even on a brief visit, can bring rewards.

For birds, one of the most obvious attractions is the river itself and the trees and scrub which provide cover along its banks and on the islands. Winter brings Little Grebes to the river, usually only in very small numbers although up to 10 or so birds have been counted. Great Crested Grebes also occasionally stray into the area from nearby gravel pits outside the breeding season. Ducks typically comprise just Mallard and Tufted Duck, and resident Mute Swan, Canada Goose, Coot and Moorhen complete the line-up of common waterfowl, but in winter watch out for occasional visitors such as Wigeon, Gadwall, Teal and even Pintail.

Careful scanning through binoculars of the vegetated fringes of the islands in winter may reveal the presence of a Water Rail if its squealing call has not already given it away; try looking from the west bank just south of Five Arch Bridge. Another occasional speciality at this time of year is Green Sandpiper, with inaccessible marshy margins of the river just downstream from the most northerly bridge probably being the most likely spot. Other waders except over-flying Lapwings are unlikely, though the Cray and its valley have attracted occasional oddities including Wood Sandpiper, Curlew and Dunlin. Kingfishers may be present anywhere along the river, as always often first detected by call as they flash past in search of a suitable fishing perch, and Grey and Pied Wagtails are also seen throughout the year.

The wide open green areas adjacent to the river, especially the playing fields of the school at the northern end of the west side of the meadows and Goldsmiths' College on the opposite bank, prove particularly attractive to gull flocks which in winter can contain numbers of all five regular species – Black-headed, Common, Herring, Lesser Black-backed and Great Black-backed. For several years until the early 1990s a Mediterranean Gull returned to this same area in consecutive winters, and the species was again found in winter 1994/95.

Overhead, locally-breeding Kestrels and Sparrowhawks can be seen throughout the year, and the quieter patches of woodland are home to a few pairs of Stock Doves. Little Owl has been seen here, raising the prospect of breeding nearby, but these unobtrusive birds are easily overlooked and are not recorded regularly. Far more conspicuous are the noisy posses of Ring-necked Parakeets which flash bright apple-green as

Ring-necked Parakeets

they chase each other in and out of the trees or call noisily from inside the leafy canopy; they might be encountered anywhere in the area, though the trees around the main car park seem to prove particularly attractive. Less predictable are the passage appearances of Turtle Dove and Cuckoo, though regular coverage at such times may bring other rewards – one fortunate observer found a Hoopoe here in March 1994. Other migrants include hirundines moving along the river valley in spring and autumn together with regular Meadow Pipits and other commoner species, but more sporadic in their appearances in this parkland landscape are local scarcities such as Yellow Wagtail, Wheatear and Nightingale. Warblers include passage Reed and Sedge and breeding Garden among the commoner species, while in 1990 a much rarer Marsh Warbler in full song for a day in May was an excellent find here. Spotted Flycatcher occurs in summer and on migration, when up to 14 have been present at one time.

The woodland, though not extensive, is suitable enough for both Green and Great Spotted Woodpeckers, and the unobtrusive Lesser Spotted is also seen occasionally and may breed in the area. Nuthatch, tits including Coal and Long-tailed and the three common thrushes all breed. Remarkably, a pair of Fieldfares also nested in the area in 1991, the first recorded breeding of this species in the London area. More typically, this thrush is encountered in winter in small groups along with Redwings, often on the playing fields where Mistle Thrushes may also be numerous.

The woodland holds the usual urban array of corvids, with Jay, Magpie and Carrion Crow joined in this outer London site by the occasional Jackdaw, which has yet to establish itself further into the urban zone of the southeast suburbs. Good numbers of the commoner finches are resident, with Chaffinch, Goldfinch and Greenfinch joined in winter by Siskin and Redpoll. Bullfinches are possible in the quieter areas, and Brambling has also been seen here. Back along the river, do not forget to check for resident Reed Buntings in vegetation along the banks or on the islands to complete your list of noteworthy birds at this site.

Timing

The woodland is quiet outside the breeding season, but with the chance of passage migrants in spring and autumn and interesting wintering species along the river including occasional wildfowl of note, a visit at any time of the year can be worthwhile. If possible visit early in the morning and on a weekday, as just like every other parkland site in the capital this area is well used by dog walkers, joggers, family outings and most other forms of disturbance known to urban birds.

Access

Foot's Cray Meadows lie in the Cray Valley immediately east of Sidcup. From inner London follow signs for Folkestone and the A20/M20, turning north off the A20 east of Sidcup onto the A224 Cray Road at Foot's Cray. Arriving from the M25 to the east, this turning is about four miles (6.4 km) west of junction 3. Continue straight over the crossroads at Foot's Cray High Street into Rectory Lane, following it round to the left but then turning off right to park in the main car park at the sign marked 'Pavilion', just before the road becomes single lane. Check the trees around this car park for Ring-necked Parakeets before walking east to the river or north to the woods to commence a circuit of the area, for which you should allow up to three hours.

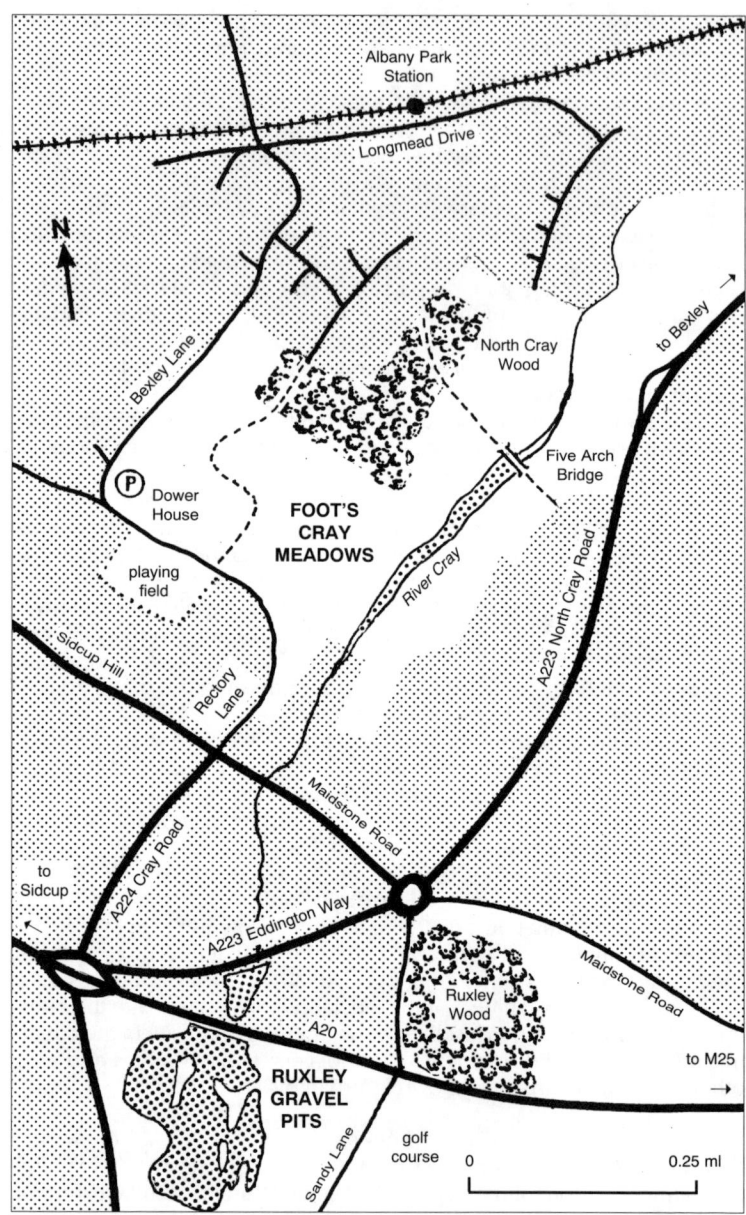

Alternatively, leave the A20 north at the same junction but instead take the A223 Edgington Way, which crosses the north side of Ruxley Gravel Pits. At the roundabout, take the second exit to continue on the A223, now North Cray Road, up the east side of the Cray valley for about a mile (1.6 km) until you reach Leafield Lane, from where there is easy access to Foot's Cray Meadows. If arriving on foot, there are numerous access points to the area, including those signed 'Cray Riverway footpath' near All Saints Church in Rectory Lane.

By bus: numbers 21 (from Moorgate in central London via New Cross, Lewisham and Eltham), 233 (from Swanley), 492 (from Dartford) and the Bromley-Sidcup services R1 and R11 serve Foot's Cray. *By train:* Albany Park station (overground from central London), one stop east from Sidcup, is half a mile walk north from North Cray Wood along St Andrew's Road and Kimberley Drive.

Calendar

All year: Stock Dove, Ring-necked Parakeet, Green and Great Spotted Woodpeckers, Kingfisher, Grey Wagtail, Long-tailed and Coal Tits, Nuthatch, Jackdaw.

Winter (November–March): Little Grebe, Water Rail, Green Sandpiper, gull flocks on the playing fields, Fieldfare, Redwing, Goldcrest, Siskin, Redpoll.

Spring (March–May): Migrants including Turtle Dove and Cuckoo, Yellow Wagtail, Meadow Pipit, perhaps Wheatear and other chats, Reed and Sedge Warblers, Spotted Flycatcher.

Summer (June–early August): Garden Warbler, Lesser Whitethroat and other warblers, common breeding species.

Autumn (mid-August–October): Returning wintering species including Little Grebe and Water Rail, gull numbers building up, passerine migrants such as Meadow Pipit and wagtails, occasional Wheatear and perhaps other chats, Redwing and Fieldfare arriving from October, warblers, Goldcrest, Spotted Flycatcher, occasional Brambling (from October).

OTHER SITES IN THE AREA

16A RUXLEY GRAVEL PITS

OS ref: TQ 473700
Map p. 94

Situated just south along the river valley from Foot's Cray Meadows, Ruxley Gravel Pits established a reputation through regular coverage over many years as a site with good potential for interesting birds. Unfortunately, however, its importance has diminished in recent years, partly since construction of the A20 flyover across the site, but also through its heavy amenity use for fishing. Its significance is maintained to a certain degree through management as a nature reserve, and with farmland and a golf course abutting the eastern side of the site it is not completely without attractions.

The pits are still home to breeding waterfowl, including around nine pairs of Great Crested Grebes and one of Greylag Goose, while in winter dabbling duck usually include Mallard, Gadwall and Teal in company with good numbers of diving duck. These have included the occasional Goosander and Smew, along with other oddities including Mandarin Duck and even Black-necked Grebe. Bittern has also been seen here in winter when Green Sandpiper, Jack Snipe and especially Snipe are occasional visitors, and several Water Rails are often also present.

Spring passage can bring interesting migrants to the area, including Hobby, Turtle Dove and Black Tern. One of the more notable earlier records here was London's first Red-rumped Swallow in April 1964. Kingfisher and Grey Wagtail breed in the vicinity, and there are a few pairs of both Reed and Sedge Warblers. Chiffchaffs occasionally winter, and in 1977 these included two of the Siberian race *tristis*. Tree Sparrow no longer breeds but is very occasionally still seen in the area, as are Bramblings in winter.

There is no general access at present to these gravel pits, which are managed as a nature reserve by the Kent Trust for Nature Conservation. However, special visiting arrangements may be possible by contacting the warden in advance (via KTNC headquarters on 01622 662012). Ruxley Gravel Pits lie off the A20 east of Chislehurst, west of junction 3 of the M25; for directions see Foot's Cray Meadows above, but turn south instead of north off the A20. The main pit lies immediately southeast of the junction of the A20 and A224; there is a smaller pit on the north side of the A20, immediately east of the A223.

17 SOUTH NORWOOD COUNTRY PARK

OS ref: TQ 353684

Habitat

Veterans of the London birding scene will best recall this site from early *London Bird Reports* as 'Elmers End SF'. In its sewage farm hey-day its potential for birds was well-documented, with the first account published in the *LBR* for 1944 detailing the results of a three-year study between the wars. While never on a par with the larger sewage farms at Beddington and Perry Oaks, it nonetheless attracted observer attention and produced a fair crop of interesting records of waders and other species before closure in the mid-1960s. Also known as South Norwood Sewage Farm, its geographical position on the borough boundary between Bromley (Kent) and Croydon (Surrey) means that it has variously appeared in either section of the *LBR*. In its latest guise of South Norwood Country Park, the whole site was brought under the jurisdiction of the latter borough in April 1994.

In this landscaped guise since 1988 the area has undergone a number of important habitat changes. There is still quite an extensive area of rank vegetation and scrub in much of the central and northern area, though in other parts the land has been cleared and re-seeded to form meadows. A new lake was thoughtfully designed with shallow margins and an island, and there is an adjacent wetland area to the south which includes a regularly flooded field outside the summer months. There are belts of trees but no woodland *per se,* with the densest stands bordering the country park on its eastern, northern and northwestern flanks. Elsewhere there are a few small areas of willow, the site otherwise being characterised by the short grass tracts of playing fields, a pitch and putt course and the Croydon Arena.

The diversity of habitats available to resident and migrant birds is varied enough to have established a list of some 148 species since 1989. With another 16 species recorded before that date, this site is clearly one of the major ornithological attractions of the southeastern sector of Greater London.

Species

The lake has provided the focus for wetland birds in recent years, though in overall terms there is now less inducement for most species of wildfowl and waders to linger here. Great Crested Grebes attempted breeding for the first time here in the early 1990s but failed to succeed and, if anything, have become less regular in recent years; in contrast Little Grebes remain sporadic in their appearances. Cormorants are regular in small numbers outside the breeding season, and one or two Grey Herons can also be expected around the lake.

Wildfowl are restricted largely to small numbers of the familiar dabbling and diving species, with Mallard the commonest but Pochard and Tufted Duck both also in double figures outside the breeding season; the latter has recently begun breeding in very small numbers. Teal, Shoveler and Gadwall all occasionally visit the lake, but other duck are much rarer: there have been several records of Mandarin and Wigeon, and even Goldeneye and Goosander have been reported. Canada Geese, as at many lakes in the London area, are a dominant feature with up to 200 present in summer and autumn, and the occasional Greylag, Mute Swan or perhaps even Shelduck is also likely.

The recovery of Sparrowhawks is indicated by the year-round presence here of the species, in stark contrast to the absence of records between the 1960s and the 1980s when it hit a national low. One or two pairs of Kestrels are also resident, and from spring to early autumn sky-ward eyes should be on the lookout for passage Hobbies here; one observer even had the good fortune to watch a Red Kite passing over in March 1990. Grey Partridges are now history with no recent records, but several pairs of Pheasants breed; they can sometimes be seen roosting in the hawthorns and elders by the stream. Impressively, migrant Quail have been found in three recent years, perhaps a better recent track record than for any other London site and no doubt due to the suitability of habitat.

Water Rail is possible around the lake in winter. A few Snipe and perhaps one or two Jack Snipe may also be present in the damper areas, though neither now occurs in large gatherings; in the early 1960s up to 700 of the former and 41 of the latter were recorded using the area. Lapwing has similarly been reduced in status from a former breeder to an occasional visitor. Little Ringed Plovers sometimes visit on passage, almost invariably singly and typically in spring, with the most likely other waders being Redshank, Greenshank and particularly Common Sandpiper which can be present in small numbers in spring and autumn. Recent studies have shown that the latter species is also the only wader likely to stay for prolonged periods, other species dropping in for just a few minutes before moving on. This must be a far cry from the site's sewage farm days when many now-absent waders were regular and there was a good chance of something more out-of-the-ordinary. However, there have been recent records of Oystercatcher, Avocet, Bar-tailed Godwit and Spotted Redshank among others, and with plans in place to naturalise the stream near the cemetery and develop a scrape there, perhaps there are prospects for a brighter future.

Black-headed Gull is the dominant gull species, with up to 200 present around the lake or on the playing fields in winter, and there are smaller numbers of Common Gulls and often a few Lesser Black-backs. Since the closure of the rubbish dump Herring and Great Black-back have become more infrequent, but sharp-eyed observers have found Mediterranean and Yellow-legged Gulls and even Kittiwake in recent years. Terns are decidedly irregular here with only Common at all likely, though on the notable day of 2 May 1990 no fewer than 30 Common, 17 Arctic, two Little and six Black were all logged moving through.

What the area is now lacking in wetland attractions it has partly made up for with landbirds, and the combination of resident and migrant species means there is generally something of interest at most times of the year. Ring-necked Parakeets are a relatively recent addition to the local avifauna. As well as resident Woodpigeons and Stock Doves, wandering Collared Doves and passage Turtle Doves are occasionally encountered, and migrant Cuckoos can similarly be hoped for in spring and early autumn, when juveniles are sometimes found. Owls are represented by Tawny, a pair of which seems to reside in the cemetery, and the very occasional straying Short-eared or Little. Kingfishers have become increasingly regular visitors to the lake, mainly in late summer and autumn but also in winter, while both Green and Great Spotted Woodpeckers are resident in the area and there is a chance of Lesser Spotted – the latter was suspected of breeding here in 1991.

Spring brings migrating parties of hirundines and Swifts to the area, the latter also breeding locally along with a few pairs of House Martins. Within the country park boundaries are a few nesting pairs of Skylarks, but this species is more numerous in winter when flocks of up to 50 may be present in the rougher areas. Meadow Pipits also occur in parties at this season, though they do not breed, and even Rock Pipit has been recorded on two recent occasions – the latter occurrence in April 1992 referring to a bird of the Scandinavian race *littoralis*. Yellow Wagtails no longer breed but do appear regularly on passage in both seasons, either moving straight through overhead or in small parties around the lake, where the occasional migrant White Wagtail might also be found. Both Pied and Grey Wagtails breed and are present year-round, though in very small numbers.

The rough grassland and scrubby terrain is perfect for Whinchats on passage, and in autumn a few birds may be present for prolonged periods in suitable habitat. Wheatears also find the site to their liking though are more regular in spring, when migrants may include the occasional Greenland race individual. Now lost as a breeding species, Stonechat is confined mainly to passage and overwintering, while both Black Redstart and Redstart remain highly erratic visitors. That other rough country specialist, the Ring Ouzel, has made enough showings in both passage periods to make it well worth seeking out in April or October, and Redwing and Fieldfare are also distinctly possible in autumn or winter.

Most of the commoner warblers are represented in the breeding season, with several pairs of Reed and Sedge around the lake margins and Willow Warbler, Blackcap, Lesser Whitethroat and especially Common Whitethroat in suitable habitat elsewhere. Garden Warbler and Chiffchaff are passage migrants here, as is the occasional Grasshopper Warbler which might reveal its presence with its characteristic 'reeling' song in spring. Less predictable are the occasional appearances of 'oddities' such as the singing male Marsh Warbler for two weeks in June 1993, a Dartford Warbler on Christmas Eve in 1990 or the two spring visits paid by

Firecrests to the area. Goldcrest nests in the cemetery, but Spotted Flycatchers have never succeeded in establishing themselves and are confined to appearances on migration.

Aside from the commoner tit species and corvids, the remaining passerine attention focuses on the gatherings of seed-eaters outside the breeding season. This used to be a stronghold of the Tree Sparrow, but as everywhere the species has undergone fluctuating fortunes and its erratic breeding and winter occurrences may now be consigned to history. Instead, one of the chief features is the winter residence of Corn Buntings, a scarce species in much of the London area. Up to 70 were recorded in the mid-1980s but 10–20 are far more likely; these birds are best searched for either early in the morning before they have dispersed or towards dusk when they come in to roost. Reed Buntings are resident, but Yellowhammer is a scarce straggler in winter when feeding flocks of up to 200 Linnets congregate. Similar numbers of Goldfinches occur in late summer and autumn, though most disperse and leave the area before winter. Chaffinches also occur in flocks, notably in the winters of 1988/89 and 1989/90 when soil disturbance during landscaping work attracted up to 200 birds; these gatherings also drew in a few Bramblings. Other winter surprises have included a long-staying Great Grey Shrike, four altogether more brief Waxwings, a Twite and in one recent winter up to six Bearded Tits; who knows what else might be discovered with more coverage?

Great Grey Shrike

Timing

A visit at any time of the year may produce something of interest, with the familiar caveats about disturbance at weekends and in summer applying. Early morning is usually the best time of day before dog walkers have flushed the overnight arrivals from the lake, although many good sightings have occurred mid-morning. Allow three or four hours at least to do the whole area justice.

Access

There is pedestrian access at all times to the site from various points around the periphery (except on the eastern side which is bordered by the railway), but the gates to the car park near the pitch and putt course are not opened until 9 am and are locked at night. The car park by the Croydon Arena is usually open at all times and cars can be parked on various roads nearby. Numerous paths and tracks criss-cross the area and give almost unrestricted access. There is now a visitor centre on the site (open most afternoons during summer and usually on weekend afternoons in winter, depending on the availability of volunteers) with toilet facilities (open during the day); records of interest should be left there for the attention of the site recorder, John Birkett.

By car from central London, follow the A23 Brighton road to just south of Streatham, then turn left (east) along the A214 Streatham Common

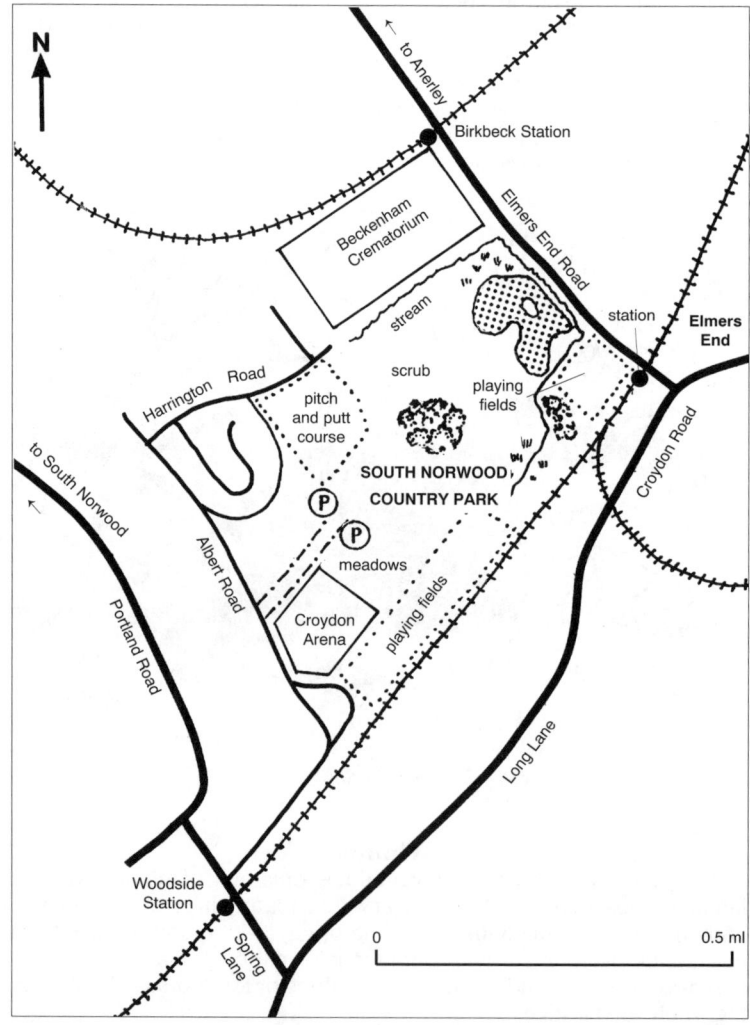

North. Follow this road through for just over four miles (6.4 km) to Elmers End via Norwood, the southern side of Crystal Palace Park and Penge. South Norwood Country Park is on the right-hand side just before Elmers End station and the junction with the A222 Croydon Road. *By bus:* number 197 from Croydon via Norwood Junction and number 312 from Peckham via Dulwich and Forest Hill run along Portland Road between South Norwood and Woodside; several other routes serve the Elmers End area. *By train:* Elmers End station (trains from London Bridge) is situated in the northeast corner of the park.

Calendar

All year: Grey Heron, Kestrel, Sparrowhawk, Pheasant, Tawny Owl (in the cemetery), Green and Great Spotted Woodpeckers, Reed Bunting.

Winter (November–early March): Cormorant, Water Rail, Jack Snipe, Snipe, Kingfisher, Meadow Pipit, Grey Wagtail, Stonechat, Redpoll, Corn Bunting.

Spring (mid-March–May): Hobby (late spring), Little Ringed Plover, Redshank, Greenshank, Green Sandpiper, Common Sandpiper, Turtle Dove, Cuckoo, hirundines, Yellow Wagtail, Whinchat, Wheatear, chance of Ring Ouzel, warblers including Grasshopper and Garden.

Summer (June–July): Swift, House Martin, Grey Wagtail, Sedge Warbler, Reed Warbler, Lesser Whitethroat, Whitethroat, Blackcap, Willow Warbler.

Autumn (August–October): Hobby (until September), Redshank, Greenshank, Green Sandpiper, Common Sandpiper, Turtle Dove, Cuckoo (early autumn), hirundines, Yellow Wagtail, Whinchat, Wheatear, chance of Ring Ouzel, warblers and other migrants.

18 OTHER SOUTHEAST LONDON SITES

Habitat, species and access

Although there is something of a lack of noteworthy birding sites away from the Thames in this sector of the capital, there are a number of parks, woodlands and other undeveloped areas which retain a few interesting breeding birds and regular visitors. A selection of these is detailed below.

About three miles (4.8 km) southeast of Blackheath along the south side of the A207 at Shooters Hill is Oxleas Wood (TQ 450686), an isolated tract of ancient woodland made famous after a high-profile conservation battle finally saved it from new road development in the early 1990s. Though not on the well-trodden circuit of London birding sites, this woodland does have a good range of breeding species including woodpeckers, Nuthatch, Treecreeper, a selection of warblers in spring and summer and the commoner tits and finches. The more open areas hold Skylark, and commoner migrants such as Meadow Pipit, Wheatear and perhaps Stonechat are possible in spring and autumn. Other interesting reports include singing Wood Warblers on two dates in 1993 and the occasional passing Hobby, and there are also records of Pied Flycatcher and Brambling. Bus number 89 stops on Shooters Hill along the north side of the wood, and the B16 runs along Rochester Way on the south side near Falconwood, which is the nearest overground station (trains connect to London Bridge).

Two miles (3.2 km) northeast of Oxleas Wood, and divided from each other by the A206, are Lesnes Abbey Woods (TQ 480785) and Bostall Woods (TQ 467778), two underwatched but productive stretches of woodland which ought to merit attention. Records from both are scanty, but species found here have included all three woodpeckers, common breeding warblers, Long-tailed and Marsh Tits, Nuthatch and, at the former site, Nightingale. Bus number 99 runs from Woolwich to Erith via Bostall Hill, and route B11 from Bexleyheath Broadway runs along the west side of Lesnes Abbey Woods along Knee Hill, at the northern end of which is Abbey Wood station (services from London Bridge).

Due south of Blackheath, against the unlikely backdrop of Catford in the London Borough of Lewisham, the cemetery at Hither Green (TQ 398729) has a sizeable roost of Ring-necked Parakeets which sometimes numbers the best part of 100 birds. Access is from Verdant Lane SE6, reached from Catford via Brownhill Road (bus numbers 160, 202 and 261 stop nearby; Grove Park station is the nearest overground connection, with frequent trains from London Bridge). A short distance to the west, Ladywell Fields (TQ 372740) has occasional visiting Kingfishers and Grey Wagtails but put itself firmly on the map with the discovery of a Yellow-browed Warbler in September 1990. Access is from Malyons Road off Ladywell Road SE13; bus numbers 284 and P4 run from Lewisham, or take the overground to Ladywell station from London Bridge. Slightly further west still, the under-watched high ground of Forest Hill, with its spectacular views across the capital, offers excellent opportunities for the pioneering migration watcher; diurnal passage can be observed overhead in the right conditions in spring and autumn, and the slopes of One Tree Hill (TQ 355743) and the adjacent allotments along Honor Oak Park could well be worth searching for grounded migrants. Honor Oak Park station lies immediately east of the site; bus number P4 runs along Honor Oak Park.

Two miles (3.2 km) to the south is Crystal Palace, another site benefiting from its position along a ridge of high ground and visible for miles with its landmark television transmitter aerials. The park here (TQ 347707) slopes down from the ridge on its western boundary with the A212 Crystal Palace Parade, and though the national recreation centre and sports arena dominate the open areas, the more vegetated sections here and at nearby Dulwich Park (TQ 335735) and Dulwich Woods (TQ 340725) occasionally attract migrants of note. Chief among these is perhaps Firecrest, which is virtually annual in the area; in March 1996 up to four were present around the TV transmitter at Beaulieu Heights, at the southern end of the A212 Church Road. Other passerines of note to have occurred include Black Redstart, Wood Warbler and Pied Flycatcher. There are numerous access point to Crystal Palace Park from the A212 or from the A214 Anerley Hill, A234 Crystal Palace Park Road, and from a number of adjacent residential roads; bus routes serving Crystal Palace include 2, 3, 63, 122, 137A, 157, 202, 227 and 249, and Crystal Palace station lies immediately adjacent to the south side of the park on Anerley Hill.

Further southeast, in the midst of the outer suburbs just west of Orpington, lies the area known as Crofton Heath (TQ 435665). This actually comprises several interesting sites, including Sparrow Wood, Roundabout Wood and Gumping Common. The Kyd Brook flows through the middle of the area, the East Kyd Brook runs along its eastern border and numerous footpaths permit straightforward access. The habitat, which includes a 56-acre SSSI rich in insect and plant life, is mostly oak woodland with hazel coppice and some stands of birch. Green, Great Spotted and Lesser Spotted Woodpeckers all breed, as do Nuthatch and Treecreeper, and other residents include Stock Dove, Tawny Owl and Goldcrest. In summer, warblers are represented by Blackcap, Garden Warbler, Willow Warbler and Chiffchaff, while Whitethroat, Lesser Whitethroat and Wood Warbler have been noted on passage. In winter Grey Wagtail may occur along the East Kyd Brook and Siskins may be present in stream-side alders, while Redpolls are perhaps still resident in the area. Willow Tit has occurred. Access to the general area from central London is straightforward via the A21 Hastings Road just south of Bromley Common; bus numbers 61, 261, 358, 366, 402, R1 and R2 all run along Hastings Road. The nearest station is at Petts Wood a quarter of a mile (0.4 km) to the north, beyond which lie Petts Wood (TQ 445670), St Paul's Cray Common (TQ 451690) and, north of the A208 St Paul's Cray Road, Park Wood (TQ 095890). These sites hold a broadly similar range of regular species along with breeding Ring-necked Parakeet, and occasional scarcer migrants have been noted including Ring Ouzel, Crossbill, Wood Warbler and, exceptionally, Marsh Warbler. To the west, Bromley Common (TQ 415655) also has all three woodpeckers, commoner warblers in summer and breeding Little Owls.

SOUTHWEST LONDON

19 BEDDINGTON FARM OS ref: TQ 290662

Habitat

This former sewage farm immediately south of Mitcham Common has been well watched for many years and, despite problems of access, is undoubtedly one of the capital's most important birding attractions. As well as a fair selection of interesting breeding birds, Beddington has regularly attracted a good range of migrant species which have included many that are scarce elsewhere in the region, as well as a respectable number of national rarities: the resulting total of 240 species recorded at the site is probably higher than anywhere else in the London area. Its position in the 'outer circle' of south London's extensive suburban districts at first appears to be outside any recognised avian fly-way, but it is thought that the high ground of Crystal Palace to the east, its position close to the River Wandle and the green 'corridor' formed with Mitcham Common to the north and Beddington Park to the south may all combine to 'funnel' birds through the area.

At present the site consists largely of disused sewage settling beds, most of which recently been refilled with sludge and some of which retain varying levels of water for part or all of the year. Those in the southeast corner have become overgrown by a variety of weeds and other vegetation which provide an important source of cover and food for various passerines. Chief among these is the Tree Sparrow, which here has what may be its largest breeding colony in Britain. The open landscape of the area is broken by significant stands of trees only around its margins and in Beddington Park, immediately to the south. A works road dissects the sewage farm area from east to west, and midway along the western boundary there is a sizeable lake with islands which provides additional habitat for wildfowl and waders; in the southeast corner there is an active filtration works.

Beddington's future importance for birds remains to be seen. Thames Water's management of the site has so far included supporting the financing of nestbox schemes, publication of the local bird report and other initiatives, but at the time of writing plans are in place to alter radically the existing landscape through gravel extraction and landfill activities. Although opposed by the local bird group, residents and conservation bodies in the area, planning permission has been granted and it seems likely that the nature of the site will be permanently altered. On a positive note, Thames Water's stated long-term goal is to transform much of Beddington Farm into a 132-hectare conservation area with permanent habitats of wet grassland, pools and reedbeds, as well as maintaining important existing habitats on which some of the scarcer breeding birds depend. These impending changes therefore mean there is no guarantee that Beddington's hitherto well-documented birdlife is any indication of the future potential of the site, so the following account should be read with that caveat in mind.

Species

For waterbirds the lake at the Hackbridge end of the site is the main focal point. Great Crested and Little Grebes are both regular and have attempted to breed in recent years with varying results. Other grebes and divers are unlikely to occur, though there have been several records of Black-necked Grebe and one recent occurrence of Red-necked. Instead, the waters are preferred by Cormorants and Grey Herons, and occasionally something rarer; back in the 1950s Little Bittern occurred no fewer than three times, including a pair which stayed for a month in 1956, and more recently both Purple Heron and Spoonbill have been noted.

As with all sites in the London area reports of wild swans and geese are at best scarce, though in recent years there have been a number of sightings of flocks of Brent Geese, presumably moving to or from regular sites on the south coast or during hard-weather movements in winter, and several of Bewick's Swans. Interesting wildfowl are far more likely to comprise Wigeon, Gadwall, Shoveler and Teal, all of which occur well into double figures each winter, while Garganey makes annual appearances, mainly in late summer. Diving ducks are generally unremarkable, with Ruddy Duck regular (especially in spring and summer) but otherwise only Goldeneye at all likely to be discovered among the regular Pochard and Tufted Duck.

Sparrowhawk and Kestrel are the only raptors known to breed in the area, but Hobby has become an almost daily sight hawking over the lake in recent summers and may well nest nearby. Other raptors are rare but not out of the question: there has been a spate of Marsh Harrier and Peregrine records in recent years, and more fortunate observers have also logged Red Kite, Osprey, Goshawk, Hen Harrier and Merlin.

One or two Water Rails are usually present in winter around the edge of the lake, and back in the site's sewage farm hey-day in the 1950s there was also a record of an unidentified small crake here – either London's first Baillon's or second Little. It was in that era that Beddington became well known for its attractiveness to waders, which included nesting Lapwing and Redshank. When the new works were built and topsoil was removed, Little Ringed Plovers colonised the gravel areas; all of these three species still usually nest in small numbers today. In recent years regular or numerous passage migrants in spring and autumn have included Ringed Plover, Dunlin, Ruff, Curlew, Whimbrel, Greenshank and Common and Green Sandpipers, the latter also occurring in winter when good numbers of Snipe and one or two Jack Snipe may be present. Other less common migrant shorebirds recorded most years include Golden and Grey Plovers, Little Stint, Curlew Sandpiper, Black-tailed Godwit, Spotted Redshank and Wood Sandpiper, with coastal species such as Knot, Sanderling, Turnstone and Bar-tailed Godwit generally more irregular in their appearances. Beddington also has a fair list of rarer waders to its credit, including Black-winged Stilt, Avocet, Killdeer, Lesser Yellowlegs, Temminck's Stint and no fewer than six Pectoral Sandpipers.

Aside from the omnipresent commoner gulls, a few Mediterranean and Little Gulls are recorded annually and occasional Kittiwakes have been noted on the lake or passing through. Common Tern is the most regular passage tern but does not breed, while smaller numbers of Arctic and Black Terns are recorded most years, with oddities such as Sandwich and Little much less expected.

Stock Dove is resident and often recorded in sizeable flocks in winter, but Turtle Dove is restricted to passage migrant status. Cuckoo is regular in spring and late summer but does not breed. Of the owls, Little and Tawny nest in the area but are heard more often than seen, whereas the formerly regularly-wintering Short-eared is now decidedly irregular; conversely, Long-eared has appeared intermittently in recent winters. Kingfishers make occasional visits to the area, as do all three woodpeckers which breed in close proximity to the farm.

The flat, rough landscape of Beddington used to be conducive to Skylarks, though numbers of this resident have declined in recent years through disturbance and change in habitat use. Good numbers of this species and Meadow Pipit are often logged on spring and autumn migration, when the possibility of scarcer species is also greatest. A Short-toed Lark was found at Beddington in April 1966, there have been two autumn records of Richard's Pipits and, more recently, three different Tawny Pipits, including two together in September 1992. Tree Pipit is a scarce but annual migrant, and unusually for an inland site, Rock Pipit appears to be regular on passage, especially in autumn. Water Pipits are also expected from October through to spring, and on occasion numbers have reached double figures in late winter. Pied, Grey and Yellow Wagtails all breed, and during migration times parties of the latter should be scrutinised for one of the continental races – Blue-headed appears most years, and birds showing characters of Grey-headed and Syke's Wagtails have also been reported recently. Claims of the latter subspecies in the 1960s were proved to be hybrid Yellow x Blue-headed Wagtails, when birds ringed as young were retrapped in later years. Rarest of all the wagtails here was London's first Citrine Wagtail, found among Yellows and Pieds at the lake in August 1993.

Stonechats are present outside the breeding season and migrant Whinchats and Wheatears find the rough, weedy terrain much to their liking on passage, but Black Redstart and Redstart are rather less regular. With luck Ring Ouzels can also be encountered on passage here, with perhaps early spring offering the best chance of a lone migrant, while from autumn through to spring parties of Redwings and Fieldfares are often in evidence. In late April and early May the first migrant Reed and Sedge Warblers arrive, with a few pairs usually staying to breed. In spring 1994 a singing male Marsh Warbler also spent a month holding territory, and the following year a pair of this nationally scarce species were present and perhaps bred – if so for the first time in the London area for many years – but unfortunately no birds returned in 1996. Perhaps surprisingly, Grasshopper Warbler is something of a rarity here, and there have been no further records of Aquatic Warbler since the single August birds of 1959 and 1965. Whitethroat, Blackcap and occasionally Lesser Whitethroat breed, but Garden generally occurs only on passage. Willow Warbler breeds nearby and a pair may have done so recently at the lake, but the species is much more numerous on passage. Chiffchaffs also appear on migration and in winter, when several individuals may be present, and two of the three Dartford Warbler records in recent years have been of long-staying birds at the latter season. Goldcrest, occasionally Firecrest and Spotted Flycatcher are also passage visitors, and more rarely small parties of the irruptive Bearded Tit have been noted in late autumn. Great Grey Shrikes have twice recently appeared in the Beddington and Mitcham Common area at this time of year, while midsummer 1994 brought a Golden Oriole to the site.

Among the passerines, pride of place must surely go to the Tree Sparrow. This nationally-declining species, which has disappeared from the large majority of its former London haunts, still nests here in good numbers. Supported by a nestbox scheme, around 90 pairs continue to raise over 300 young annually – perhaps the largest single-site population in the country. Outside the breeding season this species often joins with mixed feeding flocks of finches, which include good numbers of Goldfinch, Greenfinch and Linnet and in winter the occasional Brambling. Reed Buntings are also numerous, but both Corn Bunting and Yellowhammer have now been reduced to the status of scarce visitors. Rarer still are the likes of Lapland, Snow and Ortolan Buntings, each of which has been recorded on just a handful of occasions, while remarkably both Little and Rustic Buntings were found overwintering in early 1993 – the latter being the first British record of the species at this season.

Tree Sparrows and Spotted Redshank

Timing

Beddington is probably at its quietest between wader passage periods in midsummer and especially midwinter, but as records show the site is clearly worth scouring year-round for interesting birds. For passerines mornings are often best, as at most sites, but with interest primarily focused on the lake and settling beds and the possibility of passage waders dropping in throughout the day, a visit at any time might produce rewards. As a working site Beddington is at its busiest during weekdays; however, although there is no public access, the area is sometimes subject to heavy disturbance by trial-bikers, particularly at weekends.

Access

At the time of writing there is no public access to Beddington, and the only birdwatchers authorised to enter the site are key-holding members of the local bird group and their guests, and members of Croydon RSPB group, which also retains a key. This seems an unnecessary and avoidable restriction, and in the longer term things may change once development of the area gets underway and Thames Water's plans for more amenity-based usage become effective. In the past occasional open days have been held and special public access has sometimes been negotiated by the local bird group when rarities have been discovered on site. In the meantime, just about the only public viewpoint across any significant part of the area is from the railway bridge at the Hackbridge end of Mile Road near the lake on the western side.

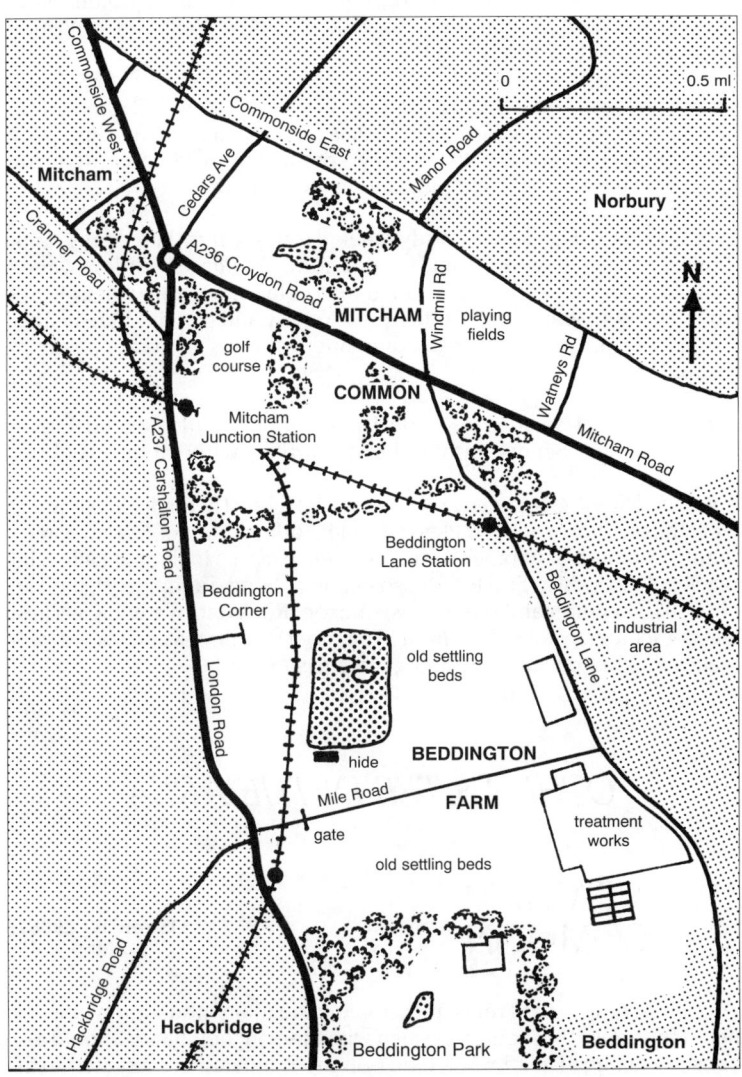

To reach the area by car from central London, take the A24 as far as Tooting Broadway, turn left to Mitcham, then right onto the A237 Carshalton Road (becoming London Road) for 1.5 miles (2.4 km), parking near Hackbridge station and entering the site if access is possible via the keyholders' gate on adjacent Mile Road. *By bus:* numbers 127 and S1 stop at Hackbridge. *By train:* trains run regularly through Hackbridge station, on the western edge of the site, from London Bridge and Victoria stations. *By underground:* the nearest station is Tooting Broadway (Northern line), from where bus route 127 connects to Hackbridge.

Calendar

Resident: Great Crested Grebe, Little Grebe, Teal, Shoveler, Pochard, Tufted Duck, Sparrowhawk, Kestrel, Pheasant, Lapwing, Redshank, Stock Dove, Little Owl, Tawny Owl, Skylark, Meadow Pipit, Grey Wagtail, Jackdaw, Tree Sparrow, Reed Bunting.

Winter (November–February): Wigeon, Gadwall, Water Rail, Snipe, Jack Snipe (scarce), Green Sandpiper, occasional Mediterranean Gull, Long-eared Owl (irregular), Water Pipit, Stonechat, Fieldfare, Redwing, Chiffchaff, chance of Brambling among finch flocks.

Spring (March–late May): Ruddy Duck, Hobby (from late April), Little Ringed Plover, Ringed Plover, Dunlin, Ruff, Whimbrel, Curlew, Greenshank, Common Sandpiper, chance of coastal or scarce waders, Turtle Dove, Cuckoo, Water Pipit (until April), Yellow and (rarely) Blue-headed Wagtails, Whinchat, Wheatear, commoner warblers and other passerine migrants.

Summer (late May–June): Ruddy Duck, Hobby, Little Ringed Plover, Yellow Wagtail, Sedge Warbler, Reed Warbler, Whitethroat, Blackcap.

Autumn (July–October): Garganey (scarce), Hobby (late July–September), Little Ringed Plover, Ringed Plover, Dunlin, Ruff, Whimbrel, Curlew, Greenshank, Common Sandpiper, scarcer waders perhaps including Little Stint, Black-tailed Godwit, Spotted Redshank and Wood Sandpiper, Little Gull (scarce), Common and other terns, Cuckoo, Rock and Water Pipits (from late September), Stonechat (from September), Whinchat, Wheatear, warblers and other migrants including scarcities.

OTHER SITES IN THE AREA

19A MITCHAM COMMON

OS ref: TQ 290675
Map p. 109

Though Beddington Farm is undoubtedly the main attraction of this corner of the capital, visitors to the area with time on their hands should also consider taking in nearby Mitcham Common, situated immediately to the north. Despite being fragmented by a number of roads and subject to much disturbance from heavy public usage, there are some interesting areas of thickets, scrub and open ground, several ponds and a golf course which between them manage to attract some interesting species, including a few unlikely to be found at Beddington.

Aside from commoner waterbirds the ponds have on occasion attracted more interesting visitors, including Little Grebe, Mandarin Duck, Gadwall and Teal, and occasionally waders such as Greenshank and Green and Common Sandpipers. Sparrowhawk probably breeds in the golf course woods, and migrant Hobbies are occasionally reported. Pheasant and Stock Dove are resident, and Little Owls have been seen near the boundary with Beddington Farm. Green and Great Spotted Woodpeckers breed and Lesser Spotted is occasionally reported. Skylarks still nest in small numbers in the more open areas, hirundines, Meadow and Tree Pipits and Yellow Wagtail occur on passage, and wintering species have included Stonechat and flocks of Redwing and Fieldfare. Whitethroat, Lesser Whitethroat, Blackcap, Willow Warbler and possibly Garden Warbler all breed, and Reed and Sedge Warblers, Chiffchaff and Goldcrest occur on passage. Tree Sparrows are occasionally seen along the Beddington boundary, Redpolls occur in winter and Bullfinch and Reed Bunting are both resident.

A number of unusual species have also been recorded at this site, including Short-eared Owl, Waxwing and a well-watched Great Grey Shrike which overwintered in 1991. The adjoining electricity generating station, gas works and industrial areas between Beddington Lane and the A23 Purley Way have attracted Black Redstarts in the breeding season.

General directions are as for Beddington Farm, but from Mitcham bear left onto the A236 Croydon Road which runs through the middle of the common. Alternatively, from the A23 London–Brighton road on the east side of the common, turn off at the Lombard roundabout and head northwest along Mitcham Road, which eventually becomes Croydon Road. Additional bus routes serving this area include 118, 152 and 264; by train, both Mitcham Junction and Beddington Lane serve the common.

20 RICHMOND PARK   OS ref: TQ 200730

Habitat

Richmond Park is by far the largest of the capital's royal parks, and at times its 2350 acres (940 ha) and 8-mile (12.8 km) radius feel much like a rambling country estate. There is enough space here to avoid clashes of interest, and picnickers, horseriders, joggers, dog walkers, birdwatchers and many others manage to co-exist peacefully alongside the roaming herds of red and fallow deer in a very attractive setting.

The gently rolling landscape is dominated by rough grassland and some extensive areas of bracken, with stands of pollarded oak and other mature trees fairly evenly distributed across the park. There is little understorey in these areas of open woodland, with the densest tracts of vegetation being found in a number of wooded enclosures, of which perhaps

Isabella Plantation is the best known. A number of small streams in the more open areas trickle towards the Pen Ponds in the centre of the park. These two waters provide valuable habitat for a range of species, and the western pond, complete with reedbed and adjoining damp woodland, can be particularly interesting. To the west the park is bordered by Petersham Meadows, Sudbrook Park and Ham Common, and to the north by Barnes Cemetery and East Sheen Common.

Richmond Park has a good range of birds year-round, with around 45 species breeding each year, a selection of regular winterers and enough habitat diversity to produce a fair range of migrants and the occasional rarity; the result is a list of around 100 species recorded annually. With an area this size and relatively few regular observers, searching for something special may seem like looking for a needle in a haystack, but the park has consistently produced some good finds.

Species

For waterbirds of various kinds the Pen Ponds are the only serious attraction, and it is here that the visiting birder should expect to find a reasonable range of species. Great Crested and Little Grebes breed and Cormorants and Grey Herons are regular visitors. Worthy of historical note here was London's second-ever Little Bittern, an immature which stayed for at least four days back in August 1954 and constituted one of the capital's earliest 'twitches'. Wildfowl include the colourful Mandarin Duck, a pair of which finds the wooded margins of the Pen Ponds suitable for breeding, but the origins of the Red-crested Pochards seen here from time-to-time are generally treated with suspicion. Duck numbers peak in winter, when totals of Wigeon and Gadwall may each approach three figures; the latter species has also been seen in summer. Diving duck can be relatively numerous, and the sometimes large rafts of Tufted Duck and Pochard are worth checking for occasional scarcer visitors such as Goosander.

Regular birds of prey comprise the ubiquitous duo of Sparrowhawk and Kestrel, and as in most parts of the capital Hobby is the next most likely species. Wandering Common Buzzards have also very occasionally been noted moving through in autumn and winter. Pheasants breed and Grey Partridges were apparently introduced into the park, though are no longer reported. Water Rails often winter in the reedbed at the Pen Ponds and have even bred, but although suitable for wildfowl these waters and their lack of muddy margins do not prove attractive to waders – recent records of Little Stint and Curlew are the exception rather than the norm. Gulls use the ponds as a bathing and loafing spot, especially in winter when numbers of the commoner species may be quite high, but more unusual gulls and terns are decidedly unlikely here.

Stock Doves are common, particularly around the oaks, and there is a reasonable chance of Cuckoo, especially in spring. As in much of this sector of the capital Ring-necked Parakeets are never far away, and here they look decidedly out-of-place against the backdrop of wooded grasslands with roaming deer herds. All three woodpeckers are resident and Tawny and Little Owls breed, though the latter can be difficult to locate despite its less nocturnal habits.

Swifts and all three hirundines can be numerous at passage times, especially around the Pen Ponds. The rough grassland terrain is ideal for Skylarks and Meadow Pipits, but just one pair of Tree Pipits has bred in recent years. The habitat is also well-suited to chats, with a few pairs of nesting Stonechats as well as passage Whinchat and Wheatear regularly

Little Owl

in spring and autumn; both Redstart and Black Redstart have also been recorded. Thrushes can include sizeable gatherings of family parties of Mistle Thrush in autumn, and numbers of the three commoner species are augmented in winter by flocks of Redwings and Fieldfares.

From late April onwards listen out for the song of Reed and perhaps Sedge Warblers in the reedbed at the Pen Ponds, and for other common warblers in the scrub and woodland on passage and during the breeding season; Bog Lodge is said to be particularly attractive to migrant species, and it was here in September 1985 that a Barred Warbler was found. Also noteworthy were the Dartford Warblers which wintered in the park in 1991/1992 and 1994/95. Goldcrest and Spotted Flycatcher breed, and in spring and particularly autumn there is a possibility of the occasional migrant Pied Flycatcher. Late autumn also brings the an outside chance of Bearded Tit, with this species having turned up in the reedbed at the Pen Ponds – though not for some years.

Noteworthy at the best of times, let alone in London, male Golden Orioles have put in recent appearances here – in May in both 1992 (two different birds) and 1993. Shrikes of any kind are also irregular in the London area, but Richmond hosted an overwintering Great Grey in the Seventies and, back in spring 1953, a rare wandering Woodchat Shrike. More recently, London's only Isabelline Shrike, apparently dead for some time, was brought in by a cat in a local garden in March 1994. Jackdaws avoid much of urban London but breed in numbers here in what are clearly ideal surroundings. Unfortunately the same cannot be said for Tree Sparrow, which despite the wealth of seemingly good habitat has recently been lost as a breeding species. As in most of the London parks common finches are generally well represented, and there can be some sizeable post-breeding flocks of Goldfinches and other species from late summer. During the winter months, Siskin and Redpoll may also be present in favoured stands of alder and birch. Reed Buntings can be numerous, but are the only likely member of their family to be encountered. Of the other buntings to have occurred, a male Ortolan for three days near the Pen Ponds in May 1993 is perhaps the most notable.

Timing

There is enough ornithological interest to justify a visit at any time of the year, though as always the woodlands are busiest in spring and early summer and the Pen Ponds perhaps at their best outside the breeding season. The park can get very crowded on bank holidays and at weekends, particularly in summer, so the earlier a visit is timed the better; a morning should produce a good range of species, though the park is big enough to roam for a whole day.

Access

Richmond Park is open from 7 am (7.30 in winter) until dusk. At other times the gates are locked to both pedestrians and traffic.

From central London, the most direct route to Richmond is via the A4 to Hammersmith, then the A316 to Richmond. The park is signposted from the town centre, bringing you through Richmond Gate on Star and

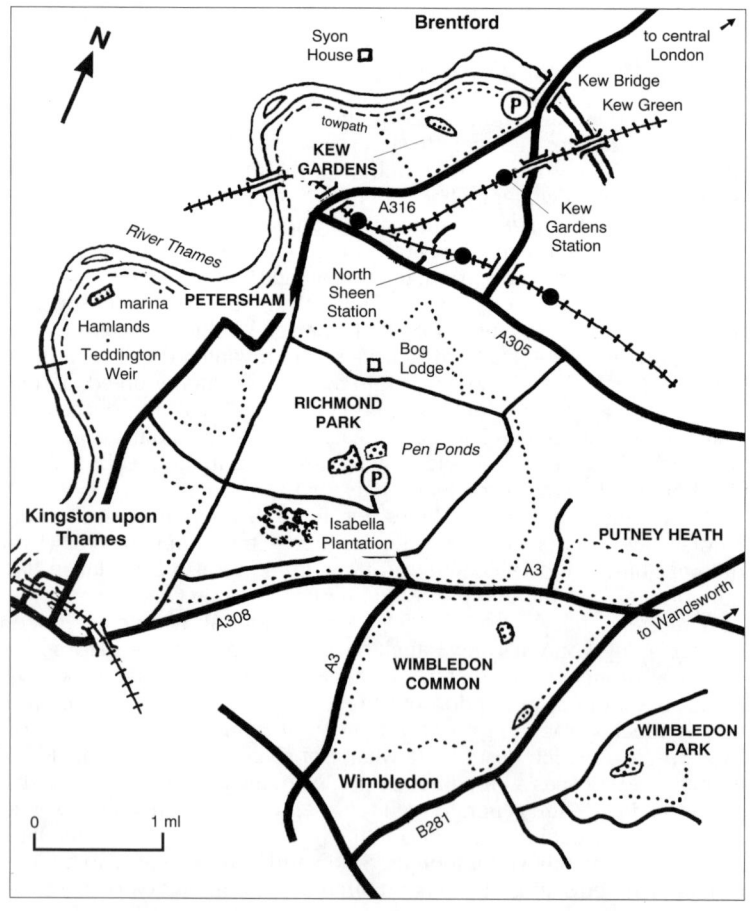

Garter Hill. On entering the gate, follow the road left or right depending on which way you want to take the perimeter road around the park; bear right for the Pen Ponds, following signs which eventually lead along a dead-end road to a car park just southwest of the ponds. If approaching the park from the south, take the A3 as far as its junction with the A308 Kingston Vale, and enter the park via Robin Hood Gate. There is no stopping or parking in Richmond Park except at designated parking areas.

By bus: routes 65, 90, 190, 337, 371, 391, 427, H22, R61, R68 and R69 serve Richmond town centre, and numbers 33 and 290 run along the A316 Richmond Road/Upper Richmond Road; the 65 and 371 also pass along the western edge of the park through Petersham and Ham. *By underground:* from Richmond station (District line), walk south for about 1.5 miles (2.4 km), through the town centre along The Quadrant, George Street and Hill Street, then up Richmond Hill to Richmond Gate. *By train:* overground trains run to Richmond station from Waterloo, and also from North London via the suburban Gospel Oak line.

Calendar

Resident: Great Crested Grebe, Little Grebe, Mandarin Duck, Tufted Duck, Pochard, Sparrowhawk, Kestrel, Pheasant, Stock Dove, Ring-necked Parakeet, Tawny Owl, Little Owl, Green Woodpecker, Great Spotted Woodpecker, Lesser Spotted Woodpecker, Skylark, Goldcrest, Nuthatch, Treecreeper, Jackdaw.

Winter (November–March): Gadwall, Wigeon, chance of other duck, gulls, Redwing, Fieldfare, Redpoll, Siskin.

Spring (April–May): Chance of Hobby, occasional Common Sandpiper and Common Tern at the Pen Ponds, Stock Dove, hirundines, Reed Warbler, Blackcap, Wood Warbler, Chiffchaff, Willow Warbler, Spotted Flycatcher, occasional passerine migrants.

Summer (June–August): Swift, Tree Pipit, Stonechat, Reed Warbler, Blackcap, Willow Warbler, Chiffchaff, Spotted Flycatcher.

Autumn (September–October): Occasional wader at Pen Ponds, commoner gulls, hirundines, migrants.

OTHER SITES IN THE AREA

20A WIMBLEDON COMMON AND PUTNEY HEATH

OS ref: TQ 247723/230739
Map p. 114

Somewhat overshadowed by the size and ornithological attractions of Richmond Park immediately to the west, the merits of the 1200-acre (480 ha) area comprising Wimbledon Common and Putney Heath are perhaps not always given the attention they deserve. Though much breeding census work has been carried out at this site and there have systematic observations of breeding and visiting species for many years, interest seems to have been greatest among local observers rather than visiting birders. This is a shame, as a well-timed tour of this area of common and heath with birch scrub and woodland can prove very productive.

Spring and early summer are the best times to visit, with resident species augmented by passage migrants and summer visitors. All three woodpeckers breed, as do Nuthatch, Treecreeper and the commoner tits, which until recently included the declining Willow Tit. Warblers are well represented, with breeding species including Whitethroat, Lesser Whitethroat, Blackcap, Chiffchaff, Willow and good numbers of Garden, while even Wood Warbler, usually recorded here on passage, has once stayed to breed. Spotted Flycatcher nests and Meadow Pipit retains a toehold in the area, though sadly Tree Pipit is nowadays likely only on passage. Other occasional passerine migrants include Whinchat, Wheatear and Pied Flycatcher, the latter being most likely in autumn when there is just a chance of something rarer turning up – in October 1988 London's fourth Yellow-browed Warbler was found here. The few ponds in the area are of no special ornithological interest, but Grey Wagtails may sometimes be found along Beverley Brook which runs along the western boundary of the site. Winter is the quietest time of year, with birds of most interest likely to comprise small flocks of Siskin and Redpoll, parties of Redwing and Fieldfare, and perhaps an occasional Woodcock, though exceptionally Waxwings have wintered in the area.

Green Woodpecker

On a historical note, the site's former importance for breeding species is underlined by the presence of breeding Red-backed Shrike and Redstart as recently as the 1960s. Even more remarkably, a male Cirl Bunting held territory from March to July 1967, an event unlikely to ever be repeated in the London area.

Access from central London is straightforward via the A3. Putney Heath lies to the north of the A3 Kingston Road just west of its junction with the A219. Wimbledon Common can be accessed by various footpaths or

Windmill Road from the A219 Wimbledon Park Side (becoming Parkside further south), from numerous residential roads along the southern side, or from a number of points along the A3. Overground trains run to Wimbledon station (walk northwest up Wimbledon Hill Road and High Street to the common) from Waterloo. The underground (District line) serves Southfields station (walk west along Augustus Road and Inner Park Road to Wimbledon Park Side), or alternatively travel one stop along to Wimbledon Park station for the local park (entrance in Wimbledon Park Road SW19), which has held Shoveler and Goosander on the lake in winter, turned up a Mediterranean Gull one recent autumn and attracted passerine migrants including Pied Flycatcher. Numerous bus routes serve the area, including numbers 57, 72, 85, 93, 200, 265 and 718.

21 KEW GARDENS

OS ref: TQ 182769
Map p. 114

Habitat
The Royal Botanic Gardens at Kew lie along the south bank of the River Thames about two miles (3.2 km) downstream from Richmond. A popular tourist attraction, the 300-acre (120 ha) gardens comprise a substantial collection of trees set out in a large area of lawns and borders containing exotic and native shrubs, an ornamental lake, a temperate house, a palm house and pond, an 18th-century pagoda, and Queen's Cottage, the grounds of which are managed as a 'wild' woodland. A towpath runs along the western boundary of the gardens by the Thames, with views across the river to Syon Park (home to a small heronry), and to the south there are sports fields and an extensive golf course in the Old Deer Park, which is also home to Kew Observatory.

For the visiting birdwatcher Kew mainly offers a range of commoner birds typical of London's inner suburbs, as well as a few woodland species which include the rather localised Lesser Spotted Woodpecker. The large captive collection of wildfowl may help to attract occasional scarcer wild visitors, while the Thames has over the years also produced various waterbirds, waders and overflying migrants. Despite the relatively small number of breeding species and regular visitors, no fewer than 128 species were recorded here between 1978 and 1992.

Species
Although breeding waterbirds are restricted to commoner species such as Great Crested Grebe, Canada Goose and Tufted Duck on the lake and the palm house pond, other species may join them outside the summer months. Wigeon, Gadwall, Shoveler and Pochard are the most likely, though the status of all of these is confused by birds in the collection. The same is also true for Mandarin Duck, with numbers of the captive residents being augmented in winter by visitors from the naturalised population which has its stronghold in nearby Surrey and Berkshire. It can sometimes be difficult to establish whether the birds on view are wild or tame – unless they start begging for food! Other wildfowl in the collection which could pose a trap for the unwary include Barnacle, Pink-footed and Greylag Geese, Shelduck,

Red-crested Pochard and Eider, but a wild Garganey on the lake one August and a hybrid male Ring-necked x Tufted Duck on nearby Kew Green Pond prove that more unusual wild wanderers may put in an appearance.

On the adjacent River Thames, however, birding is thankfully more straightforward, and outside the breeding season – especially during hard winter weather – it may be possible to see a range of species here. Typical birds such as Cormorant, Grey Heron and Mute Swan, which are present throughout the year, are joined by Great Crested and Little Grebes in winter, when there is also a regular small flock of Teal (try looking at Brentford Ait near Kew Green), the chance of scarcer ducks such as Goldeneye and Goosander, and oddities such as Shag may occur. Much more rarely, Red-necked Grebe, Ruddy Duck, Common Scoter and Guillemot have been seen here. Aside from Common Sandpipers along the tidal mud, Snipe on Syon Marsh and the occasional overflying Lapwing, waders of note are equally unusual. Of the gulls Black-headed is the commonest, but all of the other four regular species – Herring, Lesser Black-backed, Greater Black-backed and Common – may be present in varying numbers. From late summer it may be worth checking the larger gulls for Yellow-legged, which in recent years has occurred as far upstream as Barnes, and among the larger numbers present in winter there has been one record of a 'white-winged' gull, either Glaucous or Iceland. Common Tern is the only member of its family at all likely to be seen along the river.

A walk along the towpath could well produce a Grey Wagtail or perhaps a Kingfisher, both of which occasionally visit the lake, while scanning across the river towards Syon Park may be rewarded with occasional views of Ring-necked Parakeet, Kestrel or Sparrowhawk. A migrant Hobby is the only other likely raptor here – a pair even summered in Syon Park in 1992 – but both Red Kite and Common Buzzard have been recorded passing over.

Sparrowhawk

Back in the gardens themselves, much of the ornithological interest centres on the more secluded glades of Queen's Cottage grounds, in the south-west corner. Remote enough to escape the attentions of most of the visiting crowds, this woodland is divided north-south and east-west by paths and provides good opportunities to see a range of species, some of them at close quarters. The harsh two-note call of Pheasant denotes the presence of this species at one of its closest points to central London (take no notice of the Golden Pheasants in Rhododendron Dell – another species introduced by the park authorities). Woodcock is a possibility here in winter and Stock Doves can be seen in spring and summer, while the fortunate visitor may hear a rare migrant Cuckoo in late April or early May. Tawny Owls breed in the woods and the Little Owls which have been seen on the nearby golf course are presumably resident in the area. Both Green and Great Spotted Woodpeckers are likely in Queen's Cottage grounds, and Lesser Spotted also breeds though is certainly the scarcest of the three; listening out for its longer bursts of drumming or distinctive *pee-pee-pee* call in early spring, before the leaf cover on the trees gets too dense, offers the best chance of detection.

Unusual chats and thrushes are just that at Kew – unusual. With only irregular sightings of migrant Wheatears and single records of Redstart and Ring Ouzel, hopes of connecting with one are slim at best. Instead, resident commoner thrushes are joined in hard weather by variable numbers of Redwing and, usually in very wintry weather, Fieldfare. In spring and summer a few pairs of Blackcap and Willow Warbler will be on territory, but the latter is scarcer and occurs chiefly on passage; the only other regular breeding warbler in the area is Reed Warbler across the river in Syon Park, with Lesser Whitethroat, Garden and Sedge Warblers also confined to migration times. Goldcrest is resident, and there have been a handful of records of Firecrest. Spotted Flycatcher has declined and no longer breeds annually; migrant Pied Flycatchers have now been seen on four occasions in recent years and, exceptionally, a Red-breasted Flycatcher was found in early November 1989.

More typical of Kew's birdlife are the commoner woodland species in Queen's Cottage grounds which delight visitors with their tameness. Blue, Great and Coal Tits, and even Nuthatch, can be particularly confiding, coming to feeders along the path and occasionally taking morsels from outstretched hands, while Long-tailed Tits are fairly common and Tree-creeper is also resident. In addition to the commoner finches, Siskins visit in winter and are best looked for in the alders around the lake, while Redpoll may be found in stands of birch, though this species no longer breeds at Kew. With such a variety of trees in the gardens, the locality can occasionally attract specialist species such as Hawfinch (which still bred here 25 years ago). Buntings, however, are extremely rare, with single records only of Yellowhammer and Reed Bunting.

Timing

In botanical terms the gardens are at their best during spring and summer, and on weekends and during school holidays in these seasons they can become very crowded. For visiting birdwatchers an early morning or weekday visit to Queen's Cottage grounds is probably most rewarding between March and June, though the feeding activities of tit flocks can make winter trips also worthwhile. At this time there may also be ducks and other wintering waterbirds both on the lake and palm house pond and on the Thames. The river is also worthy of attention during spring and autumn, when tidal mud may offer the best chance of a wader in this area.

Access

Kew Gardens can be reached from central London via the A4 westbound through Hammersmith. Turn off at the Chiswick roundabout, where the A4 meets the elevated section of the M4 at its junction with the A406 North Circular Road and Chiswick High Road, and head southwest, bearing left after half a mile over Kew Bridge. The main entrance is on the right at Kew

Green, just after the bridge; there is parking near the gate or in the riverside car park, reached from Kew Green via Ferry Lane. There is another entrance further south along the A307 Kew Road (bear right at the lights after Kew Green), but parking is often more limited. The gardens are open from 9.30 am daily except on Christmas Day and New Year's Day, with last admission at 5.30 pm. Admission charges are currently £4.50 for adults, £3.00 for senior citizens and other concessions, and £2.50 for children; family tickets are available at £12.00.

By bus: numbers 7, 65 and 391 stop near the main entrance at Kew Green, with R68 running on Sundays only to Kew Gardens station from Richmond. *By underground*: from Kew Gardens station (District line), cross over Sandycombe Road and walk along Lichfield Road to the entrance on Kew Road. *By train*: Kew Gardens station is also on the small suburban line running from Richmond to Gospel Oak in north London.

Calendar

Resident: Great Crested Grebe, Cormorant, Grey Heron, Tufted Duck, Mute Swan, Sparrowhawk, Kestrel, Pheasant, Ring-necked Parakeet, Tawny Owl, Little Owl, Green Woodpecker, Great Spotted Woodpecker, Lesser Spotted Woodpecker (scarce), Grey Wagtail, Goldcrest, Nuthatch, Treecreeper.

Winter (November–March): Little Grebe, Mandarin Duck, Teal, Gadwall, Wigeon, Shoveler, oddities on the Thames, chance of Woodcock, Snipe (Syon Marsh), gulls, Redwing, Kingfisher (scarce), Fieldfare (hard weather), Redpoll, Siskin.

Spring (April–May): Chance of Hobby, occasional Common Sandpiper and Common Tern along the Thames, Stock Dove, hirundines, Reed Warbler (Syon Park), Blackcap, Willow Warbler, Chiffchaff, Spotted Flycatcher, occasional migrants including Skylark, Meadow Pipit and commoner warblers.

Summer (June–August): Swift, Reed Warbler, Blackcap, Willow Warbler, Spotted Flycatcher (declining).

Autumn (September–October): occasional Common Sandpiper and Common Tern along the Thames, commoner gulls, hirundines.

22 BUSHY AND HAMPTON COURT PARKS

OS ref: TQ 160690/166676

Habitat

These two parks, often treated ornithologically as a single unit, lie to the southwest of Richmond Park on the north side of the Thames where the river follows a broad U-course at Kingston and Surbiton. To the north is the larger Bushy Park, whose 435 hectares mainly comprise open grassland with bracken cover, along with some enclosed areas of managed woodland and copses and avenues of lime and horse chestnut. Most of the ornithological interest lies in the less disturbed western half of the park, which also has the best plantations and a small area of agricultural land; of the ponds here, Heron Pond and Leg of Mutton Pond prove most attractive to waterbirds. Hampton Court Park, lying to the south on the other side of the A308 Hampton Court Road, covers some 283 hectares in the shadow of Hampton Court Palace and Gardens. The landscape here is mainly one of open grassland with more avenues of limes and horse chestnuts, but with the additional attractions of the kilometre-long Long Water and Hampton Wick Pond, two of the most productive bodies of water in the area.

The parks are steeped in history, having been created by Cardinal Wolsey as a deer enclosure to surround Hampton Court Palace when it was built in the early 16th century. The palace subsequently passed to Henry VIII and was used by royalty until the mid-18th century. Bushy Park still retains its status as a royal park to this day, and together with Hampton Court Park benefited from regular coverage by official observers appointed by the Committee for Bird Sanctuaries in the Royal Parks until its abolition in 1979. A total of 150 species has been recorded between the parks over the years, of which around 95–100 are seen annually and some 45 breed.

Species

For waterbirds interest centres around Long Water and Hampton Wick Pond in Hampton Court Park and Heron and Leg of Mutton Ponds in Bushy Park, with the other ponds being too small or disturbed to warrant much attention. A pair of Great Crested Grebes has bred or attempted to do so in several recent years, but Little Grebe no longer does so and is now an uncommon winter visitor. Cormorants are occasionally noted, usually passing straight over, but Grey Herons are fairly regular visitors and can be seen fishing along undisturbed banks. Mute Swans breed but reach maximum numbers in winter, when Canada Geese are also at their most conspicuous. Mallard and Tufted Duck nest and Pochard has done so, but other ducks are most likely in winter; Shoveler is usually the most numerous visitor, but Teal has become increasingly regular and small numbers of Goosander are possible early in the morning, particularly on Long Water. Wigeon and Mandarin Duck are scarce visitors, the latter having also bred on four occasions, but other species such as Gadwall, Garganey, Pintail, Scaup and Smew have appeared very rarely indeed.

Of the raptors only Sparrowhawk and Kestrel breed, but Hobbies have been noted with increasing frequency, especially in late summer. There are also a handful of records of Common Buzzard and two of Merlin. Pheasant and Grey Partridge breed in small numbers, though at least some of the latter probably originate from a pair released in Bushy Park in 1992. Water Rail is occasionally recorded in winter but is not annual, and apart from regular flocks of Lapwing, occasional wintering Snipe and the odd Common Sandpiper on passage, waders are generally equally rare. An exception is Woodcock, at least one or two of which are recorded most winters in Bushy Park; Waterhouse Plantation and Keeper's Wood are said to be particularly favoured. Black-headed and Common Gulls can be fairly numerous in winter, but the larger gulls are generally scarce. Common Tern is the only member of its genus at all likely to occur, either at passage times or in summer when birds might wander from nearby Walton Reservoirs where they breed.

Stock Doves nest in both parks and are occasionally seen in small flocks in winter, but both Turtle Dove and Cuckoo occur only as passage migrants, especially in spring. Ring-necked Parakeets breed in small numbers. Unusually for a site in the London area Little Owl possibly outnumbers Tawny, with perhaps as many as 10 pairs of the former representing a high concentration across both parks. Kingfishers are occasionally seen, especially in autumn, but do not now breed. All three woodpeckers can be found in reasonable numbers.

Skylark and Meadow Pipit both breed and are present throughout the year, and likewise Pied and Grey Wagtails are also resident although the latter may not always nest. Aside from Stonechat, up to three of which often winter near Heron Pond in Bushy Park, chats are generally scarce: Wheatear is recorded most years, and Whinchat occasionally appears on passage, usually in season. Good numbers of both winter thrushes are present in season, though Redwing usually outnumbers Fieldfare. Of the warblers, Whitethroat, Blackcap, Chiffchaff and Willow all breed, and Lesser Whitethroat and Garden Warbler occur on passage and may occasionally stay to nest; somewhat rarer migrants are Sedge, Reed and Wood. Goldcrest also breeds and a handful of pairs of Spotted Flycatcher are present in summer. All of the commoner tits are well represented, as are Nuthatch and Treecreeper, but neither Marsh nor Willow Tit has occurred since the mid-1980s. Jackdaw joins the line-up of commoner corvids breeding here, with small numbers nesting in both parks. Formerly a numerous resident, Tree Sparrows have declined greatly and are nowadays usually only reported in winter, when numbers in Hampton Court Park may reach double figures. The commoner finches are joined by variable numbers of Siskin and Redpoll in winter, though Brambling remains somewhat irregular. Reed Bunting breeds most years but is generally uncommon.

Over the years coverage of both of these parks has produced a number of unusual visitors. Perhaps the rarest was London's third Black Kite which flew over Bushy Park in April 1986, but other notable finds have included a Woodchat Shrike in May 1992, a pair of Golden Orioles in May 1984, a Bittern in January 1982, two Hoopoes, Waxwing, overwintering Dartford Warblers in at least three years (including two together in 1994), and a selection of scarce migrants including Black Redstart, Ring Ouzel, Grasshopper Warbler and Firecrest.

Timing

A visit at most times of the year is likely to produce results. Any time from March to June will see woodpeckers and other woodland birds at their most active, and spring and, perhaps to a lesser extent, autumn bring the chance of migrant passerines and other species. In winter wildfowl should be looked for early in the morning, before disturbance becomes too great. Hampton Court is a very popular tourist attraction and the area can be flooded with crowds of visitors, particularly during the summer months and at weekends.

Access

The most direct route to Bushy and Hampton Court Parks from central London is the A3 and A308 via Kingston, but Kingston town centre can become very heavily congested with traffic. Alternatively, take the A316 from Hammersmith as far south as Hanworth, and turn left at the roundabout onto the A312 and then take the A313 towards Teddington. Soon after Hampton Hill station on Park Road turn right onto the A311 High

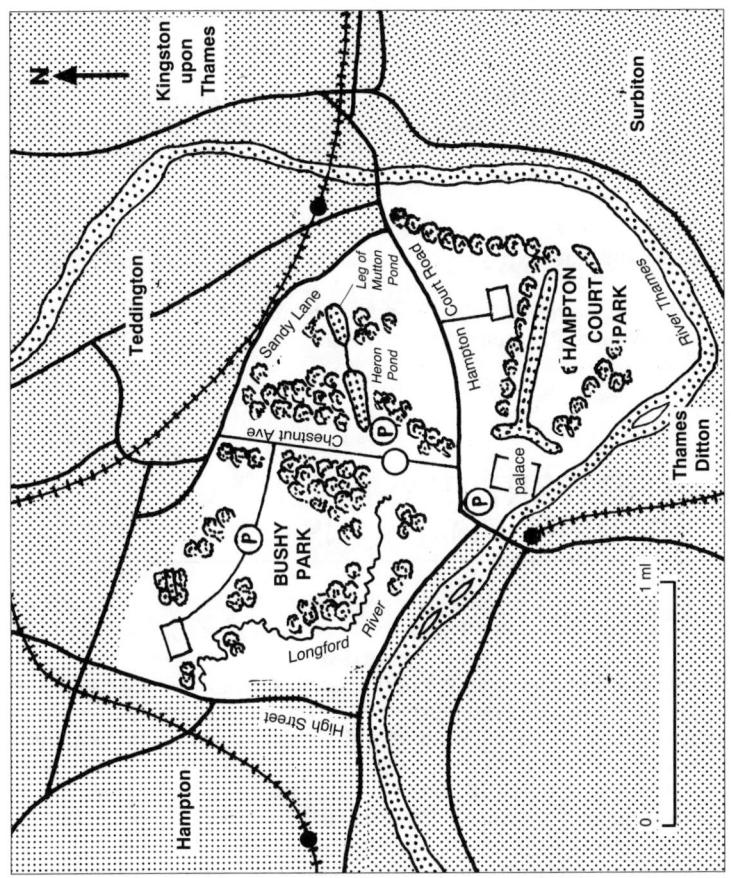

Street, and the northwest corner of Bushy Park is on the left. For the main entrance to Bushy Park and for Hampton Court Park, follow this road to the T-junction at the end, turn left and continue east along the north side of the river to Hampton Court Palace; park as signposted.

By bus: the area is well served by bus routes, including numbers 111, 131, 216, 267, 415, 431, 440, 572, 582, 726 and R68. *By train*: from Teddington station Bushy park is a short walk south along Park Road into Chestnut Avenue, which runs north-south through the middle of the park. For Hampton Court Park there are stations at Hampton Wick (northeast corner) and Hampton Court (southwest corner). There is no local underground station.

Calendar

Resident: Grey Heron, Tufted Duck, Pochard, Sparrowhawk, Kestrel, Grey Partridge, Pheasant, Lapwing, Ring-necked Parakeet, Tawny Owl, Little Owl, Green Woodpecker, Great Spotted Woodpecker, Lesser Spotted Woodpecker, Skylark, Meadow Pipit, Grey Wagtail, Goldcrest, Nuthatch, Treecreeper.

Winter (November–March): Little Grebe (uncommon), Cormorant, Shoveler, Teal, Goosander (scarce), chance of other wildfowl including

Mandarin Duck, Lapwing, occasional Snipe, Woodcock, Stonechat, Fieldfare, Redwing, Tree Sparrow, Redpoll, Siskin.

Spring (April–May): Great Crested Grebe, chance of Hobby, occasional Common Sandpiper, possibility of passage Turtle Dove and Cuckoo, hirundines, perhaps Wheatear, migrant warblers including Lesser Whitethroat and Garden Warbler.

Summer (June–August): Chance of Hobby (especially late summer), Whitethroat, Blackcap, Chiffchaff, Willow Warbler, Spotted Flycatcher.

Autumn (September–October): Kingfisher, hirundines, chance of Wheatear and Whinchat, commoner warblers.

23 THE NORTHEAST SURREY COMMONS

Habitat

The inclusion of sites from the northeastern sector of Surrey might seem out of place in a guide dealing with London, but all the locations included under this heading fall within the M25 'inner circle' and together form a discontinuous buffer zone of areas of ornithological interest between the outermost suburbs of southwest London and rural Surrey proper.

This is the leafiest fringe of the capital, and selecting any one area for inclusion would be to ignore the attractions of the many others. Instead, this account deals with a range of locations which comprise broadly similar habitat types, extending in the west from West End Common (TQ 125632), on the east side of the Mole Valley between Weybridge and Esher, through Esher Common (TQ 135625), Arbrook Common (TQ 145630), Fairmile Common (TQ 125617), Oxshott Heath (TQ 140614) and Prince's Coverts (TQ 160610), these sites known collectively as the Elmbridge Commons, to Ashtead Common (TQ 175595), Horton Country Park (TQ 190627), Epsom Common (TQ 190605) and as far east as the Banstead area, some 10 miles from the Mole Valley.

Much of this land is still wooded, although the northernmost tip of the North Downs encroaches a little into the east of the area and significant tracts of heathland and common can be found elsewhere; in ancient times more extensively wooded, the practice of clearance here has been traced back some 6,000 years. The result is a patchwork of open areas dominated by heather, gorse and various grasses and surrounded or linked by belts of ancient woodland which largely comprise oak, silver birch, sweet chestnut, beech and a few conifers, including Scots and Corsican pine and larch; more than 1,000 varieties of fungi are said to occur. Fragmentation of this habitat by a large number of roads and paths means that its attractiveness to some heathland speciality birds associated with southern England has been reduced, but it remains an important area for several locally notable breeding species.

Species

The combination of mixed woodland and heathland provides favoured habitat for one of the London area's scarcer breeding birds, the Hobby. Only a handful of pairs are known from the Surrey sector of the capital, but with a fair amount of patience and luck this attractive migrant falcon may be seen during summer; Epsom Common is as good as any a place to try. Sparrowhawk and Kestrel occur much more widely, while both Tawny and Little Owls also breed.

Another speciality of mature woodlands in the area is Woodcock, which may be heard squeaking and grunting during its peculiar roding flight at dawn and dusk. Numbers are never high and appear to fluctuate, but in recent years the species has been reported from West End Common, Esher Common, Prince's Coverts and Epsom Common during the breeding season; birds are also occasionally noted in winter. That other crepuscular speciality, Nightjar, is now so infrequent here that birders hoping to see this species would be much better advised to visit the southwest Surrey commons, where it is much more numerous. All three woodpeckers occur, with Great Spotted and smaller numbers of Lesser Spotted in the woods and Green typically in the more open areas. Cuckoo is present in summer.

Woodcock and Roe Deer

Skylarks and hirundines may pass through in numbers in spring and autumn, while perhaps surprisingly both Meadow and Tree Pipits occur in the area only on passage; higher vantage points on the downs can sometimes provide views of these and other diurnal migrants on the move. Similarly, Wheatear and Whinchat are restricted to passage periods, as is Redstart which does not breed despite the availability of apparently suitable ancient oak pasture woodland in areas such as Ashtead Common. In spring, occasional bursts of Nightingale song may be heard emanating from dense cover in the area, although this species also does not breed locally. Aside from the commoner thrushes, Redwing and

Fieldfare are present in winter and Ring Ouzel is an outside chance on the downland and commons on passage.

All of the commoner scrub and woodland warblers breed, and Blackcap, Willow Warbler and Chiffchaff can be particularly numerous. This is one of the best places in the London area to listen out for the distinctive song of Wood Warbler in spring, and migrants may appear in any suitable habitat in late April and early May; Arbrook and Fairmile Commons seem particularly favoured, and in 1994 a pair stayed to breed at West End Common. Dartford Warblers, which after breeding season records in the early years of the century were absent for many decades, have again recently bred at one site; in line with the current national increase in numbers, this species could perhaps re-establish a permanent population in this area with overspill from other nearby localities in Surrey. Conversely, while Grasshopper Warblers retained a toehold in the area as recently as the early 1990s, this species now seems to have been lost completely as a breeding bird. Goldcrest is resident and small numbers of Spotted Flycatcher are present in summer. Nuthatch and Treecreeper both occur widely, and in addition to the commoner tits both Marsh and Willow Tit are said to be present; in view of their rapidly declining fortunes, however, this now needs confirmation.

Finches include the occasional party of Brambling, Redpoll and Siskin in winter, but Hawfinches remain surprisingly rare visitors to what seems to be suitable habitat and are not recorded annually. Crossbills are likewise irregular visitors. Both Yellowhammer and Reed Bunting breed, and it is worth noting here that in the earlier years of the 20th century some of the last breeding records of Cirl Bunting in the region came from the Banstead and Epsom areas. This species, along with the likes of Woodlark and Red-backed Shrike, has sadly long since disappeared.

Areas of water of any size are few and far between in this area, so aquatic species typically comprise expected breeding birds. The 'stew ponds' on Epsom Common – Stew and Great Ponds – hold nesting Great Crested and Little Grebes, and Mandarin Duck has also recently colonised this site. Other ducks are generally unremarkable but may include small numbers of Teal, Gadwall and Shoveler outside the breeding season along with breeding Tufted Duck, and Garganey has been recorded on passage. Common and Green Sandpipers are the most likely of the few waders which have occurred, and there may be Lapwing on the nearby downs from midsummer onwards; scarcer species such as Wood Sandpiper and Little Ringed Plover are only very infrequently recorded. Kingfishers are resident, as are Grey Wagtails which might be encountered on ponds and streams in the area at any time of year.

Smaller waters such as the stew ponds are rarely likely to attract notable migrants, let alone rarities, but proving the exception to the rule was the male Little Bittern there in late May and early June 1996. Other rarities in the general area have been widely scattered in date and location and few in number, but have included a Roller at Oxshott for seven days in May 1959, a wintering Yellow-browed Warbler in Epsom in early 1991, a Red-breasted Flycatcher at Banstead in August 1958 and a Woodchat Shrike at Oxshott in June 1970.

Timing

With woodland providing the dominant interest, the period from late winter to early summer is the best time to visit. From midsummer birdsong becomes noticeably quieter, and by August many summer visitors will have fallen silent or already moved on. Autumn can still provide interest, particularly for birders prepared to try stints of migration-watching from higher vantage points on the downs. Winter is generally the quietest time, although thrushes, finches and the occasional oddity can still make a trip worthwhile. The whole area is popular with dog walkers and family outings, so unless you arrive early be prepared to share your chosen route with others, particularly on fine spring and summer days. Equally, make sure you avoid the Epsom area on Derby day each spring, when racecourse traffic jams local roads.

Access

This extensive area of commons, woods, heath and downs can be accessed from a variety of points. From junction 8 of the M25 near Redhill, the A217 runs alongside Banstead Heath to the east of Epsom Downs and north to Banstead Downs. Six miles (9.6 km) further west, from junction 9 the A24 runs northeast through Ashtead to Epsom, with Ashtead and Epsom Commons on the left about two miles (3.2 km) north of the motorway; coming from the opposite direction this route is the most direct to the area from central London (follow signs for the A3 from the City or West End and join the A24 southbound at Clapham). Alternatively, head northwest from junction 9 on the A243 towards Surbiton, turning left onto the A244 at the roundabout just north of the M25 towards Oxshott and Esher to reach sites including Oxshott Heath and Esher and Arbrook Commons. These same sites and Fairmile and West End Commons can also be reached from the west via the A3 and junction 10 of the M25. There are numerous car parks throughout the area, many of which have display boards detailing local wildlife and other information, and there is an extensive network of paths and trails giving access to the more interesting areas.

By bus: various bus routes serve this extensive area, with numbers 218, 415, 427, 437 and 527 stopping at or near West End, Fairmile and Esher Commons, 513 for Oxshott and, along with the K3, at Claygate Common just to the north of Princes Coverts, 465 for Ashtead Common, numbers 293, 498 and K9 for Epsom Common, and routes 420, 422, 520 and K8 for the Banstead area; additionally, number 516 links Epsom, Ashtead and Leatherhead. *By train*: the most convenient stations are at Belmont (for Banstead Downs), Epsom Downs, Epsom (for Epsom Common and Horton Country Park), Ashtead, Oxshott (the station entrance is immediately opposite the southeast corner of Oxshott Heath) and Claygate (for Arbrook Common); trains run mainly from Waterloo and Victoria, but some stations are also served by Thameslink services from Hertfordshire. There are no underground stations in the area.

Calendar

Resident: Great Crested Grebe, Little Grebe, Mandarin Duck, Tufted Duck, Sparrowhawk, Kestrel, Woodcock, Kingfisher, Green Woodpecker, Great Spotted Woodpecker, Lesser Spotted Woodpecker (scarce), Skylark, Grey Wagtail, Yellowhammer, Reed Bunting.

Winter (November–March): Teal, Gadwall, Shoveler, Redwing, Fieldfare, Brambling, Redpoll, Siskin.

Spring (April–May): Chance of Nightingale, occasional Redstart, Whinchat, Wheatear, Wood Warbler.

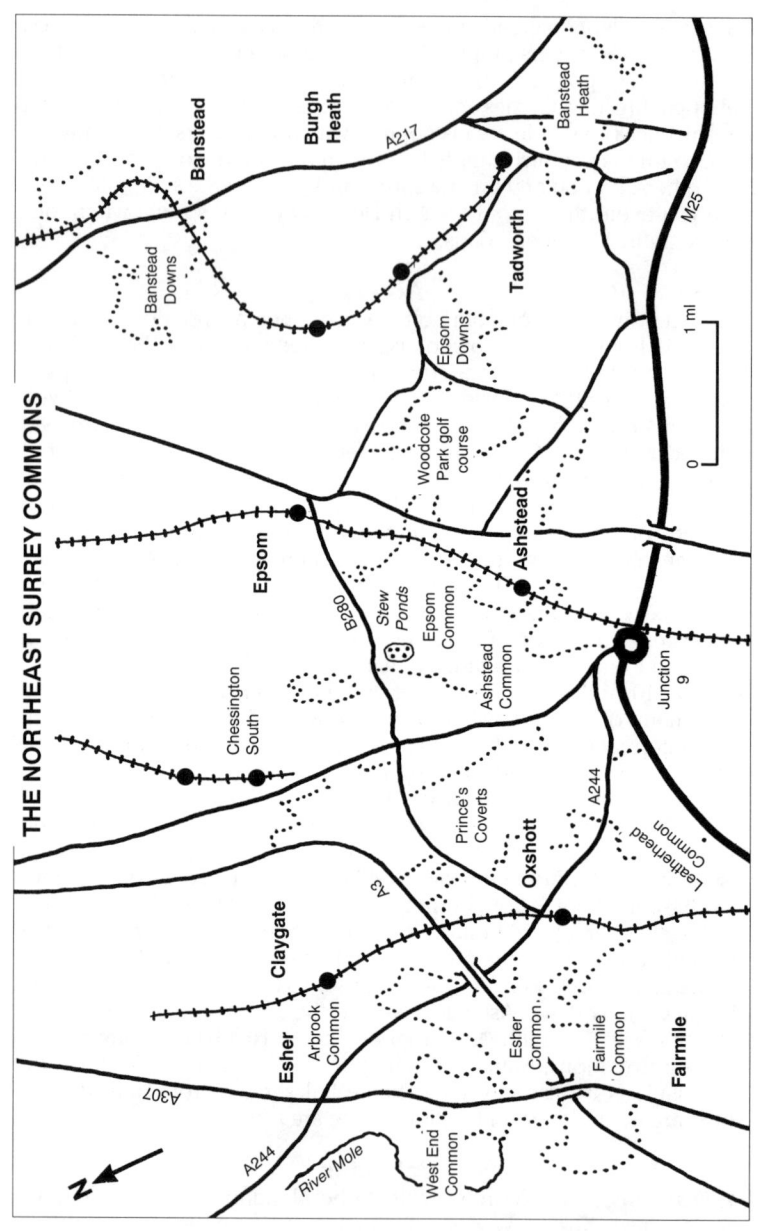

Summer (June–August): Hobby, Cuckoo, chance of Nightingale, commoner warblers and occasionally Wood, Spotted Flycatcher.

Autumn (September–October): Migrants including Skylark, pipits, chats and warblers.

THE THAMES RESERVOIRS

24 BARN ELMS
OS ref: TQ 228770

Habitat

This site overlooks the River Thames from its south bank close to Hammersmith Bridge and the Harrods Furniture Depository, a famous local landmark. Now decommissioned following the modernisation of London's water storage and supply infrastructure, the four former reservoirs and adjacent filter beds and land have been disposed of by Thames Water in a deal which has seen the development of a small part of the site for new housing.

The sale of this land has provided funding for one of the most important conservation initiatives in London in recent times – much of the rest of the area, including all of the four reservoirs, is being transformed into a new 100-acre Wildfowl and Wetlands Trust reserve. This will entail major landscaping, including the replacement of the symmetrical, raised-bank basins with naturally-edged ponds and lagoons, the establishment of islands to attract nesting waders and terns, and the creation of new reedbed habitat. There will be a visitor centre with a wide range of facilities and a collection of captive wildfowl will also be established, no doubt to help draw large numbers of visitors to this new inner-city attraction. The whole project will be a very important development for London's birdlife, particularly in this more urban inner quarter, but at the present time it is impossible to anticipate exactly which birds might be expected to occur.

In its pre-redevelopment days Barns Elms hosted important numbers of wintering wildfowl, and with its position on the Thames fly-way also attracted a good variety of passage waders. Perhaps more surprisingly for a site just four miles (6.4 km) from Westminster in the heart of the capital, it has an enviable list of rarer visitors, including a good number of unusual passerine migrants. The account that follows therefore highlights some of the more interesting records from past years, which if nothing else will serve to illustrate the potential of a wetland habitat in this location in years to come.

Species

When the reservoirs were full the water level was of sufficient depth to attract good numbers of Great Crested Grebes in winter. Scarcer grebes appeared annually, especially Red-necked Grebe, with one individual returning for five consecutive winters during the 1980s. Up to 100 Cormorants were often present in winter, with small numbers frequenting the nearby Thames throughout the year. Teal, Shoveler and Tufted Duck sometimes numbered more than 100 each in winter, usually in company with smaller numbers of Mallard, Gadwall, Wigeon, Pochard, Goldeneye and very occasionally Pintail. At one time Barn Elms was one of the best places in Britain for wintering Smew, with flocks in the 1950s approaching almost 100 birds, but as at many other sites numbers of this species have since declined dramatically. Garganey, Common Scoter, Goosander and Red-breasted Merganser have all turned up from time to time.

The reservoirs have consistently attracted waders in both numbers and variety, and regular migrants in spring and autumn have included Lapwing, Ringed and Little Ringed Plovers, Dunlin, Ruff, Redshank, Greenshank and Green and Common Sandpipers, the latter also occurring in winter. Other scarcer or more typically coastal species including Grey Plover, Sanderling, Little Stint, Curlew Sandpiper and Turnstone have put in occasional appearances, and there are also records of Temminck's Stint and Pectoral Sandpiper. Rarer still were the Buff-breasted Sandpiper found here in October 1981 and London's second-ever Spotted Sandpiper, a full summer-plumaged bird, in May 1988.

Interesting gulls and terns are a feature of this Thames-side site, and there have been some notable passage movements in spring and autumn. Yellow-legged Gulls may wander this far upriver from late summer, Little Gull is regular on migration and even Kittiwake has put in a number of appearances. London's only Bonaparte's Gull paid a brief visit back in January 1983 and Ring-billed Gull has also been recorded, while more ocean-going species such as Sabine's Gull, Long-tailed Skua and Grey Phalarope have all been logged here, usually in the wake of strong westerly weather in autumn. Other species such as terns may follow the Thames upstream from the east, and on occasion numbers can be spectacular. Parties of Common Tern are the most likely, but Black has appeared regularly and in September 1992 an impressive 265 birds of this species were noted during a single movement which affected much of southeast England. Arctic and Sandwich Terns have also been observed, and there are single records of White-winged Black Tern and, most unusually, Gull-billed Tern.

Among passerines, Black Redstart bred for several years by the Harrods Depository and has since occurred on passage, while regular observations have shown that Whinchat, Stonechat, Wheatear and Yellow Wagtail all

Male Black Redstart

pass through, sometimes in numbers, on migration. Small numbers of White and Blue-headed Wagtails and Rock Pipits have also been noted. Skylark and Meadow Pipit are regular winter visitors, and in spring and autumn most of the commoner warblers have been regularly recorded on passage, with only a few pairs of Reed Warbler and one pair of Blackcaps breeding in the area. The site list of vagrants is impressive, and includes Alpine Swift, Shorelark, Richard's, Tawny and no fewer than three Red-throated Pipits, Melodious Warbler, Serin, Ortolan Bunting and, most exceptionally of all, London's only Desert Wheatear, a male in April 1989.

Access and timing

At the time of writing construction work is in progress and access to the site for the general public is not possible. Once this new wetland reserve has been opened, it is likely that winter will remain the best time for numbers

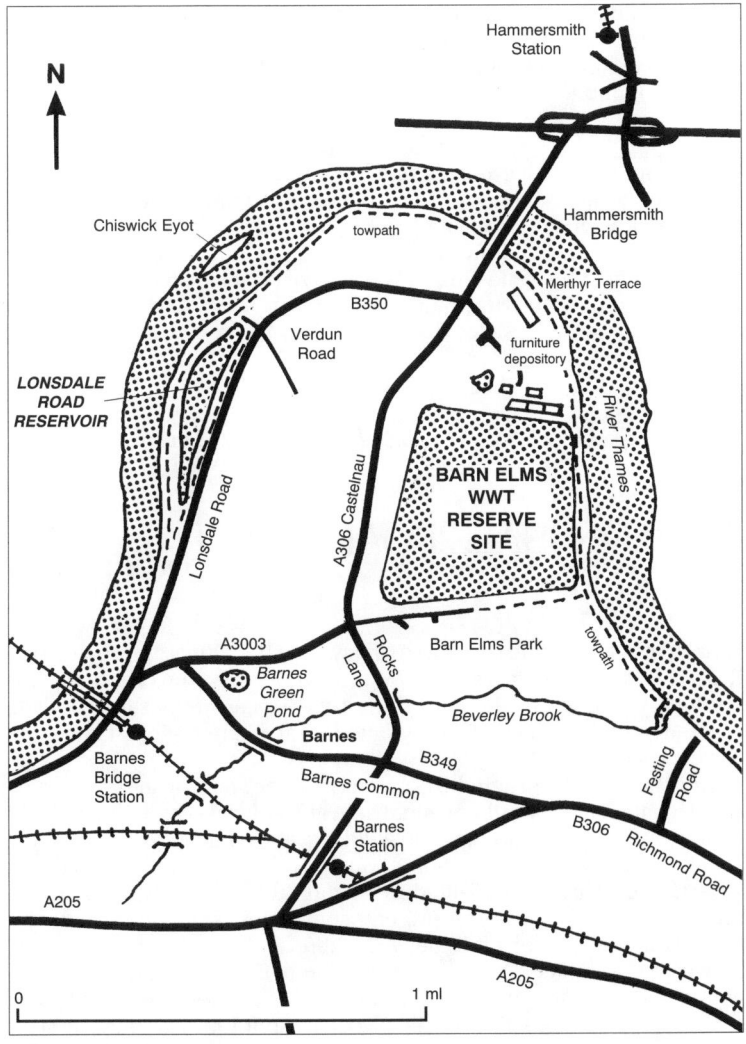

of wildfowl, and spring and autumn for waders and many other species. What used to be the main entrance to Barn Elms Reservoirs lies at the end of Merthyr Terrace SW13, the fourth turning on the left along the A306 Castelnau Road just south of Hammersmith Bridge. Exact access instructions may vary once construction at the site has been completed. From other areas of London, Hammersmith can be reached by the M4/A4 (which also connects with the A406 North Circular Road at Chiswick to the west) and the A40(M) (connecting to Marylebone Road via the M41 to Shepherd's Bush and the A219 Shepherd's Bush Road to Hammersmith). *By bus:* routes 9, 9a, 33 and 72 run along Castelnau Road between Barnes and Hammersmith, the R69 from Hammersmith stops near the junction of Merthyr Terrace and Lonsdale Road, and numbers 10, 211, 266, 267, 283, 290, 391 and H91 serve Hammersmith Broadway, 10 minutes' walk to the north of Barn Elms along Hammersmith Bridge Road. *By underground:* Hammersmith station (District, Hammersmith & City and Piccadilly lines) is in the Broadway next to the bus terminus. *By train:* services run from central London to Barnes station, just over a mile (1.6 km) to the south in Rocks Lane SW13, the continuation of Castelnau Road at Barnes Common.

Calendar

For obvious reasons it is not possible to provide details of birds expected at Barn Elms after a period of such significant change. The new reserve has been specifically designed to attract and retain various wetland species, especially wildfowl and waders, at particular times of the year, but it is likely to be some time before a list of established regular species in each season can be drawn up.

OTHER SITES IN THE AREA

24A LONSDALE ROAD RESERVOIR

OS ref: TQ 218775
Map p. 131

Situated just half a mile (0.8 km) to the west of Barn Elms, Lonsdale Road Reservoir (also known as Leg o'Mutton Reservoir) runs more or less north-south along the southern side of the Thames opposite Chiswick. Disused since 1960, it was finally granted local nature reserve status some 30 years later.

The reservoir is bordered by a variety of trees and bushes and has a small reedbed at the northern end. There are artificial islands that provide loafing places for Cormorants and wildfowl, and a pair of Common Terns usually nests in summer. Breeding waterfowl include Great Crested and Little Grebes, Mute Swan, Tufted Duck and Ruddy Duck, while in winter other wildfowl may also be present, sometimes in numbers although there is movement of birds between here and Barn Elms; up to 180 Shoveler, 130 Tufted Duck and small numbers of Pochard have been counted. Red-crested Pochard are annual, though most are very likely of suspect origin, while a Ring-necked Duck in April 1992 was only the sixth record for London. Water Rail is a possibility in winter. Yellow-legged Gulls have been noted on the Thames foreshore south of the reservoir. The trees along the western side support roosting Tawny Owl during the winter months, and in summer Kestrel, Sparrowhawk and up to two pairs of Stock Dove breed. Great Spotted Woodpeckers also nest, and Ring-necked Parakeets recently appear to have colonised the area from the other side of the river. Goldcrest and Reed Warbler, Blackcap and Willow Warbler all breed, and other warblers, especially Chiffchaff, are occasionally noted on passage. In spring and autumn the wooded margins of the reservoir may hold other interesting migrants, and both Pied Flycatcher and Nightingale have been discovered here in recent years. Siskin and Redpoll are possible in winter in the trees along the towpath by the Thames.

There is open access to the reservoir, which can be viewed easily from public footpaths or from Lonsdale Road itself. The Thames towpath can be reached from Lonsdale Road via Ferry Lane, by the northern entrance to the reservoir; park nearby in Verdun Road. There is another entrance at the southern end, with parking in Walnut Tree Close. Directions to the general area are as for Barn Elms Reservoirs, but from the south side of Hammersmith Bridge turn right (west) into Lonsdale Road and continue for half a mile (0.8 km) until you reach Verdun Road on the left. Public transport is also as for Barn Elms, but bus number R69 stops along Lonsdale Road; the nearest overground station connecting to central London is Barnes Bridge, half a mile (0.8 km) along the towpath to the south.

25 WALTON RESERVOIRS   OS ref: TQ 122685

Habitat

This group of reservoirs lies on the south side of the river between Hampton Court Bridge and Walton-on-Thames. Usually defined as comprising the Molesey Reservoirs (also known as Lambeth and Chelsea Reservoirs) between the Thames and the A3050 Hurst Road and Bessborough and Knight Reservoirs on the south side of the same road, the nearby Queen Elizabeth II Reservoir immediately to the south and Island Barn Reservoir a short distance to the east are also included here for geographical completeness.

The main reservoirs are relatively deep concrete basins with raised sides which are attractive to various waterbirds but offer little in the way of habitat to other species. In keeping with the landscape shared by most of London's main basins, rough pasture and a few isolated stands of trees are essentially all that the surrounding landscape offers in the way of other habitat – with the notable exception of Island Barn Reservoir, which is bordered around much of its circumference by more extensive scrub, including good areas of hawthorn, willow and elder, and rough pasture, weedy fields and a stream.

The smaller Molesey Reservoirs are no longer in service and are currently proving quite attractive to birds; the site clearly has potential and would benefit from rumoured plans for redevelopment as a nature reserve. The larger, deeper waters of Bessborough, Knight, Queen Elizabeth II and Island Barn Reservoirs that can also prove productive for birding, especially outside the breeding season when wintering wildfowl and passage waders are among the main attractions.

Species

Divers and the scarcer grebes are most likely to turn up at the deeper waters in winter, and some have stayed for prolonged periods; individuals occasionally commute between the different waters. As everywhere, Cormorant numbers have increased, and at peak times in winter approaching 200 birds may be present. Walton's rarest visitor was certainly the Mediterranean Shearwater found here in August 1984, still the only record for the London area. Grey Herons call in regularly from the heronry across the river in Kempton Park, and in 1995 a Little Egret reportedly paid a brief visit to Island Barn Reservoir.

Numbers of commoner waterfowl begin to build up in the autumn, when more than 50 Great Crested Grebes may be present along with perhaps several hundred each of Wigeon, Teal and Shoveler; up to almost 600 of the latter species were counted here in November 1994. Small numbers of some species, including Teal and Gadwall, may remain into the summer and Ruddy Duck is resident, while migrant Garganey have been noted in autumn. Diving duck can also be numerous, with 200 or so each of Tufted Duck and Pochard often present in winter, and Goldeneye numbers rising to between 30–40 late in the season. Goosander are less numerous, often barely reaching double figures, and Smew are nowadays a distinct rarity here. Other odd wildfowl have included Scaup, Long-tailed Duck, the occasional Common Scoter in summer and irregular Pintail.

Water Rail is a possibility in winter in suitable habitat. Waders are not likely in the area in numbers, but regular species on the reservoirs include Dunlin, Redshank and Green and Common Sandpipers. In recent years the range of other shorebirds noted on passage has included Oystercatcher, Avocet, Grey Plover, Little Stint, Ruff, Black-tailed Godwit, Whimbrel and Greenshank, while in August 1995 a White-rumped Sandpiper was found here. A short distance to the south at Hersham Gravel Pits (TQ 128663), Snipe are regular in some numbers and one or two Jack Snipe are recorded annually.

All of the commoner gulls form roosts on Queen Elizabeth II Reservoir in winter, and these can sometimes comprise spectacular numbers of birds. In 1993 the count of over 40,000 Black-headed Gulls was the highest in London for several years; a decade earlier almost twice that number were present. Common Gull is the next most numerous species, with in excess of 1,800 recently recorded. Scarcer species are occasionally noted, especially Little Gull and Kittiwake, and there has been one recent record of Glaucous Gull. Up to 12 pairs of Common Tern nest at Queen Elizabeth II Reservoir, and such is the attraction of this group of reservoirs in the Thames fly-way that Arctic, Sandwich, Little and Black have all been recorded moving through on passage recently.

Large counts of Swifts and hirundines are occasionally made at migration times, but the paucity of good habitat means there is often little else of interest around the reservoirs. Rock Pipit and White Wagtail have been noted and Yellow Wagtails can sometimes gather in small flocks on passage, but the only other noteworthy passerines in much of the area are likely to be the occasional migrant Wheatear or Whinchat in spring and autumn and, with luck, the possibility of a Black Redstart in winter. Also worthy of mention is the large roost of Ring-necked Parakeets at nearby Elmbridge Leisure Centre (TQ 107678). This introduced species is present in the area throughout the year, but sizeable numbers gather together in winter and this roost held as many as 697 birds in December 1994 – probably an all-time British record.

Timing
Walton Reservoirs offer good wildfowl watching from autumn through to spring, and during the winter months the gulls roosts on Queen Elizabeth II Reservoir can be very impressive. Waders and terns are best during spring and autumn; this group of reservoirs is at its quietest in midsummer. Bear in mind that the view from the entrance to Bessborough and Knight Reservoirs looks south into the sun, so earlier or later visits may offer easier birding.

Access
At present a complicated policy towards access means that entry is possible with a Thames Water permit to the Walton Reservoirs, but Queen Elizabeth II and Island Barn Reservoirs are only accessible by special permission (usually only for wildfowl counters). Even with a permit to the Walton Reservoirs, advance notice may be necessary for weekend visits.

Walton-on-Thames can be reached from junction 1 of the M3, or from the A316 from central London at the same intersection, by turning west onto the A308 and then south onto the A244. Leave the town centre north on the A3050 Terrace Road, becoming Hurst Road; the entrance to Walton Reservoirs is just over a mile (1.6 km) along this road. For Queen Elizabeth II Reservoir, turn right onto the B369 Walton Road immediately south of Knight Reservoir, follow this to the end, turn right again into Molesey Road and park nearby for the main entrance. For Island Barn Reservoir continue down Molesey Road for another quarter of a mile (0.4 km), turning left into Island Farm Road and right down Ray Road to the entrance.

To reach Elmbridge Leisure Centre for the Ring-necked Parakeet roost, turn off west from the A3050 Terrace Road at the roundabout about three-quarters of a mile (1.2 km) north from Walton town centre. The leisure centre is 200 metres along this road by the river.

By bus: number 718 runs along the A3050 past Walton Reservoirs and Elmbridge Leisure Centre, and the 431 stops along Walton Road between Walton Reservoirs and Queen Elizabeth II Reservoir. Routes 131, 451, 461, 501 and 561 serve Molesey Road for the entrance to the latter site and for Island Barn Reservoir. *By train:* overground services from Waterloo call at Hersham station (connecting with bus 501 along Molesey Road) and Walton-on-Thames. There is no local tube service.

Calendar
Resident: Cormorant, Ruddy Duck, Ring-necked Parakeet.

Winter (November–February): Great Crested Grebe, Wigeon, Teal, Shoveler, Tufted Duck, Pochard, Goldeneye, Goosander, large numbers of roosting gulls, possibility of Black Redstart (irregular).

Spring (March–May): Lingering wildfowl, passage waders, Common Tern, chance of passerine migrants including Yellow Wagtail, Whinchat and Wheatear.

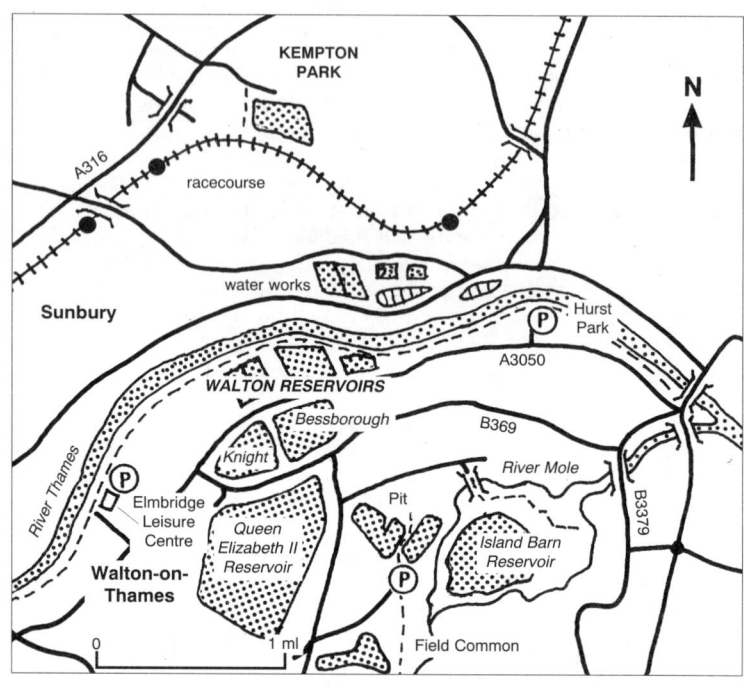

Summer (June–July): Common wildfowl perhaps including Teal and Gadwall, occasional passage waders, Common Tern.

Autumn (August–October): Possibility of Garganey, Dunlin, Redshank, Green Sandpiper, Common Sandpiper, other waders, Common Tern, chance of passerine migrants including Yellow Wagtail, Whinchat and Wheatear.

26 KEMPTON PARK

OS ref: TQ 122702
Map above

Habitat, species and access

Kempton Park lies to the north of Walton Reservoirs just across the Thames between Hampton and Sunbury. The area is best known for its racecourse, but in ornithological terms is important because of the disused reservoirs, gravel pit and other habitats which between them hold a good range of breeding, migrant and wintering species. One of the two main reservoirs which used to provide much of the focus for birds, Kempton Reservoir West, was drained in 1983 and has since been all but levelled; Thames Water is in the process of building an advanced water treatment plant on this part of the site. The other main basin, Kempton Reservoir East, has been earmarked by the company for the development of a 50-acre waterfowl refuge. Other elements of the 134-acre site include Kempton Park Gravel Pit, the Stain Hill Reservoirs, several other smaller bodies of water and, to the south and east, some small belts of mature woodland and an area of damp pasture.

Because of the changing nature of the site, it is not possible to anticipate accurately which species might be expected at particular times of year in the future. However, Thames Water's planned reserve will aim to retain existing wetland visitors such as the large numbers of Teal, Wigeon, Shoveler and Gadwall in winter and regular Garganey on passage, while the introduction of purpose-designed habitats for waders may attract Ringed Plovers to breed alongside the Little Ringeds which currently nest. Many other waders have been attracted to the muddy margins of Kempton Reservoir East over the years, including regular Snipe and Lapwing in winter and occasional breeding Redshank, and commoner passage waders such as Greenshank and Common Sandpiper are often present in spring and autumn. There is a thriving heronry which contained 35 pairs in 1994.

Greenshank

Other less regular visitors to the area in the past have included Black-necked and Red-necked Grebes and various wildfowl including Pintail, Scaup and Smew. In addition there have been many records of rare visitors, including Spoonbill, Spotted Crake, Black-winged Stilt, Temminck's Stint, Mediterranean Gull, Firecrest and London's first Common Rose-finch. Scarce species are still sometimes recorded, and in May 1996 Hoopoe, Pectoral Sandpiper and a pair of Avocets were all logged here – the latter staying to nest and making history by becoming not only

London's first breeding pair, but also the first to successfully raise young at an inland site anywhere in Britain.

Parts of the area have unlimited access, but the only means of entry to the east reservoir at present is by special Thames Water permit. However, with the development of this part of the site as a nature reserve the declared intention is to open it up to the public, with access to new hides and a raised terrace for birdwatching.

To reach the area from central London, join the A316 at Hammersmith and follow it southwest as far as the Sunbury roundabout, just north of junction 1 of the M3 (or from outer areas, via the M3 which connects at junction 2 with junction 12 of the M25). Turn east at this roundabout along Nallhead Road and continue for a third of a mile (0.5 km) as far as the school. Park where convenient, walk south down the public footpath which runs along the west side of Kempton Reservoir East and explore the area.

By Bus: local bus routes serving the area include numbers 290, 440 and H25. *By train:* services from central London stop at Kempton Park station, near the southwest corner of the site. There is no local underground service, although bus 290 connects with the District line at Richmond.

27 QUEEN MARY RESERVOIR

OS ref: TQ 070695

Habitat

Lying to the north of the Thames between Shepperton and Ashford, Queen Mary Reservoir constitutes the largest single body of water in the London area. In places more than one mile (1.6 km) across, its vast surface area is almost divided in two by a causeway which extends from the northern bank for three-quarters of a mile (1.2 km) out across the middle of the reservoir. Sailing is popular, especially in the area west of the causeway. Due to its size and depth Queen Mary rarely freezes over, a feature which used to be very attractive for wintering waterbirds forced off the surrounding waters during harsh weather.

However, in ornithological terms the reservoir is only a shadow of its former self. The decline in its importance has been brought about by the constant extraction of gravel over the last 15–20 years. It is almost certainly far too deep now, and the constant stirring up of the mud and gravel means that it holds little or no underwater vegetation and is probably relatively sterile. Consequently, many of the past records for the site are no longer an indication of what is likely to occur now, with formerly regular species either no longer using the reservoir or appearing only rarely. A good example of this is Goldeneye, up to 100 of which used to be regular in the 1970s: this species is now something of a rarity here. The same is true for Goosander, and even commoner species such as the diving ducks and Great Crested Grebe have plummeted in number. Not surprisingly, many of the rarer waterfowl used to turn up among the more numerous species – now they go elsewhere. In short, it is rapidly becoming a birdless zone.

Charlton Gravel Pits, on the eastern side of the area, are viewable from the embankment of the reservoir, although they are partially obscured by trees. On the western side lie the more productive Queen Mary Gravel Pits, which are surrounded by belts of thick scrub with a small pocket of woodland at the southern end. This area can also be observed from the reservoir embankment.

Species

Queen Mary Reservoir, perhaps more so than most other reservoirs and gravel pits in the West London area, can be particularly productive in lengthy cold spells when other shallower waters freeze over. Despite degradation of the habitat for waterbirds, oddities are still occasionally found among the commoner species. Most winters these include a diver, usually Great Northern or Red-throated, and individuals may stay for protracted periods. Scarcer grebes such as Red-necked and Slavonian are also a possibility, though neither is annual. Throughout the winter there are usually large congregations of Great Crested Grebes, with numbers from August through until March sometimes exceeding 300.

Cormorants occur in some numbers here outside the breeding season, with more than 100 birds present at peak times. There have been occasional winter records of Shag, while more unusually Little Egrets have twice been found on neighbouring Charlton and Queen Mary Gravel Pits, and in July 1986 the latter site also attracted a Spoonbill.

Red-throated Diver

Shelduck has bred in several recent years. Winter wildfowl numbers have declined markedly and dabbling ducks are generally unremarkable, with few large recent gatherings of species such as Shoveler and Teal, and only the very occasional record of more unusual species such as Garganey and Pintail. Diving duck are also much less numerous, with wintering Goldeneye peaking at only around 20 in recent years, and Goosander now absent from the reservoir and just the occasional party reported on Queen Mary Gravel Pits – a far cry from the gathering of 440 birds counted on the reservoir in the cold weather of January 1985.

The lack of exposed mud means that Queen Mary Reservoir is not best suited for passage waders, but species occurring occasionally in small numbers around the banks include Oystercatcher, Lapwing, Little Ringed Plover, Dunlin, Redshank, Greenshank, Green Sandpiper and especially Common Sandpiper. Other less regular species, often noted moving straight through, include Black-tailed Godwit, Curlew, Whimbrel, Grey and Golden Plovers and Knot.

The reservoir has a good record for attracting storm-blown seabirds, usually after strong westerly winds in autumn, and these have included Leach's Storm-petrel, Long-tailed Skua, auks and Grey Phalarope. During the great storm of October 1987, this reservoir alone held three Grey Phalaropes, four Sabine's Gulls and over 20 Little Gulls. The latter species is a fairly regular migrant in smaller numbers, usually in autumn, and both Kittiwake and Mediterranean Gull have occurred from time to time, though both are more erratic in their appearances. In spring and autumn, migrating terns also use the reservoir, occasionally in large numbers. Although no longer a breeding species, Common Tern can be expected any time from April to September, and on passage parties of Arctic and Black Terns may sometimes be present. Wandering Sandwich and Little Terns have been recorded, and remarkably there were no fewer than 11 records of White-winged Black Tern here between 1961–1978, though none has occurred since.

Queen Mary can sometimes prove productive for other species. Birds of prey include Sparrowhawk, which is often seen hunting around the banks and may breed locally, the ubiquitous Kestrel and, from April to September, regular Hobby. Rarer species such as Osprey and Merlin have occurred and, perhaps the most astonishing of all records from this site, London's first Gyr Falcon turned up here briefly in early March 1971. Other species occurring in the surrounding area include resident Ring-necked Parakeet, Kingfisher and Great Spotted Woodpecker.

Of the passerines, Meadow Pipits and good numbers of Pied Wagtails favour the weedy concrete banks of the reservoir outside the breeding season, and in spring and autumn sizeable parties of Yellow Wagtails may be present. Rock and Water Pipits and White Wagtail have also occurred on migration, but are irregular here. Neighbouring Charlton and Queen Mary Gravel Pits have breeding Reed Warblers and sometimes attract interesting passage migrants such as Pied Flycatcher, Redstart and Nightingale, and there is a recent record of Waxwing from the latter site.

Timing

Early morning visits reduce the chances of disturbance from water sports activities, which may force any wildfowl present to move off to other quieter waters in the area. The large surface area and extensive perimeter of this reservoir may mean that species such as wildfowl and waders can be spread out over a considerable distance and take some searching for. Late autumn through to early spring sees the highest numbers of duck present and the chance of other scarce waterbirds such as a diver or rare grebe, while spring and autumn are, as always, best for passage waders and terns. After severe westerly weather in the latter season, this and the large reservoirs in the nearby Colne Valley are the best positioned in the London area to receive storm-driven seabirds.

Access

Entry to the reservoir is by Thames Water permit only, between 7.30 am and 4.30 pm from Wednesday to Sunday. Thames Water is currently working to improve access around the reservoir, especially to benefit disabled visitors. Both gravel pits are private but can be viewed in part from the reservoir embankment.

The main entrance to Queen Mary Reservoir is situated at the northeast corner, adjacent to the junction of Ashford Road and the A308 Staines Road West south of Ashford. Leave the M3 west at junction 1 at its intersection with the A316 and head west for 1.25 miles (2 km) to this junction; alternatively, from the west leave the M25 at junction 13 eastwards on the A30 to Staines, and continue southeast on the A308 to the reservoir. Park in the car park inside the main entrance and walk up the embankment to view.

By bus: numbers 290 and 592 stop almost opposite the main entrance, and number 440 runs along the A308 on the north side of the reservoir.

By train: services from Waterloo call at Ashford station, from where bus 592 connects with the reservoir.

Calendar

All year: Great Crested Grebe, Cormorant, Sparrowhawk, Kestrel, Ring-necked Parakeet, Kingfisher, Great Spotted Woodpecker.

Winter (December–February): occasional divers and scarcer grebes, wildfowl including Goldeneye (uncommon), outside chance of Mediterranean Gull and Kittiwake.

Spring (March–May): Hobby (from late April), Common Sandpiper and other passage waders, Little Gull (scarce), Common, Arctic and Black Terns, Swift and hirundines, Pied and Yellow Wagtail, other migrant passerines including occasional White Wagtail.

Summer (June–July): Shelduck (most years), chance of Hobby, occasional Common Tern, Reed Warbler (gravel pits).

Autumn (August–November): Hobby (until September), Shoveler, Goldeneye (few from October), Common Sandpiper and other passage waders, Little Gull, Common, Arctic and Black Terns, Pied and Yellow Wagtails, other migrant passerines (especially gravel pits).

OTHER SITES IN THE AREA

27A BEDFONT LAKES COUNTRY PARK
OS ref: TQ 078726

This underwatched area lies just over one mile (1.6 km) to the north of Queen Mary Reservoir on the other side of Ashford, and a short distance east from Staines Reservoirs. The site comprises two landscaped water-filled pits, Bedfont Lake and Princes Lake, both of which are surrounded by rough grassland. The deeper Princes Lake is leased to the Princes Water Ski Club and despite disturbance is still favoured by wildfowl, partly because of the cover afforded by its well-vegetated islands. During periods of excessive water sports activities birds tend to relocate onto Bedfont Lake, the more secluded of the two waters. Designated as a local nature reserve and managed by the London Borough of Hounslow, this 190-acre (76 ha) lake and its margins have undergone a major transformation since the redevelopment of the area from a landfill site in the early 1990s, and the reserve supports good areas of woodland with willow carr and a reedbed fringe.

Up to three pairs of Great Crested Grebe and one or two pairs of Little Grebe usually nest, while breeding wildfowl include Pochard and Ruddy Duck. Gadwall, Shoveler and Teal are regular outside the breeding season, and the full sawbill complement of Goosander, Red-breasted Merganser and Smew has been recorded here in recent winters. Water Rail and Snipe are also possible at this time of year. Little Ringed Plover has attempted to breed, and the fringes of the lake have attracted passage Ringed Plover, Lapwing, Redshank, Greenshank, Common and Green Sandpipers and even Wood Sandpiper on a number of occasions. Common Terns are regular in spring and autumn, and oddities have included Little Gull and Sandwich Tern.

In winter Short-eared Owls have occasionally hunted over the surrounding grassland, in which a few pairs of Skylark and Meadow Pipit still breed. The reedbeds were once heavily used by large numbers of hirundines, Yellow Wagtails and Reed Buntings for roosting, and in September 1982 a total of 327 Yellow Wagtails was caught and ringed at the roost here – about one-sixth of all the Yellow Wagtails ringed in the UK that year. Around 20 pairs of Reed Warbler breed in the area and Chiffchaff is occasionally recorded in winter, while migrant passerines occurring either here or at nearby Bedfont Cemetery have included Nightingale, Redstart, Ring Ouzel, Grasshopper Warbler and Pied Flycatcher. Rarer still were records of Quail in June 1994 and Bittern in February 1995.

To reach the site from Queen Mary Reservoir, take the B378 Convent School Road into Ashford and leave the town centre north on the B3003 Clockhouse Lane. This road runs between Princes and Bedfont Lakes north of the railway and just south of the junction with the A30/A315 Staines Road. Park in the reserve car park and check in at the information centre to enquire about access to the nature reserve. Princes Lake is private and can be viewed from Clockhouse Lane. Bus numbers 116 and 419 run along Staines Road; Heathrow Terminal 4 underground station (Piccadilly line) is about a mile (1.6 km) walk to the north across the A30/A315 roundabout along Great South West Road, and Ashford overground station is about one mile (1.6 km) to the west back through the town centre.

27B THORPE PARK   OS ref: TQ 030681

The unlikely inclusion of the home of one of Britain's biggest amusement parks in a birdwatching site guide can be attributed largely to the possibility of finding one species: Smew. While by no means guaranteed here, this rare wintering duck has appeared in several recent seasons, and as many as 26 birds were counted here in February 1996. Along with the gravel pits in the Colne Valley and at nearby Wraysbury, just outside the M25, this makes Thorpe Park perhaps one of the more likely possibilities for locating this species around London between late November and mid-March. Birds are especially likely to appear in southeast England following severe weather in the Low Countries, and ice-free waters in the West London area are typically among those benefiting from influxes at such times.

There are other ornithological attractions that can be taken in while searching for Smew. Divers and scarce grebes such as Red-necked and Slavonian have occasionally turned up in winter. Several species of wildfowl winter in numbers, with Gadwall and Wigeon sometimes totalling more than 100 each, and Goldeneye often get into double figures here. Beware of Red-crested Pochards often reported: these birds are part of the collection. In summer Great Crested Grebes nest, and there are good populations of wetland passerines such as Reed Warbler and Reed Bunting.

Thorpe Park lies just northeast of the M3 and M25 intersection at Thorpe, and access is well signposted from the A320 between Staines and Chertsey. Many of the pits have been given over to water sports, but quieter areas can be checked from the main car park at the amusement park (open from late March to late October) and from the public footpath which runs from St Mary's Church in Coldharbour Lane to the A320. Other pits in the area can be viewed from the A320 or from adjacent minor roads, including Ten Acre Lane north of Thorpe. Bus numbers 436, 440, 451, 561 and 718 run along the A320, with the 290 service extended beyond Staines (connecting with the overground station) on summer Sundays to Thorpe Park.

THE COLNE VALLEY

28 STAINES RESERVOIRS OS ref: TQ 051731

Habitat

Staines Reservoirs is one of the best known birding sites in the London area and, along with Beddington Farm and Rainham Marsh, must also rank among the best in terms of the total number of species recorded within its boundaries. Designated as an SSSI, the attractions of these two basins in the Colne Valley fly-way just south of Heathrow Airport include good numbers of wintering wildfowl, a wide range of passage birds (including several regionally and nationally scarce species) and an enviably long list of rarities.

Completed in 1902, the reservoirs occupy a total of 424 acres (170 ha), with the south basin reaching a depth of 29 feet (9 m) and the north basin 38 feet (12 m). These two elevated concrete-banked bodies of water are divided by an east-west causeway which has been designated as a public footpath, affording excellent access to panoramic views across both reservoirs. Occasionally, one or both of the basins is drained, creating an excitingly rich habitat of shallow lagoons and pools with muddy margins, shingle bars and gravel islands that prove extremely attractive to wildfowl, waders and other species; however, there is no set pattern as to when the draining occurs, and effectively it is not much more often than once every few years.

Habitat for landbirds is largely provided by the few areas of trees, hawthorn scrub and bramble tangles around the rough pasture on the outer banks, while there is also more limited cover along the banks of the causeway which sometimes attracts commoner migrants and the occasional scarcer visitor.

Species

The reservoirs in this sector of London seem to attract one or two divers most winters, and while Staines is not always favoured, Great Northern, Red-throated and Black-throated have all been recorded in the past (though less frequently in recent years). Among the grebes Black-necked is the real speciality: this site is the most reliable for the species in the London area, with small numbers occurring in autumn and usually also in spring. Occasional Slavonian and Red-necked Grebes are also found most years, and good numbers of Great Cresteds can be present outside the breeding season. Some large counts of Cormorants have been made in recent years, and occasionally one or two Shags may put in an appearance in the winter months. Grey Herons can be quite numerous if water levels are low, and exceptionally rarer herons have been noted – there are records of both Purple Heron and more recently Little Egret.

Black-necked Grebes

From early autumn through to spring wildfowl are a dominant feature of the reservoirs. Canada Geese and other species in the Staines area seem to favour the local gravel pits and Staines Moor, but in passage periods parties of Brents occasionally drop in on the reservoirs, presumably en route to or from wintering areas on the south coast, and in autumn 1984 London's first Black Brant – the vagrant North American form of Brent Goose – made a prolonged stay here. Shelduck occur regularly, and seem to be most numerous when the reservoirs are drained; at such times when conditions are right the species has bred here.

Among the dabbling duck, Teal are present in variable numbers, occasionally in the low hundreds, while Wigeon may peak at over 200 birds in December and January. A similar number of Shoveler can also be present, but Gadwall is typically less numerous. All of these species may occasionally occur during the breeding season in small numbers, particularly if the basins have been partially drained. Pintail are scarcer but regular visitors from September to April, while Garganey are irregular on passage and best hoped for when the water level is low. Among the diving species Tufted Duck are well represented, with peak counts in late summer reaching up to 1,000 or more birds in recent years, and numbers in winter sometimes exceeding 2,000; the largest congregations occur after the reservoirs have been drained, allowing vegetation to grow and provide an abundance of food once the basins have been refilled. Accompanying the Tufted Duck can be even greater numbers of Pochard – 3,200 were present in December 1994 – and Staines often logs good counts of Goldeneye, especially during early spring when numbers may well exceed 100 birds. Wintering flocks of Ruddy Duck sometimes total 150 or more birds, but though regular, Goosanders occur in much smaller parties. Scaup are rare but seem to put in an appearance most years during autumn or winter, while other less expected wildfowl visitors have included Red-crested Pochard, Ferruginous and Long-tailed Ducks, Common and Velvet Scoters and even Eider. Smew are very unlikely here and best searched for at nearby Wraysbury Gravel Pits (TQ 015735), just west across the M25 from Staines Reservoirs.

In spring and autumn the reservoirs regularly attract migrating waders, some pausing to rest and feed and others moving straight through. Lapwing, Golden, Ringed and Little Ringed Plovers, Dunlin, Redshank, Greenshank and Common Sandpiper are among the many species that can be seen at these times, and if the basins are being drained the commoner species can occur in sizeable flocks. Some species may also breed if conditions are right, and during 1994 when both basins were drained at least six pairs of Ringed Plover and eight pairs of Little Ringed Plover were present. Other passage waders which may exploit this excellent habitat at such times include Grey Plover, Curlew Sandpiper, Little Stint, Wood and Green Sandpipers, Spotted Redshank, Ruff and Snipe, while more typically coastal species such as Sanderling, Turnstone, Knot and Bar-tailed Godwit may also appear. Black-tailed Godwit is also a possibility, and Curlew and Whimbrel usually pass through in one and twos most years. When not drained, passage waders often seem to favour the west bank of the north basin. Part of the appeal of Staines is that anything can turn up at any time, and rare waders seem to appear almost annually. Red-necked Phalaropes have been seen in several recent years, and in 1992 a fly-over party of three summer-plumage Dotterel was the site's third record of the species. There have also been many true vagrant waders, including Collared Pratincole, Sharp-tailed, Pectoral and Buff-breasted Sandpipers, an overwintering Baird's Sandpiper, Long-billed Dowitcher, three Lesser Yellowlegs and two Wilson's Phalaropes.

In autumn strong southwesterly weather has produced notable records of ocean-going species such as Grey Phalarope, Leach's Storm-petrel and Sabine's Gull, and very infrequent visits from skuas have included a single record of Long-tailed. This is the best site for Little Gull in the London area, with spring and autumn passage being the prime times to connect and numbers sometimes being impressive: in late April 1995 a major influx brought 186 birds. Much smaller parties are the norm in both passage periods, while singletons are occasionally also seen in summer and winter. Kittiwakes appear almost annually, though seemingly as often on passage as due to adverse coastal weather conditions. Outside the breeding season good numbers of commoner gull species form pre-roost gatherings here, providing the chance to search for a Mediterranean Gull or, more rarely, one of the larger 'white-winged' species – in recent years Iceland has tended to be more regular than Glaucous, though either would be notable. Rarer still was London's second Ring-billed Gull here in November 1982.

Tern passage is often healthy in both spring and autumn, and usually involves Common, Arctic and Black Terns. Up to 50 pairs of Common Tern have bred on specially-constructed tern rafts in recent years. Careful examination of migrant terns has produced occasional Sandwich and Little, both London scarcities, and there have been records of genuine rarities such as Caspian, Whiskered, White-winged Black and – perhaps the most remarkable of all of Staines' rarities – Sooty Tern.

While waterfowl, waders, gulls and terns provide much of the focus at various times of the year, the possibility of other interesting species should not be ignored. Birds of prey include resident Sparrowhawk and Kestrel in the area, and from late April to early September Hobby is quite likely. Merlin occurred more regularly during the 1980s but has become very rare in recent years, while Peregrine, Marsh and Hen Harriers, Osprey and even Goshawk have also occurred.

In spring and summer passage periods gatherings of Swifts and hirundines can be very large indeed. Other migrants at these times include good numbers of Meadow Pipits and Pied Wagtails, and parties of Yellow Wagtails are often present in the latter season. This species should be checked carefully, as males of the Blue-headed and Grey-headed continental races have also occurred in recent years, as has White Wagtail, the continental race of Pied. Rock and Water Pipits are irregular but are very occasionally noted foraging around the edges of the concrete banks. A Black Redstart used to winter regularly around the towers at the western end of the causeway, but this species is now only a scarce migrant at Staines. More rarely recorded here have been oddities such as Woodlark, Grasshopper Warbler and Snow Bunting, while the long list of landbird rarities over the years includes such gems as Alpine Swift, Roller, Bee-eater, Hoopoe, Wryneck, Tawny and Richard's Pipits and Icterine Warbler.

Timing

Staines Reservoirs are likely to offer the broadest range of species and the greatest chance of something more unusual during spring and autumn migration. However, winter visits are worthwhile with large numbers of wildfowl present and often the possibility of a scarcer duck or grebe among them. Although summer is often regarded as a quiet time for reservoir birding, Staines has a proven track record for producing good birds at this season too – especially in years when the basins are partially drained and passage waders are present almost continually. As the reservoirs are not subject to disturbance from fishing, water sports or other activities, visits made at any time during the day can be fruitful, though note that on bright days glare from the sun can hamper viewing across the south basin from the causeway.

Access

The causeway between the north and south basins is a public footpath with open access at all times, though disabled visitors may have difficulty getting wheelchairs through the kissing gates at either entrance. The large size of the reservoirs means that it can be difficult to view all birds present from the causeway, but there is no authorised access to other sections of the banks or from the B378 Park Road which runs close to the north side of the north basin in Stanwell.

The reservoirs lie immediately north of the A30 London Road, just east of the main roundabout at the junction with the A308 at Staines. To reach the area from central London, use either the A4 and the A30, or more conveniently the M4 and M25. Leave the M25 east at junction 13 onto the A30, continuing past Staines Moor and King George VI Reservoir to the roundabout. Turn left here onto the A3044 Stanwell Moor Road, and continue for about half a mile (0.8 km) until reaching the signposted public footpath up onto the reservoir causeway on the right; park sensibly on the grass verge without blocking the entrance. Alternatively, the causeway can be accessed from the eastern end in Town Lane via the A30.

By bus: numbers 216, 417, 419, 555, 556, 557, 572, 582 and 592 travel from Ashford station to the junction with the A30 at the southeast corner of the reservoirs, with routes 116, 203, 216, 417, 419, 436 and 572 running west along that road along the south side of the south basin and routes 436, 555, 556, 557, 582 and 592 stopping along Town Road for the eastern

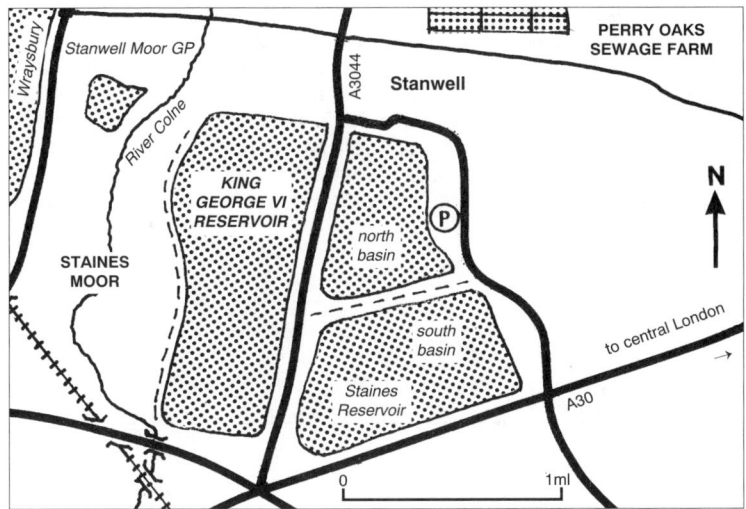

end of the causeway. Number 203 also travels along the A30 from Staines to Hounslow via Stanwell and Hatton Cross (Monday-Saturday only). No buses run along Stanwell Moor Road for the western end of the causeway. *By underground:* there are no tube stations in the immediate area, but for the Piccadilly line bus 203 connects with Hatton Cross (not Sundays) and numbers 555, 556 and 557 link to Heathrow. *By train:* Ashford overground station is about a mile (1.6 km) walk to the southeast from the eastern end of the causeway. From the station walk along Church Road and Stanwell Road, cross the A30 (the next main junction) and continue past Ashford Hospital to the reservoir entrance.

Calendar

All year: Great Crested Grebe, Grey Heron, commoner wildfowl, Sparrowhawk, Kestrel, Ring-necked Parakeet, Pied Wagtail, commoner finches.

Winter (November–February): Chance of rare grebe, Wigeon, Gadwall, Teal, Pintail, Shoveler, possibility of Scaup, Goldeneye, Goosander, Ruddy Duck, commoner waders (when partially drained), good numbers of gulls in pre-roost gatherings including chance of occasional scarcer species, Meadow Pipit.

Spring (March–May): Black-necked Grebe (scarce), irregular Garganey, lingering winter wildfowl, Hobby (from late April), Lapwing, Ringed and Little Ringed Plover, Dunlin, Redshank, Greenshank, Common Sandpiper, other waders including coastal species and chance of rarities when basins partially drained, Little Gull, Common, Arctic and Black Terns, large numbers of Swift and hirundines, Meadow Pipit, White and Yellow Wagtails, occasional chats and other migrants including oddities.

Summer (June–July): Small numbers of oversummering wildfowl sometimes including Shelduck, occasional Hobby, small numbers of late or early passage waders (and commoner breeding waders when partially drained), Common Tern, return Swift movements, breeding Yellow Wagtail when water levels are low.

Autumn (August–October): Black-necked Grebe, Garganey, returning winter wildfowl, Hobby (until early September), Lapwing, Ringed and Little Ringed Plover, Dunlin, Redshank, Greenshank, Common Sandpiper, other waders including coastal species and chance of rarities when basins partially drained, chance of Arctic Skua, Kittiwake and other storm-driven or wandering seabirds, Little Gull, Common, Arctic and Black Terns, passage hirundines, Meadow Pipit, Yellow Wagtail, occasional chats and other migrant passerines including oddities such as Rock Pipit and Snow Bunting.

29 KING GEORGE VI RESERVOIR

OS ref: TQ 041732
Map p. 149

Habitat

Situated immediately west of Staines Reservoirs, this vast concrete-banked water body shares an attraction for many of the same species and benefits from an even closer position to the River Colne, which flows across Staines Moor just to the west. Built during the Second World War by German POWs, its main drawback is access – entry is currently authorised only by special permit to a small number of wildfowl counters. However, the short account that follows is included both for the sake of completeness and in the event that access restrictions may change in the future. It also reflects the fact that the range of species likely to be encountered is broadly similar to that at Staines Reservoir, and for the same reason no seasonal calendar is given.

Species

Divers are as rare on King George VI as they are across the road at Staines, but by the same token Black-necked Grebes are a possibility on this reservoir, particularly in autumn, and occasional Red-necked and Slavonian Grebes are sometimes reported in winter. There may be some interchange between reservoirs of the same individual birds, a factor which no doubt also influences wildfowl counts for the two sites. Numbers of most dabbling duck are generally similar to those at Staines – for example in late 1994 peak numbers include 408 Wigeon, 60 Gadwall, 612 Teal and 246 Shoveler. In contrast gatherings of diving duck are typically more disappointing, with Tufted Duck the most numerous, peaking in late summer when several hundred may be present – the exceptional count of 1,049 in August 1994 was a site record. Pochard can also be well represented, and Goosander and Goldeneye favour the reservoir in winter when recent oddities have included up to 18 Smew in the very cold spell of February 1991.

Waders are a regular feature during spring and autumn migration, with a range of expected species not dissimilar to that at Staines Reservoirs, though numbers will certainly be lower if the basins across the road are being drained. Rarities in recent years on King George VI have included Long-billed Dowitcher and, on the same day in autumn 1995, Pectoral Sandpiper and American Golden Plover – the latter the first record for the London area. As with Staines there is no gull roost here, but Iceland Gull has recently occurred among the commoner species, large numbers of which may be present prior to moving off to roost in winter. Little Gulls are regular on passage, if rather less numerous than at Staines, and similarly numbers of migrant Common, Arctic, Black and the scarcer terns are perhaps also lower here.

The range of commoner passerines such as pipits, wagtails and finches is generally much as for Staines, but the more exposed sheep-grazed banks may be more likely to produce a migrant Wheatear, Whinchat or even Ring Ouzel in spring and autumn. Less observer coverage has resulted in fewer landbird records of note, but Short-eared Owl, Hoopoe, Tawny Pipit and Snow and Lapland Buntings are all among the more interesting species to have been recorded in recent years.

Timing and access

The same rules of thumb for timing for Staines Reservoirs also apply here. Access is strictly by permit from Thames Water, and then only to those carrying out wildfowl counts. Routes to the general area are as for Staines, but having turned into Stanwell Moor Road from the main roundabout on the A30, turn left again into a slip road to enter the reservoir from the southeast corner. There is no authorised access to the north embankment of the reservoir from residential roads in Stanwell Moor. Directions by public transport are also as for Staines.

OTHER SITES IN THE AREA

29A STAINES MOOR

OS ref: TQ 033734
Map p. 149

As the Colne approaches its junction with the Thames at Staines, the river meanders across a floodplain of open damp pasture bordered by willows and scrub. This is Staines Moor, an unusual piece of wetland habitat in the London area which has been granted SSSI status on account of its rare flora. Sandwiched between King George VI Reservoir to the east and the M25 to the west, and bordered by the A30 to the south and built-up Stanwell Moor to the north, this site, in spite of disturbance from dog walkers, anglers and others, often holds interesting birds.

In winter there can be a number of areas of standing water on the moor, and these can help to attract some large gatherings of Canada Geese, several hundred of which may be present at peak times. Aside from feral Greylags, grey geese – and indeed wild swans – rarely make touchdown in the London area, but Staines Moor is as likely a site as any to hold them when they do; in the past these have included small parties of White-fronted Geese. Wildfowl in winter are more likely to include parties of Wigeon or Teal, while spring and autumn the chances of other species such as Pintail or Garganey occurring increase. Between these periods Hobbies may sometimes be noted hunting in the area.

In winter Snipe are likely and there is an outside chance of Jack Snipe; this unobtrusive species is not often reported here but the habitat seems suitable. Gatherings of Lapwings may include a few Golden Plover at this time of year, though this species too is rather irregular here. In the breeding season several pairs of Redshank are often present. Passage waders may include the occasional Ruff, while scarcer species occurring in recent years – especially when there are areas of standing water still remaining – have included Wood Sandpiper and both Grey and Red-necked Phalaropes. Among the older records of notable waders are occurrences of Lesser Yellowlegs in August 1953 and Long-billed Dowitcher in October 1987, the latter bird also frequenting King George VI Reservoir and Perry Oaks Sewage Farm during its stay.

Ring-necked Parakeets can be easy to see here, especially along the public footpath immediately below the west bank of King George VI Reservoir. In the winter these noisy birds can also gather around the gardens and trees on Hithermoor Road at the northern end of the moor. Summer tends to be a quiet time, with breeding Skylarks frequenting the drier areas and Whitethroat, Lesser Whitethroat and Blackcap holding territory in the more vegetated margins. A few pairs of Reed Warbler breed in suitable habitat. In spring and autumn, migrant passerines include good numbers of Meadow Pipit and regular Yellow Wagtail, Whinchat and Wheatear, with very occasionally more notable London species which have included Water Pipit, Redstart and Ring Ouzel. London's first Short-toed Lark was a notable find here back in June 1960, when it remained for eight days, while perhaps the best recent discovery was an overflying Honey Buzzard in October 1993.

Immediately north of Staines Moor lies Stanwell Moor Gravel Pit (TQ 034744), a small site which can sometimes be productive for wildfowl, waders and other species and which is certainly worth taking in on a visit to the area. Shelduck has bred, and Garganey and Spotted Redshank are among the other species of note recorded in recent years.

Directions to the general area are as for Staines and King George VI Reservoirs. Staines Moor lies in the shadow of the latter site, just west of the main roundabout at Staines on the north side of the A30. The site can be viewed from the south from lay-bys along the A30, from numerous public footpaths which criss-cross the area, or from the northern end at Stanwell Moor. For this last access point, turn off the A30 north at the Staines roundabout onto the A3044 between King George VI and Staines Reservoirs, then take the first left after King George VI down Horton Road, turning left again at Hithermoor Road. Park near the public footpath signs at the entrance to the moor and explore this area and Stanwell Moor Gravel Pit.

29B PERRY OAKS SEWAGE FARM

OS ref: TQ 054758
Map p. 149

This area of sewage beds lies within the western edge of the Heathrow Airport complex, a mile (1.6 km) or so to the north of Staines reservoirs and just east of the River Colne and the A3044. It has amassed an enviable list of waders over the years, including a fair number of national rarities, but since the tightening of airport security in the 1970s there has been no general access to birdwatchers. Brief details of the site are included here in the unlikely event that this position might change in the near future.

Waders are without doubt the chief attraction. The patchwork landscape of sludge beds of varying degrees of dampness attracts a range of passage and wintering species and a handful of breeders. Lapwing and several pairs of Redshank are usually present in the summer, and by the end of the breeding season Little Ringed Plovers have often gathered in some numbers: in July 1993 an exceptional 56 were counted here on one day. Migrating Ringed Plovers can be almost continually present between March and September, and on good autumn days 30 or more birds may be present; this species has also bred at Perry Oaks. Dunlin, Ruff, Greenshank and Common and Green Sandpipers can all be well represented in spring and autumn, and the latter also occurs in winter when Snipe and the occasional Jack Snipe are present. Other passage species appearing annually (or almost so) include Little Stint and Curlew and Wood Sandpipers, with less regular appearances from coastal species such as Oystercatcher, Grey Plover, Bar-tailed Godwit, Knot, Sanderling and Turnstone.

Among the truly scarce and rare visitors, Temminck's Stint, Pectoral Sandpiper and Red-necked Phalarope have been recorded in recent seasons, there are records of Black-winged Stilt and Dotterel, and over the years a good list of American shorebirds has been established. This includes Long-billed Dowitcher (1987) and the first records for the London area of Lesser Yellowlegs (two in 1953 and a single in 1962), White-rumped Sandpiper (1984), Baird's Sandpiper (1950), Buff-breasted Sandpiper (1953) and Solitary Sandpiper (1977). Very few inland sites in Britain can boast such a reputation.

Gulls and terns are better represented at other Colne Valley sites, though one or two Little Gulls sometimes pass through during May or in August and September. Passerines can include good numbers of pipits and wagtails which find plenty in the way of insect food around the sludge beds. Pied and Yellow Wagtails both breed and can be present in some numbers on passage, and most years a White or Blue-headed is likely to appear among them, especially in spring. Water and Rock Pipits are erratic but both have appeared in recent autumns, while in the site's well-watched hey-day of the 1950s and 1960s there were no fewer than three records of Tawny Pipit. The same period brought a similar number of Aquatic Warblers, while much more recently a Common Rosefinch was found here in October 1995. Several pairs of Tree Sparrow still breed.

As stated above, there is currently no public access to this sensitive airport site because of security considerations. Plans have also been discussed to develop the area as Heathrow's fifth terminal, a proposal which would entail the destruction of Perry Oaks and the loss of yet another outstanding habitat for birds in London. Even if this eventuality is avoided, it seems unlikely that the access position will change.

30 BROADWATER GRAVEL PIT

OS ref: TQ 045892

Habitat

Formerly known Harefield Moor Gravel Pit, this water is the largest and deepest gravel pit in Middlesex. Its size and depth also mean that in cold winter spells it is the last body of water in this chain of pits in the Colne Valley to freeze over, and on such occasions it can attract large numbers of waterfowl displaced from elsewhere. A sailing club occupies the northern section of the lake, while at the southern end there is an unofficial wildfowl refuge which water sports enthusiasts do not enter. Within this area of the lake is a large wooded island and several much smaller vegetated islands. The pit is surrounded by a belt of woodland in which willow is dominant.

Moorhall Gravel Pit (TQ 048889), adjacent to the southern edge of the site, is strictly private but can be viewed from the perimeter path. Both pits have SSSI designation.

Species

Numbers of Great Crested Grebes at this large pit increase during winter, when there is a possibility of a scarcer grebe or diver appearing – in recent years Red-necked Grebe and Great Northern Diver have both been recorded. The first breeding of Cormorants in the London area took place here in 1987, but though now established in numbers elsewhere they have yet to recolonise this site. Grey Herons have bred since the 1970s, and the thriving heronry now holds some 40 pairs. Hard weather in winter has brought the occasional Shag and Bittern.

Large counts of Mute Swan and Canada and feral Greylag Geese are often made outside the breeding season, and one or two pairs of this last species usually nest. Bewick's Swan and White-fronted Goose have both been recorded at Broadwater in the past few years. The pit is an important refuge for moulting and wintering duck, with regularly up to 500 Mallard, 600 Tufted Duck and over 200 Pochard. All three species have bred, as has Ruddy Duck. Up to 200 or more Shoveler and Wigeon may be present in winter; the latter can be highly mobile, often feeding on farmland at Park Lodge Farm (TQ 057892) three-quarters of a mile (1.2 km) to the east in South Harefield. Teal and small numbers of Gadwall are also regular in winter, as are 20 or so Goldeneye, while more erratic visitors include Red-crested Pochard, Scaup and Smew, and even Eider has been recorded.

Smew

There is some movement of wildfowl between different waters in the area, a feature which applies not only to the commoner species but also some of the rarer visitors: a female Long-tailed Duck commuted between here and neighbouring Tilehouse Gravel Pits when it returned during several winters in the early 1990s, while a Ring-necked Duck found in May 1993 at Stocker's Lake, further north along the Colne Valley, also pitched in here during its brief stay.

Hobbies sometimes hawk over the pit during the summer months, while scarcer raptors have included Merlin, Marsh Harrier and, back in spring 1955, London's first-ever Goshawk. Winter usually brings a couple of Water Rails, a few Snipe and often one or two Jack Snipe, but other waders are generally thin on the ground as there are relatively few suitable feeding areas. During spring and autumn they may include Common Sandpiper and the occasional Redshank, while more rarely other species such as Oystercatcher have been recorded on passage. Large numbers of gulls use this pit during the winter, and pre-roost gatherings involving several hundred each of Herring and Lesser Black-backed Gulls and over 60 Great Black-backeds have been noted. Migrant Little Gulls are a possibility, especially in autumn, and Common Terns are regular in numbers on passage, with a handful of pairs breeding at adjacent Moorhall Gravel Pit. Arctic Terns are noted moving through in most years, there is always a chance of Black Tern in the area, and even Little Tern has been recorded.

Turtle Dove and Cuckoo occur on migration, and Kingfisher and Grey Wagtail are resident along this stretch of the Colne Valley. Winter brings Fieldfare and Redwing, and both Brambling and Siskin have been recorded in the past. Spring and autumn have brought oddities such as Rock Pipit, Redstart and Black Redstart among more regular migrants which include Yellow Wagtail. In summer a good variety of the commoner warblers is present, with numerous Reed and Sedge Warblers around the edges of the pit, and Whitethroat, Blackcap, the occasional Garden Warbler, Willow Warbler and Chiffchaff in the more vegetated areas. Many of these commoner species and a few others – including Grey Partridge, all three woodpeckers, Spotted Flycatcher, Nuthatch, Treecreeper and Yellowhammer – can also be found a short distance south along the Colne Valley at Denham Country Park (TQ 055865), a 70-acre (28 ha) area of wet woodland, damp meadows and lakes.

Timing

Wintering waterbirds comprise much of the interest at this site, and therefore the period October to April is perhaps the most productive. Spring and autumn bring terns and the occasional wader to this under-watched site, which is at its quietest in the summer months. Early morning visits avoid the possibility of disturbance from sailing activity, especially at weekends.

Access

Access to the site is by permit only from site owners Redland Aggregates (for details telephone 01784 437373). A private road runs along the east side of Moorhall Gravel Pit and up along the east and north sides of Broadwater Gravel Pit to the sailing club and the northwest corner. There is open access to Denham Country Park.

By road: the area can be reached via the A40 and A40(M) from central London, the M40 from the west and the M25 (exit at junction 16 for the

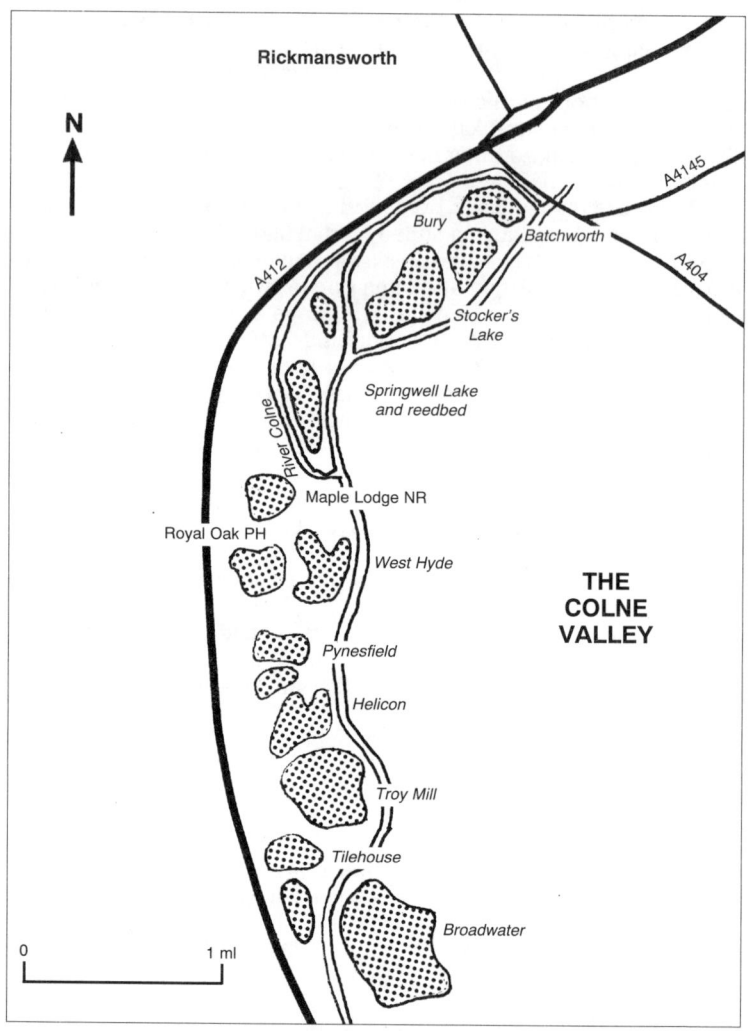

M40) from other outer areas. At the roundabout where the A40 meets the M40 at junction 1, continue northwest along the A40 at Denham, turning right for Denham Country Park down the lane to Denham Court, then right again following signs as marked to the car park. For Broadwater Gravel Pit, return to the A40 and continue northwest, turning right two-thirds of a mile (1 km) from the A40/M40 roundabout onto the A412 Denham Avenue/North Orbital Road. After another two-thirds of a mile, just beyond the railway bridge, turn east into Moorfield Road and continue for about three-quarters of a mile (1.2 km) along Moorhall Road until reaching the gravel driveway of Redland Aggregates on the left (the cement workings should be visible). Do not park in the car park designated for birdwatchers as the gates can sometimes be locked without warning. Instead, park sensibly along the lane leading to the car park and enter the site from there.

By bus: route 348 from Uxbridge runs along the A412 and then along Moorhall Road past the site entrance. The U1, also from Uxbridge, also travels along the A412 on Mondays–Saturdays; disembark at Moorfield Road and walk the remaining three-quarters of a mile (1.2 km). *By underground:* the Piccadilly line terminates at Uxbridge station, from where bus routes 348 and U1 run to or near to the site. *By train:* trains from central London stop at Denham station, just east of the A412 to the south of Moorfield Road.

Calendar

All year: Great Crested Grebe, Grey Heron, Greylag Goose, Tufted Duck, Pochard, Ruddy Duck, Sparrowhawk, Kestrel, Stock Dove, Kingfisher, Grey Wagtail.

Winter (December–February): Cormorant, Wigeon, Gadwall, Teal, Shoveler, Goldeneye, Smew (scarce), chance of wildfowl oddities such as Pintail and Scaup, Water Rail, Jack Snipe, Snipe, commoner gulls, Fieldfare, Redwing, occasional Brambling, Siskin.

Spring (March–May): Cormorant, departing winter wildfowl, Hobby (from May), occasional commoner passage waders, Common, Arctic and perhaps Black Terns, hirundines, Yellow Wagtail, commoner warblers and other migrants.

Summer (June–July): Hobby, Common Tern, Sedge Warbler, Reed Warbler, Garden Warbler, Whitethroat, Blackcap, Willow Warbler, Chiffchaff.

Autumn (August–November): Cormorant, returning winter wildfowl, Hobby (until early September), occasional commoner passage waders, Common, Arctic and perhaps Black Terns, hirundines, Yellow Wagtail, winter thrushes (from October), common migrants.

OTHER SITES IN THE AREA

30A TILEHOUSE AND WEST HYDE GRAVEL PITS

OS ref: TQ 038897
TQ 038916
Map p. 156

This string of pits extends north from Broadwater Gravel Pit to Maple Lodge, and forms part of an almost continuous chain of water bodies between Uxbridge and Rickmansworth in the Colne Valley. The majority of these waters, which straddle the boundaries of Middlesex, Buckinghamshire and Hertfordshire, are private property, but some can be viewed at least in part from roadside vantage points from the east side of the A412 Denham Way/North Orbital Road. Not all are attractive to birds mainly because of recreational use, but in general they share similar avifaunas, with a reasonable range of commoner waterfowl and a few regular waders, good numbers of gulls in winter, passage terns, Kingfisher,

Grey Wagtail and a variety of commoner passerines including warblers in summer and Yellow Wagtail and good numbers of hirundines on migration. Hobbies are regular in the area during summer.

To the northwest of Broadwater Gravel Pit are Tilehouse North (TQ 038898) and South (TQ 038896) Gravel Pits. Top of the list here is Smew, at least a few of which are usually present between December and February; they often favour the north pit, which has been designated as an SSSI. Other wildfowl can include high numbers of Gadwall early in the year, as well as Shoveler, Wigeon and Goldeneye, and these pits also shared the female Long-tailed Duck which wintered at Broadwater for several years from 1991. Little Grebe breeds, Water Rail sometimes occurs in winter and scarcer visitors in recent years have included Bittern. The pits can be viewed from the A412 Denham Way on the west side; park just south of the county boundary sign and look over the wooden fence from the embankment to view.

Immediately to the north is Troy Mill Gravel Pit (TQ 039905), which despite being home to Rickmansworth Sailing Club still manages to attract wildfowl in winter. In the past these have included impressive numbers of Goosander – a record 109 were logged in 1975 – but numbers have been much lower since. Among a range of other birds notable species including Great Northern Diver, Black Tern and, back in September 1965, London's first Alpine Swift have been recorded moving through. Jack Snipe has been found along the Colne in this area in winter. The adjoining Helicon Gravel Pit (TQ 039909) attracts fewer birds than its neighbour. Both are well served by public footpaths, including one which can be accessed from the cul-de-sac off the A412 immediately west of Troy Mill. Nearby, Tilehouse Lane cuts through farmland and hedgerows which in summer are said to hold breeding Yellowhammer and the locally scarce Corn Bunting; turn east off the A412 just south of West Hyde, adjacent to Pynesfield (TQ 038912) and Helicon Gravel Pits.

North of Pynesfield Gravel Pit is Royal Oak Gravel Pit (TQ 035914), which is separated from the private West Hyde Gravel Pits (TQ 038916) to the north by Coppermill Lane. This road runs from the Grand Union Canal in the east to Old Uxbridge Road in the west; the latter, near the junction with the A412 at its northern end, provides viewing over the farmland at Lynsters Farm which can hold large flocks of Canada and Greylag Geese – these should be checked in winter, especially in hard weather, for the outside chance of wild geese joining them. Limited views of both of the West Hyde pits are possible from the entrance to the farm. In winter the surrounding agricultural land can hold good-sized flocks of Lapwing and occasionally smaller numbers of Golden Plover. Try searching for this species in the fields at Woodoaks Farm (TQ 033933), a site which in December 1994 held a Russian-ringed Bewick's Swan.

All of these sites can be combined together in a morning's itinerary, and can be reached easily from the A412 which runs north-south roughly parallel to the River Colne to the east and the M25 to the west. The A412 connects with the motorway a short distance to the north of Maple Cross via the A405 at junction 17. Bus number U1 runs the length of the A412 from Rickmansworth in the north (Metropolitan line and overground trains from central London) to Denham (overground trains from Paddington stop at Denham Green) and Uxbridge (Metropolitan and, in peak hours, Piccadilly lines) in the south.

Habitat

Stocker's Lake, sandwiched tightly between the River Colne to the north and the Grand Union Canal to the south, is situated just south of Rickmansworth on the northwestern edge of the London area. The lake is a legacy of the extensive gravel extraction which took place in this area between the 1920s and the end of the Second World War. Its margins and islands now have well-established mature vegetation which includes significant areas of willow and alder scrub and small copses of mixed woodland. The attractive range of habitats at this SSSI has helped to establish it as one of the best birding areas in the Colne Valley.

Stocker's Lake itself occupies around 93 acres (37 ha), and is a local nature reserve managed by the Hertfordshire and Middlesex Wildlife Trust on behalf of the site owners, Three Valleys Water Services. The canal side of the reserve has developed into an area of damp woodland dominated by alder. The lake itself is very shallow, with numerous well-vegetated islands offering breeding sites for a range of species but little in the way of good habitat for waders. The lake is separated from the smaller and far more disturbed Bury Lake to the east by a causeway and meadows; the more scrubby corners of this area can be good for passerines. To the west lies the less interesting Stocker's West Lake, while on the south side of the canal the meadows around Stocker's Farm (TQ 053934) can be particularly interesting when wet.

The area has a good range of regular birds, with more than 60 species found to be breeding here during a census in the 1970s and more than 80 recorded nesting in total. In excess of 100 species are logged annually.

Species

Up to 10 pairs of Great Crested Grebe nest around the lake, though Little Grebe is only a rare breeder. Scarce grebes and divers are exceptional here, and unusual visitors in hard winter weather are more likely to come in the form of a wandering Shag or perhaps even a Bittern. There is a

Ruddy Duck

thriving heronry that is well worth a visit in late winter and early spring; from a mere three pairs in 1977, numbers had increased to 58 pairs by 1994 and appear to be growing steadily each year.

Feral geese include large numbers of Canadas and a single pair of Greylags, though numbers of the latter build up substantially later in the summer, usually peaking during September. Bury Lake is important for non-breeding Mute Swan, with counts exceeding 70 in recent years. Mallard, Pochard, Tufted Duck and Ruddy Duck all breed regularly and Gadwall has done so, while Shelduck are occasionally seen on passage and one pair has bred since the early 1990s. Winter brings good numbers of waterfowl, with particularly large gatherings of Coot and Tufted Duck and up to 300 Shoveler. Pochard and Teal rarely peak at more than 150 and Gadwall may exceed 100 early in the year, but Wigeon numbers do not normally reach double figures. Among the diving duck 20 or more Goldeneye are regular in winter, Goosander are occasionally seen and a few Smew may be present, though this is not the most reliable site for the species in the western sector of London. Among records of oddities such as Mandarin, Garganey, Pintail, Ferruginous Duck, Scaup, Common Scoter and Red-breasted Merganser are almost regular recent appearances of Red-crested Pochard, particularly in autumn and winter, but as at other sites in the London area the origin of these birds must be open to question.

Aside from regular Sparrowhawk and Kestrel, Hobby breeds not far away and may be seen over the area in the summer months. Water Rail is regular in winter and probably best looked for in damp wooded areas near the canal. In the same season large flocks of Lapwings can be present on the damp meadow at Stocker's Farm, but aside from Snipe other waders are often scarce because of the lack of extensive suitable feeding areas. Little Ringed Plover, Greenshank and Common and Green Sandpipers are among those that have occasionally been attracted to the meadow or to the rafts and islands on the lake, but aside from odd 'drop-ins' – these have included Knot and Wood Sandpiper in the past – other wader sightings may amount only to a chance encounter with an overflying migrant.

Unusual gulls are a rare find among the large numbers of commoner species present outside the breeding season, but both Mediterranean Gull and Kittiwake have been recorded recently. Numbers of breeding Common Terns have gradually increased to about eight pairs here, but perhaps surprisingly passage terns are unusual at this end of the Colne Valley: past visitors have included Black and Little.

Stock Doves are fairly common residents, with some pairs occupying nest boxes which were originally erected to try and attract Mandarin Ducks. Turtle Doves probably still breed nearby and Cuckoos regularly parasitise the local Reed Warblers. Tawny Owls are resident, Little Owls can sometimes be seen at Stocker's Farm (often on the farm buildings), and Short-eared Owl has wintered in the area. Great and Lesser Spotted Woodpeckers are occasionally noted. Kingfishers are often present in the area, and Grey Wagtails breed by the canal; try looking for this species around Stocker's Lock. Parties of Pied and Yellow Wagtails on passage have been known to contain the occasional White and Blue-headed.

The more open areas may hold the occasional migrant Whinchat or Wheatear in spring and autumn, and, especially in late winter, feeding flocks of Fieldfare and Redwing may be present. Breeding warblers include the expected commoner species, but Spotted Flycatcher now seems to appear only on passage: numbers of this summer visitor have more than halved in the London area in the last eight years. Another lost species is the declining Willow Tit, a former breeder which has not been recorded at all in recent years. Treecreepers are among the commoner nesting passerines, which are joined in winter by flocks of Siskin and Redpoll in suitable areas of habitat, while occasional oddities such as Bearded Tit have been recorded outside the breeding season.

Stocker's Lake has turned up a good number of local and national rarities. Night Heron, Little Egret, Blue-winged Teal, Ring-necked Duck, Ferruginous Duck, Black Kite and Red-necked Phalarope have all been recorded here over the years, and in early May 1992 ornithological history was made when the largest flock of Cattle Egrets ever seen in Britain was watched flying over from the bridge at Stocker's Lock. These eight birds, the first record of this species in London, remained in the area for two days and were enjoyed by many hundreds of birders who made the journey to see them.

Timing

The range of habitats means that there is enough ornithological interest at Stocker's Lake to justify a visit throughout much of the year. Wildfowl numbers are significant in winter, tailing off by spring when the first summer visitors arrive. Although there are no breeding specialities a good range of birds is present throughout summer, and in autumn when migration gets underway again chances are probably best of an interesting wader, oddity or perhaps even a rarity. Fishermen use the canal and Bury Lake fairly heavily at weekends, especially in summer, and the latter site is also prone to disturbance from water sports activities. Allow at least a couple of hours to do justice to this site, which can be easily combined in a day or half-day itinerary which includes other pits and reservoirs in the Colne Valley.

Access

Although public footpaths and roads allow access to or viewing of parts of the general area, a permit is required from the Hertfordshire and Middlesex Wildlife Trust to visit the reserve itself. There is a society called Friends of Stocker's Lake, through which members can contribute directly to the site's conservation; for details contact the Trust.

Stocker's Lake is a short drive from the M25 in Hertfordshire. Turn off the motorway south at junction 17 onto the A405, then left (northeast) at the roundabout onto the A412 Uxbridge Road. Take the second right into Springwell Lane, pass over a bridge and continue past Stocker's West Lake on the left; after a second bridge, over the Colne, turn left again and park by the river. If the limited parking space here is full, use the aquadrome car park to the east at Bury Lake (access via Harefield Road and the A404 from the A412 and Rickmansworth) and walk west alongside that site to Stocker's Lake. The latter car park has toilet facilities. Walk around the reserve along the designated paths, calling in at the two hides en route; the footpath crosses the canal at Stocker's Lock to give views over the adjacent fields around Stocker's Farm.

By bus: route U1 runs along the A412 Uxbridge Road from Rickmansworth station (Monday-Saturday). *By underground:* Rickmansworth is on the Metropolitan line. *By train:* overground trains to Rickmansworth run from Marylebone. There is also a taxi rank at the station.

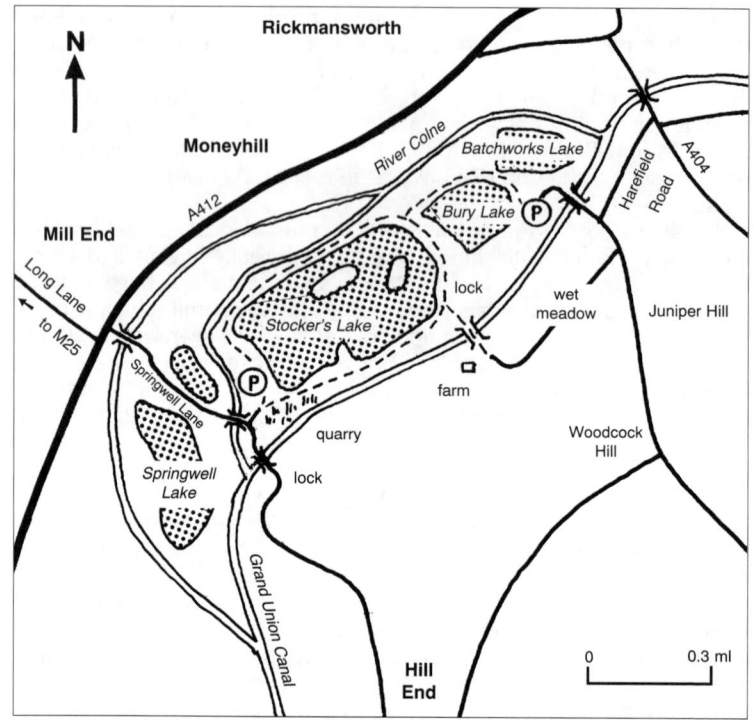

Calendar

All year: Great Crested Grebe, Grey Heron, Greylag Goose, Ruddy Duck, Sparrowhawk, Kestrel, Stock Dove, Tawny and Little Owls, Kingfisher, Great Spotted and Lesser Spotted Woodpeckers, Grey Wagtail, Treecreeper, Reed Bunting.

Winter (December–February): Little Grebe, Wigeon, Gadwall, Teal, Shoveler, occasional Red-crested Pochard, Goldeneye, Goosander, Smew (scarce), Water Rail, Lapwing, Snipe, gulls, Fieldfare, Redwing, Siskin, Redpoll.

Spring (March–May): Shelduck, lingering winter wildfowl, Hobby (from May), chance of Little Ringed Plover, Common Sandpiper and perhaps other waders, Common Tern, Turtle Dove (from May), Cuckoo, migrants including hirundines, Yellow Wagtail, occasional chats and commoner warblers.

Summer (June–July): Shelduck, Common Tern, Turtle Dove (scarce), Cuckoo, Reed Warbler, Sedge Warbler, Blackcap, Whitethroat, Lesser Whitethroat, Willow Warbler.

Autumn (August–November): Returning winter wildfowl, occasional Red-crested Pochard, Hobby (until early September), waders including Greenshank and Green and Common Sandpipers, gulls, migrants including hirundines, Yellow Wagtail, occasional chats, commoner warblers and returning winter thrushes.

OTHER SITES IN THE AREA

31A SPRINGWELL LAKE AND REEDBED

OS ref: TQ 043932/041924
Map p. 162

This site lies just southwest from Stocker's Lake, from which it is separated by the ornithologically uninteresting Stocker's West Lake. Popular with anglers, disturbance means that most duck in the area tend to prefer larger waters nearby. Since the small watercress bed on the eastern side was filled in (in its day attractive to wintering Water Pipit and Water Rail), the most interesting area is the reedbed at the southern end of the site, which at 20 acres (8 ha) is probably the largest in Greater London. As well as wetland species which include wintering Water Rail and Snipe, the reeds are used as a roost by hirundines and wagtails during passage periods and by Corn Buntings in winter. Over 100 of this last species have been counted here in the past, though currently numbers are typically between 20–30 birds.

Directions to the general area are as for Stocker's Lake, with access from Springwell Lane at Drayton Ford on the A412 Uxbridge Road. Follow Springwell Lane a short distance past Stocker's West Lake; turn off right before the Grand Union Canal to follow the circular route around the lake which passes the reedbed. There is a small car park at Springwell Lock, and an additional car park is planned on Springwell Lane near the A412. Bus number U1 runs along the A412 and connects with Rickmansworth underground (Metropolitan line) and overground stations.

31B MAPLE LODGE

OS ref: TQ 036924
Map p. 164

This attractive nature reserve of around 40 acres (16 ha), on the site of a former sewage farm south of Springwell Lake, is managed by the Maple Lodge Conservation Society under licence from owners Thames Water. A path runs around three-quarters of the site, giving access to various habitats which include woodland, wetland, farmland and two lakes. The largest of these, Marsh Lake, is ornithologically the most interesting and can be viewed from hides on the western and southern banks. There is a small reedbed where a stream enters the lake in its southeast corner, and part of this area is being cleared to make way for a wader scrape. Near the reserve entrance is a mixed plantation and an area of meadow managed to encourage wild flowers, while passerines visiting the adjacent feeding station can be observed from the comfort of a small hide.

Maple Lodge sustains an interesting range of birds within these varied habitats. Up to six pairs of Little Grebes breed and can best be seen on Marsh Lake, while nesting Great Crested Grebes tend to prefer the smaller Clubhouse Lake. Wildfowl numbers are generally low in winter, but Teal are among the most numerous and occasionally reach three figures. This species and Mallard, Gadwall, Shoveler, Tufted Duck, Pochard and Ruddy Duck also either breed regularly or have bred recently in small numbers. Scarcer wildfowl in winter have included Pintail, Goldeneye and Scaup, and Garganey has occurred on migration. Water Rail can sometimes be found in winter, usually near the mouth of the stream on Marsh Lake.

The site can also prove attractive to waders, with Little Ringed Plover and Redshank occasionally nesting in the area and a number of other species appearing on passage and in winter. As well as regular migrants such as Common Sandpiper, rarer visitors in recent years have included Black-tailed and Bar-tailed Godwits and Curlew and Wood Sandpipers. Lapwing, Snipe and Green Sandpiper are usually present in winter here and on flooded fields at nearby Lynster's Farm (TQ 034920). Common Tern does not breed but is often encountered between spring and autumn, and likewise the commoner gull species are also regular outside the breeding season.

Sparrowhawk breeds in the area and Hobby is regular, especially during late summer. Tawny Owls nest in special owl boxes, and in summer the young can sometimes be seen in trees near the box outside the wildlife centre. Kingfishers are occasional, particularly along the stream, while all three woodpeckers are resident in the area. All of the common breeding warblers are present in summer, and Chiffchaff is occasionally also noted in winter. At this time of year the reedbeds are used as a roost site by Reed Buntings, with the occasional Corn Bunting joining them. Bearded Tit has also been mist-netted here in the past. Parties of wintering Redpoll and Siskin should be looked for in the plantation, while the feeding station has on rare occasions attracted Brambling.

The reserve offers many facilities for visitors including a clubhouse, wildlife centre, car parking, toilets and excellent access for wheelchair users. Entry to the reserve is usually restricted to members of Maple Lodge Conservation Society, but non-members, groups and school parties can be accommodated by special arrangement: for details contact the society's secretary on 01923 230277. To reach the area by road, continue south from Stocker's Lake along the A412, bearing left at the roundabout, and turn off left at Maple Lodge Close. Bus route U1 runs along the A412 and connects with Rickmansworth underground (Metropolitan line) and overground stations.

WEST LONDON

32 WORMWOOD SCRUBS

Habitat

This extensive area of common land and scrub lies just north of the A40 between Shepherd's Bush and Kensal Green. Home to an imposing prison of the same name on its southern boundary, the 'Scrubs' at first sight looks unlikely to hold much attraction for birds. However, although not outstanding for breeding species, its 180 acres (72 ha) can prove very productive for migrant birds, especially passerines, during spring and autumn.

Some parts of the site offer reasonable habitat for passage and commoner breeding species. A thin strip of young woodland, dominated by sycamore, birch and plane and divided by a path, runs along the western perimeter to the northern edge of the site, along which is the enclosure known to local birders as 'chat paddock'. The wetter, extreme western corner near Old Oak Common Lane, which has some reasonable areas of scrub with stands of alder and willow, is one of the best areas for migrants, but is subject to much disturbance during summer each year when large numbers of camping tourists establish a temporary 'tent city'. In other areas the Scrubs largely comprises uninteresting short-turf parkland, and with redevelopment of part of the site as the Channel Tunnel rail depot, its attractions are somewhat limited.

Species

Ornithological interest is fairly sharply focused on spring and autumn, and when migrant passerines are present (generally after winds with an easterly element at both seasons) the area near Old Oak Common Lane can hold good numbers of the commoner species. Blackcap, Whitethroat, Lesser Whitethroat and Willow Warbler, all of which also breed in small numbers, may be well represented, and Reed, Sedge and Garden Warblers and Chiffchaff are regular on passage. Wood Warbler has also occurred here, but is irregular and best looked for in spring when Grasshopper Warbler, Black Redstart and Pied Flycatcher have also appeared.

Keeping an eye skyward, while walking east along the path parallel with the embankment north of chat paddock, sometimes pays off with passage Turtle Dove or Cuckoo. Autumn is the best time to look out for a marauding Hobby. Meadow Pipits start to appear in numbers at this time, peaking in excess of 50 birds, and migrating Skylarks, often in parties, also appear. Most of these diurnal migrants are found in the long grass between chat paddock and tent city, but they tend to disperse once the area has been mown. In autumn especially, check any migrant pipits carefully as Tree Pipit is a possibility at this time.

In recent years the Scrubs has become well known for its passage of chats, in particular Whinchat. Spring migration is fairly quiet, with perhaps the occasional individual staying for a day or two, but from mid-August birds are present on most days until at least late September. They favour the area of thistles and weeds where the bulk of the Meadow Pipits and Skylarks are also found, as well as chat paddock along the embankment. Autumn 1994 was an exceptional season for Whinchats here, with up to 18 individuals present at one time – the highest count in the London area in recent years. Wheatears should also be looked for in spring and autumn, and later in the latter season Stonechats may also appear, sometimes staying all winter.

Other regular visitors and resident species are unremarkable, but include Sparrowhawk, Kestrel, Great Spotted Woodpecker and Bullfinch.

Timing

Spring and autumn offer the best chance of finding interesting birds at this site, which is really one to repay regular coverage rather than a chance visit. The general lack of substantial cover means that the best areas can be worked fairly thoroughly in an hour or two. Early morning is the most productive time, as disturbance often forces migrants to move on. Remote-controlled model aircraft and heavy use by the general public do nothing to enhance chances of good birding throughout much of the day and at weekends.

Access

Wormwood Scrubs is easily reached from central London via Marylebone Road and the A40(M) Westway, and from the west also by the A40, which as the M40 connects with junction 16 of the M25. Turn off the A40 where it becomes the A40(M) Westway at White City, bearing north onto the A219 Scrubs Lane (which connects to the north with the A404 Harrow Road). Reaching Wormwood Scrubs on the left after a short distance, park in the pay and display car park and explore. Alternatively, the more interesting western edge of the site can be reached from Old Oak Common Lane W3 and Braybrook Street W12, both of which have ample parking.

By bus: number 220 services Scrubs Lane, and the 72 stops along Old Oak Common Lane. *By underground:* the nearest tube stations are both on the Central line, at White City station nearly a mile to the south on Wood Lane, the continuation of Scrubs Lane (bus 220 connects with Wormwood Scrubs), and at East Acton station, a short walk along Erconwald Street from Braybrook Street at the western end. *By train:* mainline services from Euston station in central London and suburban services on the North London (Gospel Oak–Richmond) line stop at Willesden Junction, just west of the northern end of Scrubs Lane in Tubbs Road NW10.

Calendar

All year: Sparrowhawk, Kestrel, Great Spotted Woodpecker, Bullfinch.

Winter (December–February): Chance of Fieldfare and Redwing, Stonechat, tit flocks.

Spring (March–May): Skylark, hirundines, Meadow Pipit, occasional Redstart, light passage of Whinchat and Wheatear, commoner warblers and other migrants including occasional local scarcities.

Summer (June–July): Whitethroat, Lesser Whitethroat, Blackcap, Willow Warbler.

Autumn (August–November): Chance of Hobby (until mid-September), Turtle Dove (scarce), Cuckoo (scarce – usually August), hirundines, Skylark, occasional Tree Pipit, Meadow Pipit, Wheatear, Whinchat, Stonechat, commoner warblers and other migrants including possible Redstart and Pied Flycatcher.

33 OSTERLEY PARK   OS ref: TQ 145780

Habitat

This 158-acre (63 ha) estate is situated in the London Borough of Hounslow, just south of Hanwell between junctions 2 and 3 of the M4. The centrepiece of the park is Osterley House, a mansion which dates back to 1575 when it was built for Sir Thomas Gresham, founder of the Royal Exchange. The attractively landscaped grounds are essentially flat, but interest is provided by areas of mature woodland and a number of lakes, with significant adjoining tracts of arable land which until recently held a variety of farmland birds otherwise scarce in urban London. Most of the area is now owned by the National Trust. Osterley Park is not outstanding in ornithological terms, but common bird census work has revealed up to 45 or so breeding species (some of which are no longer regular), while perhaps 80–90 species are likely annually.

Species

The lakes support Great Crested and Little Grebes and two pairs of the exotic Mandarin Duck among commoner breeding waterfowl. There is a small heronry, re-established in 1990 after an absence of 39 years, which has held up to eight pairs of Grey Heron in recent breeding seasons. Ducks in winter can include Shoveler among the more numerous Mallard, Tufted Duck and Pochard, but species such as Teal, Gadwall, Wigeon and Goosander are much less regular in their appearances.

Osterley Park was formerly a stronghold of Grey Partridge, but this species seems to have disappeared in recent years. Chukar x Red-legged Partridge hybrids were said to have been released in 1986–87, and these birds may account for occasional recent reports of partridges. Lapwings can be present in numbers on the farmland in winter, and flocks should always be checked carefully for the possibility of Golden Plover among them. Other waders are something of a rarity, but have included Snipe, Jack Snipe, Woodcock, Whimbrel and Common Sandpiper in the past.

Stock Doves are perhaps not so numerous as they used to be, but around 10 pairs still breed. Turtle Dove and Cuckoo are both sometimes noted on passage, and Ring-necked Parakeet is a possibility here. A small winter roost of Long-eared Owls has been recorded in the park, but

Stock Dove

this is almost certainly not a regular feature. Four pairs of Little Owl are resident and the more wooded areas hold Tawny Owl, Green, Great Spotted and Lesser Spotted Woodpeckers, Nuthatch and Treecreeper. The range of common breeding passerines includes Skylark and Goldcrest and used to feature Tree Sparrow and Corn Bunting, but perhaps only the latter of these two species now still occurs in the area. Winter visitors can include sizeable flocks of Redwing and Fieldfare and occasional parties of Siskin. Stonechat has also appeared in this season, while the rougher areas may attract Whinchat and Wheatear on passage, the latter sometimes in numbers. In addition to the commoner passage migrants are scarcer visitors such as Black Redstart, Redstart, Ring Ouzel, Wood Warbler and Pied Flycatcher, and in 1987 one of this last species held territory throughout the summer – an unusual event in southeast England. Rarities are exceptional but in 1974 a Wryneck was a notable find here, surpassed only by the immature Roller which remained for two days in August 1968.

Timing and access
Resident birds provide much of the interest here, so a visit at any season is worthwhile; as is often the case, however, spring is likely to provide the greatest range of birds, including drumming woodpeckers and passage warblers. The park is open all year from 9.00 am until 7.30 pm (or sunset if earlier). Entry is free, but there is a car park charge of £1.50 (and an admission charge of £3.70 to the house). Access to the area from central London or from the west is via the A4 Great West Road, 2.5 miles (4 km)

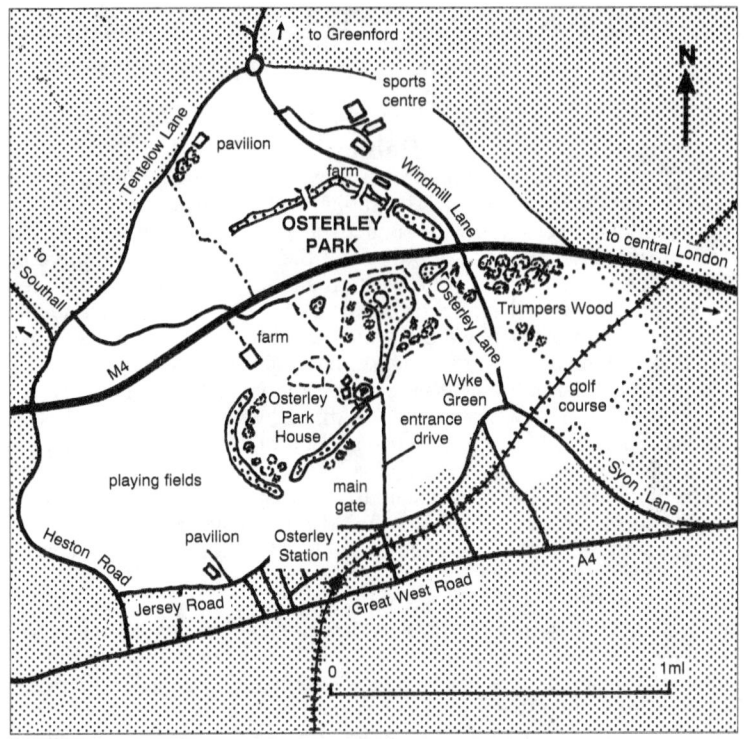

west of its intersection with the M4 at junction 2. Turn off the A4 north into Thornbury Road, then at the end of the road follow the driveway into the park to the main car park.

By bus: route H91 from Hounslow to Hammersmith runs along the A4 Great West Road every day except Sunday. *By underground:* Osterley Park station (Piccadilly line) is a short walk away from the park along Jersey Road; follow the signs on leaving the station.

Calendar

All year: Great Crested Grebe, Little Grebe, Grey Heron, Mandarin Duck, Stock Dove, Little Owl, Tawny Owl, Green, Great Spotted and Lesser Spotted Woodpeckers, Skylark, Goldcrest, Nuthatch, Treecreeper.

Winter (November–February): Shoveler (scarce), Lapwing, occasional Stonechat, Fieldfare, Redwing, Siskin.

Spring (March–May): Lapwing, arriving summer migrants including Whinchat, Wheatear and commoner warblers.

Summer (June–early August): Blackcap, Chiffchaff.

Autumn (mid-August–October): Lapwing, departing summer migrants including Whinchat, Wheatear, commoner warblers and occasional oddities, Fieldfare and Redwing (from October).

34 HOUNSLOW HEATH OS ref: TQ 123745

Habitat

This 200-acre (80 ha) local nature reserve lies about two miles (3.2 km) southeast of Heathrow Airport. The habitat is largely grassland and heath, and heathland vegetation is being actively encouraged as part of a 10-year conservation project supported by the Countryside Commission. The wooded areas towards the western side of the site have matured since the days of gravel extraction during the Second World War, and provide good nesting sites for warblers and other species. There is also a belt of oak woodland along the southeastern margin of the site.

In the northeast of the heath is an area known as 'the wetland' which consists of a small newly-created lake, fringed with reedmace and other waterside plants. This lake, which has been developed with wildlife in mind, has benefited from the creation of a scrape, and a hide has been erected. Adjoining Hounslow Heath to the west is a 60-acre (24 ha) public golf course, through which the wooded course of the River Crane flows. Hounslow Heath LNR is managed by the London Borough of Hounslow.

Species

The wetland holds meagre numbers of waterfowl but has a small breeding nucleus of Mallard, Moorhen and Coot. Teal occur during the autumn and winter in small numbers, while the reserve recorded its first Shoveler in 1992. One or two Water Rails can sometimes be heard squealing from cover around the lake in winter, particularly during cold years when this species is likely to be more widespread. Snipe are regular visitors from autumn through to spring, and one or two Jack Snipe have also occasionally been reported in winter in the wetland. Other waders are less regular, but during recent years Little Ringed Plover, Ruff, Redshank and Green Sandpiper have all been found feeding on the mud around the lake.

Woodcock have occasionally been flushed from the more wooded areas of the heath in the winter months, and there are still said to be small numbers of Grey Partridge on the reserve. Stock Dove is resident and all three woodpeckers have been recorded, with Green and Great Spotted breeding and Lesser Spotted most likely during the winter months. Turtle Dove, Cuckoo and Yellow Wagtail occur on spring and autumn migration, and in recent years Pied Flycatcher, Redstart, Whinchat and good numbers of Wheatear have been reasonably regular in these seasons. Redwings and Fieldfares can be noted on the move in autumn and spring, and in the latter season this site offers probably one of the best opportunities of finding Ring Ouzel in the London area. Though not recorded annually, there has been a succession of records of this regionally scarce migrant in recent Aprils, with a peak of at least six recorded in 1989. Stonechat is a possibility in winter.

Several species of warbler breed, with Whitethroat the most numerous at up to 30 or so pairs. Chiffchaffs nest in the woods around the margins of the site, while Willow Warbler, Blackcap and Lesser Whitethroat breed on the heath. Reed and Sedge Warblers have recently nested in the wetland and also occur on passage, as do the occasional singing Wood and Grasshopper Warblers in spring; up to three of this last species were present in late April and early May 1994. Goldcrests are apparent during the

Whitethroat

winter, when flocks of the commoner finches on the heath may include small numbers of Siskin and Redpoll.

The site has built up a varied list of casual visitors and oddities which includes Fulmar, Sandwich Tern, Barn, Long-eared and Short-eared Owls, Red-backed Shrike and Ortolan Bunting.

Timing

Much of the ornithological interest at Hounslow Heath centres on spring and autumn, when the common resident and breeding birds are augmented by a range of migrants, including several notable regular passerines and the chance of a wader or two in the wetland. Early morning is by far the best time to visit, ahead of the majority of dog walkers. The heath is busy at weekends, especially in summer.

Access

There is open access to all areas of Hounslow Heath except the wetland, for which prior arrangements must be made with the ranger service (telephone 0181 577 3664).

Hounslow Heath can be reached from central London via the A4 to the Chiswick roundabout and the A315 London Road/Staines Road to just west of Hounslow, or from outer areas via the M25 to Staines (junction 13) and the A315 eastbound. The entrance to the heath is clearly signposted from the A315 just east of North Feltham. Park in the car park and call in at the information centre for details of the various nature trails to follow.

By bus: routes 116, 117, 237, 417 and H23 travel along the A315 Staines Road past the entrance to Hounslow Heath. *By underground:* Hounslow Central (Piccadilly line) is on Lampton Road, a short distance north of the A315, just over a mile (1.6 km) east of the site. *By train:* overground services from Waterloo stop regularly at Hounslow station, from where buses 417 and H23 run along Staines Road past the heath.

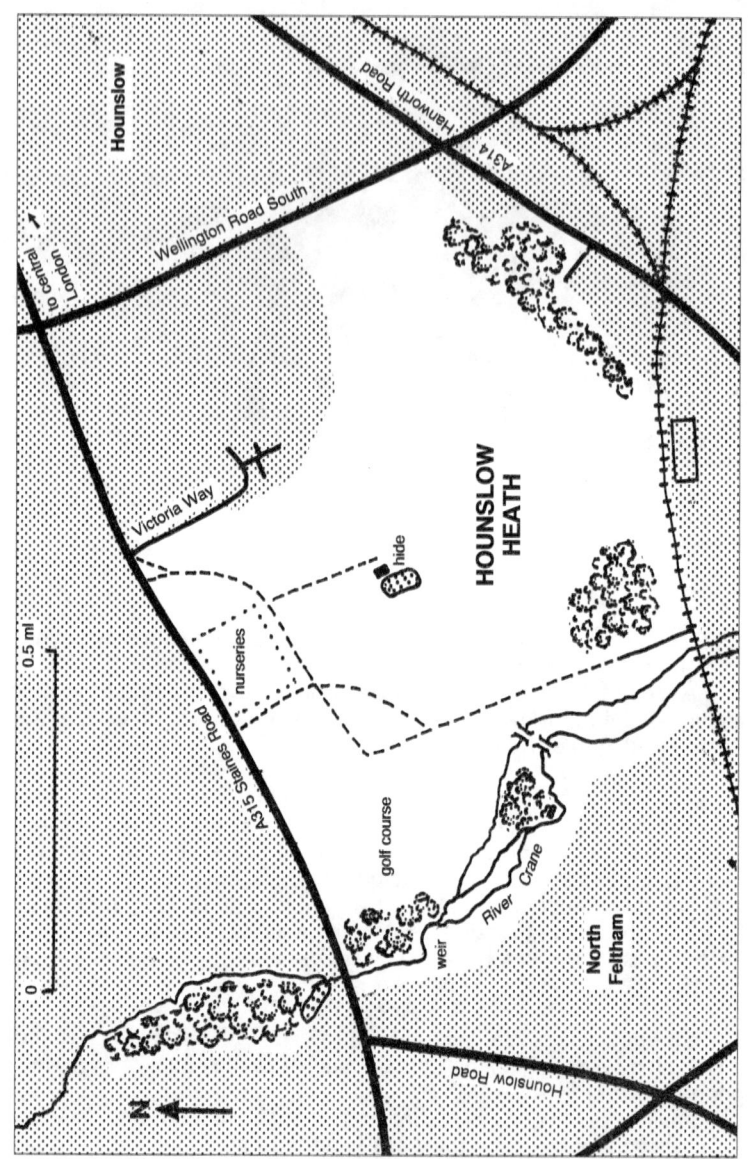

Calendar

All year: Mallard, Grey Partridge (very scarce), Stock Dove, Green and Great Spotted Woodpeckers, Skylark, Reed Bunting.

Winter (December–February): Teal, occasional Water Rail, Snipe, possibility of Jack Snipe and Woodcock, occasional Lesser Spotted Woodpecker, Stonechat, Redwing, Fieldfare, Goldcrest, Siskin, Redpoll.

Spring (March–May): Chance of waders including Little Ringed Plover, Turtle Dove, Cuckoo, Yellow Wagtail, Wheatear, Whinchat, commoner

warblers including Reed and Sedge, scarcer migrant passerines including occasional Redstart, Ring Ouzel, Grasshopper Warbler and Pied
Flycatcher.

Summer (June–July): Whitethroat, Lesser Whitethroat, Blackcap, Chiffchaff, Willow Warbler.

Autumn (August–November): Teal, Water Rail (from November), occasional waders, Yellow Wagtail, Wheatear, Whinchat, Stonechat (from
October), Redwing and Fieldfare (from October), commoner warblers
and other migrant passerines, occasional scarcer species such as Redstart
and Pied Flycatcher.

OTHER SITES IN THE AREA

34A THE CAUSEWAY NATURE RESERVE   OS ref: TQ 105754

This reserve is less than half a mile (0.8 km) northwest of Hounslow Heath
along the River Crane, and lies immediately east of Heathrow Airport.
Originally a flooded gravel pit, The Causeway NR's lake is now replenished
by surface water collected from the airfield. Over 40 years the surrounding area has developed into a mixture of grassland, scrub, woodland,
Phragmites and reedmace. Covering some 30 acres (12 ha), it is bordered
by the A312 The Causeway, the Crane and a water meadow to the north
and west, and by an industrial estate to the south.

The lake attracts breeding Little Grebe, Mallard, Tufted Duck, Pochard
and Ruddy Duck. During the winter small numbers of Great Crested
Grebe, Gadwall, Shoveler and Goldeneye can occur, and more rarely
Wigeon has been noted. Common Terns are occasionally reported
between spring and autumn. Reed Warbler, Blackcap, Lesser Whitethroat
and Willow Warbler all breed in the area, and Chiffchaffs are regular,
sometimes wintering and associating with mixed tit flocks which can also
include Goldcrest. The water meadow is worth checking for Teal and
Snipe in winter, and there is always a chance of catching a glimpse of a
Kingfisher along the river. Small flocks of Siskin and Redpoll feed in the
alders most winters. Unusual species at this underwatched site are unlikely, but a Night Heron here in June 1992 proved the exception to the rule.

The reserve is supported and funded by Heathrow Airport, and access
is strictly by prior arrangement; telephone the conservation warden on
0181 745 6594 for further details. To reach the reserve from Hounslow
Heath, turn north off the A315 Staines Road opposite the heath onto
Green Lane and follow it through to the junction with the A312 The
Causeway. Turn left and continue for a short distance to the reserve
entrance on the left, which is instantly recognisable by its high iron gates.
There is good wheelchair access around the reserve. Buses 203
(Mondays–Saturdays) and H23 run along the A30 Great South West Road
which crosses the north end of The Causeway.

35 YEADING BROOK MEADOWS

OS ref: TQ 105835

Habitat

This local nature reserve is part of the Hillingdon Trail footpath which extends for over 20 miles (32 km) through the London Borough of Hillingdon along the Yeading valley as far as Ruislip Woods to the north-east. The site, which lies in the river valley immediately south of the A40 west of Northolt, is bisected north-south by Kingshill Avenue, with the smaller eastern side managed by the London Borough of Ealing and the western area managed jointly by the London Wildlife Trust and the London Borough of Hillingdon. The Ealing side is mostly wet grazed grassland with marshier areas, with the periphery made up mostly of amenity grassland and residential areas. The Hillingdon area consists of a similar mix of habitat, but lacks the amenity grassland. A large wet pasture, grazed by horses, adjoins the eastern boundary of the nature reserve. The banks of the brook itself are well vegetated with scrub, mostly hawthorn.

Adjoining the reserve to the north is Cowslip Meadow, beyond which lies the deciduous woodland of Ten Acres Wood. To the east are two further pockets of woodland, Gutteridge Wood and The Gorse. Despite being underwatched, this well-managed habitat has a number of interesting breeding species and several notable visitors.

Species

Wildfowl and waders are rather limited in numbers and variety in this small, mainly grassland area, but Mallard and, outside the breeding season, Teal, are commonly seen in groups along the brook. Snipe favour the marshy areas and have been seen throughout the year, while Jack Snipe have also occurred in the winter months when good numbers of the commoner gulls and several hundred Lapwing may be present on the damp pasture. This last species also breeds, and with up to 14 or so pairs the population is one of the highest in the London area. Redshank are also occasionally seen during the summer, and a pair was thought to have nested in 1992.

Cowslip Meadow and the area around Ten Acres Wood are good places to search for Grey Partridge, though they can be hard to find. Stock Dove and Green and Great Spotted Woodpeckers can be found in suitable habitat, Kingfishers are sometimes seen along the brook and in winter look out for Grey Wagtail in the same area. The site's speciality birds are its owls, with up to four species present in good years. Tawny and Little Owls are resident, with the latter best looked for in the scattered oaks in Cowslip Meadow and beyond to the areas adjacent to The Gorse and Gutteridge Wood. Short-eared Owl occurs in most winters but typically ranges over a wide area; the winter of 1991–92 was particularly good for this species, with up to seven birds present. At the same time there were even higher numbers of the usually scarcer Long-eared Owl, up to 17 of which regularly roosted in favoured hawthorns; there was some interchange of birds between this roost and another some two miles (3.2 km) away at Ickenham Marsh (TQ 078858), west of Northolt Aerodrome. However, numbers of both Short-eared and Long-eared Owls in the

Long-eared Owl

London area vary greatly from year to year, and since this impressive showing there have been no further reports of sizeable roosts. Importantly, birders hoping to see these birds should ensure they avoid disturbing daytime roosts.

During the breeding season Reed Warbler, Blackcap, Whitethroat, Chiffchaff and Willow Warbler are present alongside a range of resident passerines which includes Meadow Pipit, Goldcrest, Reed Bunting and the commoner finches and tits. Singing Willow Tits have been reported in spring but the species does not appear to be established in the area, and though Redpoll and Yellowhammer have bred at Downe Barns Farm recently these species also seem irregular. Stonechat has occurred in winter, and at passage times Whinchat and Wheatear are a possibility, with occasional scarcer migrants such as Pied Flycatcher only infrequently reported.

Timing

A visit at any time of the year is likely to produce a reasonable range of regular species, with no one season particularly outstanding. The Hillingdon trail is a popular walk on fine days, and birders visiting the area are best advised to go early – or, for the possibility of hunting owls in winter, in late afternoon and at dusk when the birds are most active.

Access

There is open public access to this stretch of the 20-mile (32 km) Hillingdon Trail; the leisure services department of the London Borough of Hillingdon can give detailed information on walks and sights to see along its entire length (telephone 01895 250111).

Yeading Brook Meadows lies immediately south of Northolt Aerodrome, with straightforward access from the east or west via the A40. Turn south off the A40 at the roundabout just east of the airfield onto the A4180

West End Road, then take the right turn into Sharvel Lane where the A4180 becomes Ruislip Road. Continue past Downe Barns Farm, parking along this road and following the public footpath west past Westways Farm until you reach Charville Lane. From here, either turn right into Cowslip Meadows or take the path left, over a bridge (under which the Yeading Brook flows) into the corner of Lane Covert and ultimately into Yeading Brook Meadows.

By bus: no bus routes run along the A40 at this point, but the E2 (Mondays–Sundays) and E7 (Mondays–Saturdays) from Brentford and Ealing Broadway respectively serve the A4180 West End Lane. In the southwest corner of the site, route 195 from Southall serves the Charville Lane estate and the U2 Uxbridge–Hillingdon service stops nearby. *By underground:* the nearest tube stations are South Ruislip and Ruislip Gardens (Central line), both northeast of Northolt Aerodrome along West End Lane on the other side of the A40, or at Hillingdon (Piccadilly line), to the west along the A40 just north of the traffic lights at the next junction. There are no convenient overground train services in the area.

Calendar

All year: Sparrowhawk, Grey Partridge, Pheasant, Lapwing, Redshank, Stock Dove, Little and Tawny Owls, Kingfisher, Green and Great Spotted Woodpeckers, Skylark, Meadow Pipit, Reed Bunting.

Winter (December–February): Teal, occasional Jack Snipe, chance of Short-eared and Long-eared Owls (latter irregular), Grey Wagtail, Stonechat (rare), Fieldfare, Redwing.

Spring (March–May): Teal, Snipe, Yellow Wagtail, Whinchat, Wheatear, commoner warblers and other passage migrants.

Summer (June–July): Occasional oversummering Snipe, Reed Warbler, Lesser Whitethroat, Whitethroat, Blackcap, Chiffchaff, Willow Warbler.

Autumn (August–November): Teal, Snipe, Short-eared Owl (possible from November), Yellow Wagtail, Stonechat (rare), Whinchat, Wheatear, Fieldfare, Redwing, commoner warblers and other passage migrants.

36 RUISLIP LIDO AND WOODS

OS ref: TQ 089891

Habitat

This broad heading covers a number of interesting birding sites centred around Ruislip Lido, the largest body of water in this sector of London away from the Colne Valley. The lido was built in 1811 as a top-up feeder for the Grand Union Canal, but more recently it has become a centre for recreational activities. The concrete-sided banks are not particularly attractive to birds, though water levels vary and when low muddier margins can become exposed. Heavy amenity use means that it is not a key site for waterfowl, some of which prefer the small pond in the adjoining Ruislip Local Nature Reserve (TQ 090899).

Immediately west of the lido are the open areas of Ruislip Common (TQ 085893) and Poor's Field (TQ 088898), the latter a site known to have been in existence since 1295. These commons support a variety of plant life which includes heather and significant areas of gorse and scrub. Grassland dominates much of the rest of the habitat, but there are stands of mature deciduous trees including hawthorn and oak.

The area known as Ruislip Woods comprises several discrete tracts of ancient woodland between Harefield, Northwood and Ruislip. These are predominantly deciduous, with a wide variety of species among which beech, oak and hornbeam are numerous. East and south of the lido is the extensive Park Wood (TQ 095890); to the northwest of Poor's Field and Ruislip Common lies Copse Wood (TQ 085897); immediately west of that site is Mad Bess Wood (TQ 076895); and beyond that lies Bayhurst Wood (TQ 065892), now designated a country park. All have SSSI status and collectively occupy some 726 acres (290 ha), making them the largest woodland complex in the London area.

The woods were historically managed for gamebirds, and timber from the area was used in the construction of Windsor Castle. Today there is considerable emphasis on amenity use, and facilities include picnic areas with barbecue griddles in some of the woods. The entire area is managed by the London Borough of Hillingdon, and forms the northern end of the Hillingdon Trail.

Species

The small pond on the nature reserve holds breeding Little Grebe. Aside from common species such as Mallard and Tufted Duck, waterfowl numbers on the lido are usually very low except during cold snaps when parties of Gadwall, Wigeon, Teal and Shoveler may appear; the last two have also paid brief visits in the summer months. Other rarer species may occasionally visit the site: 17 Bewick's Swans dropped in during a cold spell in March 1988, while in April 1994 a flock of over 30 Brent Geese flew over to the northeast.

Common Sandpipers may often stop off on passage when water levels are low in spring and autumn. Other waders are rare but have included Oystercatcher, Jack Snipe and Redshank. Common Terns are occasionally noted in the summer months and a pair has oversummered, but they have yet to breed successfully. More unusual have been occasional parties of migrant Black Terns and, on one occasion, two Sandwich Terns, while a record of a Little Auk picked up from a puddle in Park Wood in February 1983 is positively bizarre.

Woodcocks are occasionally flushed in spring and autumn, and this species has also been reported in the Ruislip area in summer though probably no longer breeds regularly. Sparrowhawk and Kestrel nest locally and Hobbies are sometimes seen in the summer months. Little and Tawny Owls are resident in the area, the latter species using specially-erected nest boxes in Bayhurst Wood, and all three woodpecker species can be found. Among migrant passerines, White Wagtails have been noted on several occasions at the lido and Nightingale has occurred on Ruislip Common. Sizeable flocks of Fieldfare and Redwing are often present in the winter months, while good numbers of breeding warblers include Whitethroat, Lesser Whitethroat, Garden Warbler, Blackcap, Chiffchaff and Willow

Warbler. A migrant Grasshopper Warbler was a good find on Ruislip Common one August, while more likely are occasional singing Wood Warblers on spring passage; in 1990 a pair was found feeding young in Mad Bess Wood, but breeding of this species in the area is exceptional. Nuthatch, Treecreeper and the commoner tits are all present, though the once-resident Willow Tit is now irregular and no longer breeds. The commoner finches may be joined in winter by parties of Siskin and Redpoll, and though the secretive Hawfinch is rarely reported, it may be more regular than records suggest in this extensive area of woodland.

Rarities are exceptional in the area, but more unusual records have included an Osprey in April 1993, a singing Golden Oriole in May 1983 and a Snow Bunting in late autumn 1993.

Timing

Spring is undoubtedly the best season to work this area, for which at least a full morning should be allowed. At this time of year resident birds are joined by summer visitors and the woodlands are alive with bird song. Although less productive later in the season, autumn brings the possibility of the occasional wader or unusual passage migrant. The area is at its quietest in winter, when the woodlands are largely deserted. If you want to avoid the crowds, start early.

Access

Ruislip can be reached from the south via the M40/A40. Approaching from the east, leave the A40 just east of Northolt Aerodrome, turn right (north) at the roundabout onto the A4180 West End Road and continue for two miles (3.2 km) into central Ruislip; from the west turn left (north) off the A40 at Hillingdon, just west of the aerodrome, and follow the B466 for two miles (3.2 km) into Ruislip until it meets the A4180. Turn left and continue straight on along the A4180 (now Bury Street and then Duck's Hill Road) for another mile (1.6 km), turning right at the church for Ruislip Lido, Ruislip LNR (entry by permit only from the Ruislip Natural History Society and Park Wood, or continue along Bury Street for Copse and Mad Bess Woods, parking as signposted. The A4180 joins the A404 to the north at Northwood; this route connects with Rickmansworth and the M25 (junction 18).

For Bayhurst Wood Country Park, leave the A4180 Duck's Hill Road where it becomes Bury Street just south of the church, turning west into Breakspear Road, then right after two-thirds of a mile (1 km) into Breakspear North Road. The entrance to the wood is signposted on the left after about a mile (1.6 km); follow the signs to the large car park within the wood. Breakspear Road North continues north to Coppermill Lane at West Hyde in the Colne Valley.

By bus: route U1 (Mondays–Saturday) runs from Uxbridge to Ruislip, and during extended services to Chorleywood runs along Duck's Hill Road and Breakspear Road, providing access to or near all of the main woodlands. Numbers 114 and H13 terminate at Ruislip Lido. *By underground:* routes 114 and U1 stop at Ruislip station (Piccadilly line). There are no convenient overground services in the immediate area.

Calendar

All year: Sparrowhawk, Pheasant, Stock Dove, Little and Tawny Owls, Green, Great Spotted and Lesser Spotted Woodpeckers, Nuthatch, Treecreeper, outside chance of Hawfinch.

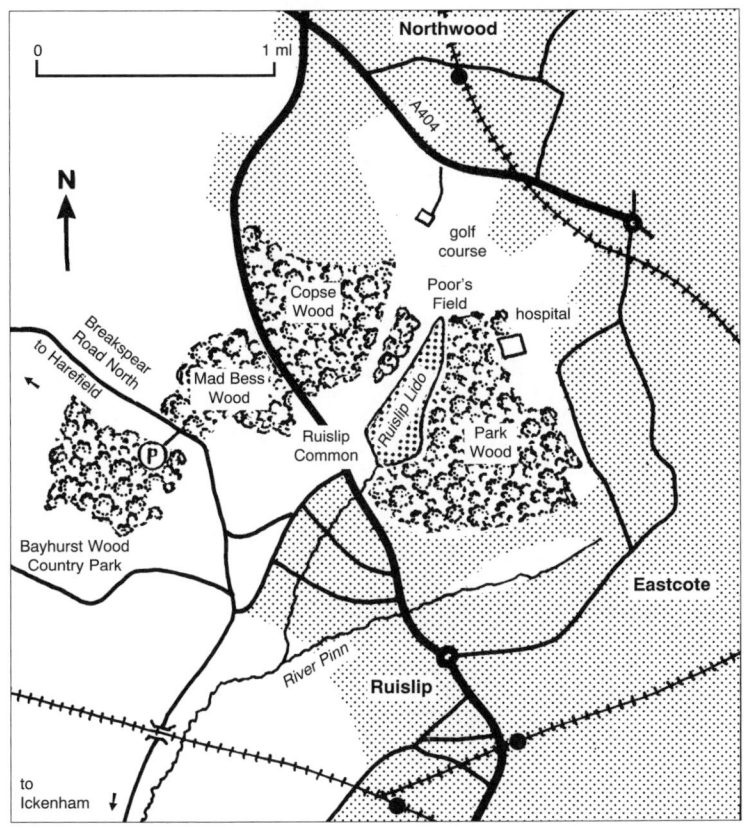

Winter (December–February): Wildfowl including oddities in cold weather, chance of Woodcock, Redwing, Fieldfare, Redpoll, Siskin.

Spring (March–May): Occasional Hobby (from late April), chance of Woodcock, Common Sandpiper, Common Tern, resident breeding birds and summer migrants including occasional Wood Warbler.

Summer (June–July): Occasional Hobby, Common Tern sometimes present, Whitethroat, Lesser Whitethroat, Garden Warbler, Blackcap, Chiffchaff, Willow Warbler.

Autumn (August-November): Occasional Hobby (until early September), chance of Woodcock, Common Sandpiper, Common Tern, regular passage migrants.

NORTHWEST LONDON

37 CASSIOBURY PARK OS ref: TQ 090970

Habitat, species and access

This 190-acre (76 ha) site on the west side of Watford holds a number of interesting species. Although much of the area is municipal parkland and subject to heavy use by the general public, early morning visits to the better corners of habitat can be productive throughout the year. The most interesting area lies between the River Gade and the Grand Union Canal, at the western end of the park. There is a good-sized tract of semi-natural woodland, dominated by willow, ash and alder, which in winter attracts flocks of Siskin and Redpoll. All three woodpeckers breed in the area, as do Treecreeper, Nuthatch and the commoner warblers and tits, though a former speciality, Willow Tit, is now extinct here.

In addition to the woodland species, the waterways have breeding Kingfisher and Grey Wagtail, and there are some disused cress beds which attract other wetland species in small numbers. Chief among these used to be Green Sandpiper and also Water Pipit, which was regular during the winter months and often lingered into early spring; however, the beds have become overgrown in recent years and this species is unlikely to occur again unless the habitat is improved. Grey Heron, Teal, Water Rail and Snipe may all be present in this area in winter, and scarcer visitors have included Bearded Tit and, on one recent occasion, Dipper.

From central London Watford can be reached via the M1/A41, and from other areas via junctions 19 and 20 of the M25. From the centre of Watford take the A412 Watford–Rickmansworth road, bearing right into Gade Avenue; there is a car park just inside the park gates at the end of this road, and numerous other local access points. The centre of Watford, a short walk away, is well served by bus routes, and Watford underground station (Metropolitan line) is a few minutes away along Gade Avenue. Overground rail services from central London and other areas serve Watford station, just east of the town centre along the A412.

There are two other sites in the area which can also be taken in during a visit to Cassiobury Park. A short distance to the northwest, on the other side of the West Herts Golf Course, is Whippendell Woods (TQ 075977), a 161-acre (64 ha) site comprising mainly oak, beech, ash and silver birch. This woodland holds a good range of commoner species, and in the past has been noted for Little Owl, Hawfinch and, in winter, Brambling, though none of these is now regular. Wood Warbler has been recorded on passage. There is good public access and two large car parks. Leave central Watford northwest on the A411 and after 1.25 miles

(2 km) bear left along the minor road by the weir at The Grove Mill; the first car park is half a mile (0.8 km) along on the left.

A short distance to the southwest lies Croxley Moor (TQ 065956), an area dominated by scrub and grassland. Despite heavy use from dog walkers and model aircraft enthusiasts, this site still manages to hold a few ground-nesting species and attract various migrants in spring and autumn. Both Skylark and Meadow Pipit breed in the open areas, Green Woodpecker is resident and the scrub holds Blackcap, Whitethroat, Willow Warbler and Reed Bunting in the summer. There is a possibility of locally-scarce migrants such as a Ring Ouzel or Redstart in spring and autumn, and Stonechat has wintered in recent years when Siskin may also be present. A Mediterranean Gull returned to winter at nearby Croxley Green for five years in the late 1980s and early 1990s. Access to the site is from Watford Road in Croxley Green; turn into Frankland Road opposite Croxley underground station (Metropolitan line) and immediately left into Field Close. There is also an overground station slightly further east at Croxley Green.

38 BENTLEY PRIORY AND THE STANMORE AREA   OS ref: TQ 155927

Habitat

Stanmore lies on the leafy northwest fringe of London in the borough of Harrow, and marks the divide between the end of the capital's more prosperous suburbs and the start of rural Hertfordshire. For birders there are several adjoining sites of interest on the northern side of Stanmore, of which Bentley Priory is perhaps the best known.

Its name probably derived from the Anglo-Saxon 'beonet' (a place covered in coarse grass) and 'leah' (a piece of cleared ground in the uplands), Bentley Priory is an undulating landscape of meadows and mature woodlands covering approximately 215 acres (86 ha). As a monastic site it dates back to the 13th century, but the original buildings were demolished and the present house, on the northern edge of the site, was built in 1775; this is now owned by the Ministry of Defence and is closed to the public. Much of the area to the south of the house is an SSSI-designated local nature reserve, with the most extensive areas of woodland at Lake Wood, within which is Summerhouse Lake and the largest oak tree in Middlesex (measuring about 30 feet (9 m) in circumference), and the oak and hornbeam-dominated Heriot's Wood. There is a cypress and pine plantation towards the southeast of the site and a private deer park in the northeast corner, but otherwise the landscape is of stands of open woodland, scattered thickets, meadows and pasture, through which several small streams flow.

Immediately northeast of Bentley Priory is Stanmore Common (TQ 156940), which includes arguably the best areas of broadleaved woodland and a number of small ponds, and beyond that lies Stanmore Country Park (TQ 175930) and golf course, while to the west of Bentley Priory is Harrow Weald Common (TQ 148933), and to the south of that

Harrow Weald Park (TQ 148920). The whole area is a mosaic of woodland and open country which has a number of interesting breeding birds, many of which can be found at most or all of these sites.

Species

With the exception of Summerhouse Lake, which holds a few pairs of commoner waterbirds, there is little standing water of significance in the area. However, the ponds on Stanmore Common are worth checking for one exotic resident, Mandarin Duck, and a pair nests most years. Sparrowhawk is resident and Hobby breeds in the area; try scanning for the latter species in the summer months from the high ground near the MOD site at Bentley Priory. Woodcock has been found roding recently at Stanmore Common, and there is an outside chance of flushing migrant or wintering birds between September and April. The extensive woodland in this area holds a good range of resident species including Stock Dove, Cuckoo, Tawny Owl and Green, Great Spotted and Lesser Spotted Woodpeckers, and of historical note was a haunt of Wryneck and Nightjar several decades ago, before both species underwent drastic declines in range and population.

Tawny Owl

In winter one or two Grey Wagtails are often present in the area, while in spring migrants range from the numerous Meadow Pipit to less regular visitors which have included Tree Pipit, Redstart, Wheatear and Whinchat; more exceptional are records of Black Redstart and, perhaps surprisingly, Nightingale. Warblers are much in evidence from spring, and though numbers are higher on passage Lesser Whitethroat, Whitethroat,

Garden Warbler, Blackcap, Chiffchaff and Willow Warbler all breed. Singing Wood Warblers are occasionally recorded in spring. Goldcrest, Nuthatch, Treecreeper and all of the commoner tit species are present, and in addition Willow Tit is still occasionally seen at Stanmore Common and Stanmore Country Park, though sightings are erratic to say the least. The expected resident finches are joined by flocks of Siskin and Redpoll in winter, and there have also been sporadic sightings of Hawfinch, though despite the wealth of apparently suitable habitat this retiring species does not seem to be resident in the area.

Timing

With interest reserved mainly for woodland species, the area is likely to be most productive in the months March to June when most species will be in song and easier to locate. Unlike many open spaces in the London area these sites often seem relatively uncrowded, and though morning visits are best for woodland birds, disturbance from other site users is generally not a problem.

Access

Stanmore lies to the west of the A5 Brockley Hill/Edgware Road about two miles (3.2 km) south of junction 4 of the M1. From the A5 take the A410 London Road west into Stanmore, and turn right (north) at the next main junction after the station onto the A4140 Stanmore Hill. Where this road becomes The Common, turn right into Warren Lane and park in the

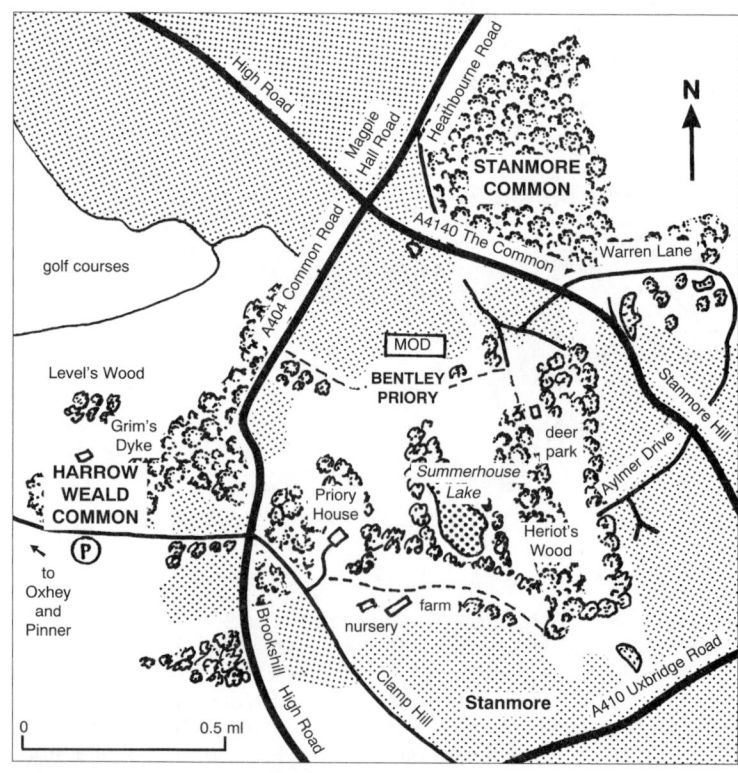

car park (closed Sunday–Friday from dusk until 9.30 am). A noticeboard here maps out two circular walks around the area, one of 4.3 miles (6.9 km) and the other of 1.7 miles (2.8 km). The first, at about two hours, takes in much of Stanmore Common and Bentley Priory, while the shorter route cuts out most of the latter area.

Alternatively, to take in more of the western side of Bentley Priory and also Harrow Weald Common, leave Warren Lane north on the A4140, turn left at the traffic lights onto the A409 Common Road and right after almost a mile (1.6 km) into Old Redding. From the car park here there is a suggested 3.2 mile (5.1 km) route around the area. Paths suitable for wheelchairs and prams are clearly signed from both car parks. Bentley Priory LNR has a voluntary warden who can be contacted on 0181 954 2918 for more information.

By bus: routes 340, H12 and 142 serve Stanmore, with the last running from the station up Stanmore Hill between the common and Bentley Priory. *By underground:* Stanmore station is on the Jubilee line.

Calendar

All year: Mandarin Duck, Sparrowhawk, Woodcock (rare), Stock Dove, Tawny Owl, Green, Great Spotted and Lesser Spotted Woodpeckers, Goldcrest, Willow Tit (very rare), Nuthatch, Treecreeper.

Winter (December–February): Grey Wagtail, Fieldfare, Redwing, Siskin, Redpoll.

Spring (March–May): Hobby (from late April), Turtle Dove, Meadow Pipit, Cuckoo, commoner warblers, Spotted Flycatcher, chance of migrants including Tree Pipit, Redstart, Whinchat, Wheatear, Wood Warbler and Pied Flycatcher.

Summer (June–July): Hobby, Cuckoo, Lesser Whitethroat, Whitethroat, Garden Warbler, Blackcap, Chiffchaff, Willow Warbler.

Autumn (August–November): Hobby (until early September), Turtle Dove, Cuckoo (rare after July), Meadow Pipit, Fieldfare and Redwing (from October), departing summer migrants including commoner warblers and perhaps Tree Pipit, Redstart, Whinchat, Wheatear or Pied Flycatcher.

39 HILFIELD PARK
RESERVOIR
OS ref: TQ 158959

Habitat

The vast majority of London's reservoirs are located in the Colne, Lea and Thames Valleys, and interest for many waterbirds naturally concentrates on these areas. There are, however, several other major bodies of water located away from these main rivers, and of these Hilfield Park Reservoir is one of the most significant.

Situated by the M1 just east of Bushey in Hertfordshire, the reservoir was constructed in the early 1950s and since 1969 has been designated as a local nature reserve, managed by the Hertfordshire and Middlesex Wildlife Trust. At full capacity the reservoir has a surface area of 115 acres (46 ha) and can hold about 600 million gallons of water. With the exception of the western bank, the margins are 'natural' in appearance and support a variety of marshland plants and several small reedbeds. There is a hide on the south bank, overlooking the bay in the southeast corner which is one of the best areas for wintering wildfowl. Surrounding the reservoir is an additional 80 acres (32 ha) of grassland and woodland, the latter including some good mixed stands originally planted as a screen around the reservoir.

The site is of local and regional significance on several counts, and has nationally important numbers of moulting Pochard in late summer. Just over 20 species breed and around 100–120 species are recorded annually, although the reservoir's significance for birds will certainly decline if proposals by site owners Three Valleys Water to allow sailing receive approval.

Species

The main attraction here is waterfowl, particularly during the winter months when impressive totals of a number of species can be present. Great Crested Grebes have on occasion reached nearly 200, though an annual peak somewhere between 40–60 is more typical. Around seven pairs breed, as do three pairs of Little Grebe which may increase in number to about 20 by autumn. Slavonian, Red-necked and especially Black-necked Grebes have all made sporadic appearances between autumn and spring, and in 1990 this last species made history by nesting here – the first breeding record for the London area. Remarkably, a pair of Slavonian Grebes was also watched displaying in April of the same year, though they did not stay. Black-necked Grebes have not repeated their success, though a displaying pair appeared briefly again in spring 1992.

A few Grey Herons are present throughout the year and Cormorants are regularly seen between September and March, though this species is much less numerous here than at most other large London waters. Much rarer are occasional winter visits by Shag, and in September 1994 the reservoir's first Little Egret was found in the southeast bay.

During autumn and winter good numbers of wildfowl are present on the reservoir. These include up to 100 or more Wigeon and around 50 each of Teal and Shoveler, while unusually Gadwall can be the most numerous dabbler with in excess of 150 recorded; in contrast Mallard may not exceed 40 at any time during the year. Species such as Sheldluck and Pintail are much more irregular, and similarly Garganey has been recorded on passage but is not annual. This deep-water site is used as a late summer moulting refuge by Tufted Duck and Pochard, and nationally significant numbers of the latter species have been recorded with up to 100 the norm. Ruddy Duck winters here in increasing numbers, with regularly well over 100 birds present, and displaying pairs are often present in summer though do not breed regularly. Up to 10 or so Goldeneye may be present between September and April and Goosander are scarce but near-annual visitors, but other species such as Smew, Red-breasted Merganser, Common Scoter and Red-crested Pochard are much less predictable.

In addition to resident Kestrel and Sparrowhawk, Hobby breeds not too far away and is occasionally seen hunting over the reservoir between May and September. Rarer birds of prey in recent years have included Osprey, Common Buzzard and Peregrine. Pheasants are sometimes seen on the reserve and this is also a good site for Red-legged Partridges, which seem to favour the dam area. The reedier margins usually attract a Water Rail in winter, though this species can be difficult to observe here. There is a healthy breeding population of Coots, and in winter numbers can rise to more than 500, making this often the most numerous waterbird on the reservoir.

The relatively high water levels and lack of exposed mud mean that this site is not ideally suited to attract migrant waders in numbers or variety. A few Little Ringed Plovers and Common Sandpipers are regular on passage, the former particularly in spring, and Lapwing breeds on the adjacent farmland, but otherwise the reservoir typically attracts just a handful of Dunlin, Redshank and Snipe annually. Other species such as Oystercatcher, Ringed Plover, Greenshank and Green Sandpiper are perhaps more likely to be recorded as fly-overs or if the water level has receded after a hot summer. Truly rare waders are therefore exceptional, but include the notable discovery of London's first Spotted Sandpiper back in September 1956. More recently, single Grey Phalaropes appeared in September 1988 and November 1995.

A notable feature of the winter months is the gull roost, one of only two in Hertfordshire. This spectacle is best viewed from the dam wall. At peak times numbers have exceeded 25,000 birds, the vast majority of them Black-headed Gulls. Over 2,000 Common Gulls may also be present, but by comparison only small numbers of Herring and Lesser Black-backs occur and there are usually fewer than 10 Great Black-backs. Sightings of Mediterranean Gulls have increased, with perhaps six different birds recorded in one recent year, and in autumn or more often spring there is a chance of Little Gull or perhaps even a Kittiwake dropping in. Occasional surprises have included Sabine's Gull and Long-tailed Skua within a week of each other in September 1988 and two Little Auks in November 1995. Spring is the peak period for tern passage, and from late April to late May respectable numbers of Common and regular Black Terns appear, sometimes also with a few Arctics; all are also possible in autumn, though perhaps in smaller numbers. Sandwich and Little Terns have also been recorded, while the site's only White-winged Black Tern record was of two birds in September 1970.

Stock Doves are resident and believed to breed in the grounds of nearby Hilfield Castle, and Tawny Owl and Green and Great Spotted Woodpeckers all nest locally, as perhaps does Kingfisher, which is seen occasionally at the reservoir and may breed at the lake in the castle grounds. In spring and early autumn large numbers of Swifts and hirundines can concentrate over the reservoir when insect prey is in abundance, and they should always be checked carefully for rarer species: Red-rumped Swallow has twice been found here, and in April 1990 an Alpine Swift appeared briefly. Passage periods bring good numbers of Meadow Pipits and regular Yellow Wagtails, and there is always an outside chance of a Rock or Water Pipit or White Wagtail appearing among them. Other passerine migrants of note are few and far between, and aside from regular Wheatears in spring and autumn, species such as Ring Ouzel, Redstart, Black Redstart and even Whinchat are rare here. In winter small numbers of Fieldfare and Redwing are usually present in the area.

During the breeding season the site attracts several pairs of Reed Warbler, but though Whitethroat, Lesser Whitethroat, Garden Warbler, Blackcap, Chiffchaff and Willow Warbler can all be encountered on passage, especially in spring, there is no firm evidence that any of these species is an annual breeder. However, there are several pairs of Goldcrest in the woodland, along with the commoner tits (including Coal Tit) and finches, and in winter a small flock of Siskin is usually present in the castle wood. Reed Bunting breeds and Yellowhammer appears to be resident in small numbers on the surrounding farmland. Although passerines are not its strong point, the site can lay claim to old records of two regional rarities: a Little Bunting in April 1960, and London's second Serin in March 1973.

Timing

Summer is the quietest season, with the variety of species increased by migrants in spring and autumn and numbers boosted by wildfowl and gulls in winter. The site can be worked on a circular route which should take no more than about two hours; in winter an afternoon visit can be rounded off with the spectacle of many thousands of gulls coming in to roost at dusk.

Access

Parts of the reservoir can be viewed from the A41 Watford By-pass Road, Dagger Lane on the east side, a public footpath alongside Elstree Aerodrome to the north and from the footbridge over the M1 motorway to the west. However, access to the reservoir banks and nature reserve is by permit only from the Hertfordshire and Middlesex Wildlife Trust, and keys are required for entry via the main gate (see Useful Addresses for contact details).

The reservoir lies about 1.5 miles (2.4 km) northwest of junction 4 of the M1, offering a straightforward route from London to the south or from

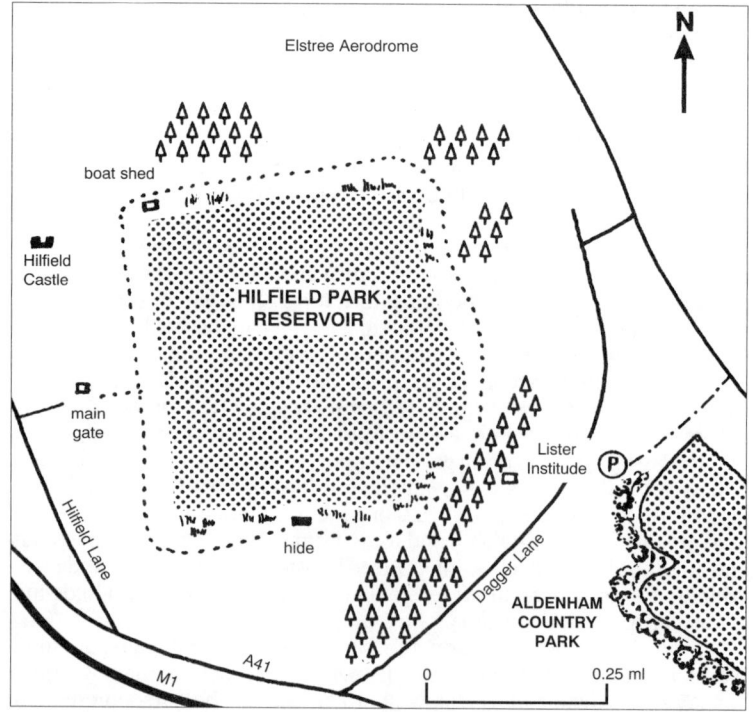

other outer areas via junctions 21/21a of the M25 which connects with the M1 at junctions 6/6a to the north. From junction 4 head northwest on the A41 Watford By-pass Road alongside the M1 towards Aldenham. Continue straight over the next roundabout, still running parallel to the motorway, and turn right after two-thirds of a mile (1 km) into Hilfield Lane. The main entrance to the reservoir is a short distance along on the right; permit-holders should park by the pumping station and walk up the concrete stairs to reach the reservoir embankment. There are no convenient public transport services in the immediate area.

Calendar

All year: Little Grebe, Great Crested Grebe, Grey Heron, Pochard, Tufted Duck, Ruddy Duck, Sparrowhawk, Kestrel, Pheasant, Red-legged Partridge, Lapwing, Stock Dove, Tawny Owl, Kingfisher, Green and Great Spotted Woodpeckers, Grey Wagtail (irregular), Goldcrest, Yellowhammer (scarce), Reed Bunting.

Winter (November–February): Occasional oddity such as a rare grebe or Shag, Cormorant, Wigeon, Gadwall, Teal, Shoveler, Goldeneye, chance of Goosander and occasional scarcer wildfowl, Water Rail (scarce), Snipe (irregular), large gull roost with occasional Mediterranean Gull, small numbers of Fieldfare and Redwing, Siskin.

Spring (March–May): Black-necked Grebe (irregular), departing winter wildfowl including occasional oddity, Hobby (from May), Little Ringed Plover, Common Sandpiper, possibility of other common waders, Little Gull, Common, Arctic and Black Terns (from April), Cuckoo, Meadow Pipit, Yellow Wagtail, Wheatear, commoner warblers on passage, outside chance of other migrants such as White Wagtail or Redstart.

Summer (June–July): Hobby (occasional), chance of odd passage waders or visiting Common Tern, Reed Warbler.

Autumn (August–October): Black-necked Grebe (irregular), arriving winter wildfowl including occasional oddity, Hobby (until early September), Water Rail (scarce, from October), Common Sandpiper and other passage waders, chance of Little and perhaps Mediterranean Gulls, Meadow Pipit, Yellow Wagtail, Wheatear, Fieldfare and Redwing (from October), commoner passage warblers, outside chance of other migrants.

OTHER SITES IN THE AREA

39A ALDENHAM COUNTRY PARK

OS ref: TQ 169995
Map p. 188

This public amenity site, located immediately south of Hilfield Park Reservoir, started life as Aldenham Reservoir. In its hey-day it provided important habitat for good numbers of wildfowl and for many other species, and a number of interesting records included London's first Bluethroat in March 1942. Today, however, with its redesignation and landscaping as a country park, the emphasis is very much on family and leisure activities, with a 'children's corner' and lakeside picnic area, extensive fishing activities and, on the southeast side of the site, a sailing club.

As a result, this body of water and its adjoining woods and farmland are much less ornithologically attractive than they used to be, and many waterbirds prefer to feed and roost on neighbouring Hilfield Park Reservoir. Great Crested Grebes are often present but wildfowl are generally unexceptional, with Teal and Ruddy Duck being the most noteworthy of the regulars in winter, and there are only occasional records of more local species such as Gadwall. Mandarin Duck has also occurred. Water Rail has been noted on occasion in winter, but with the exception of Lapwing on the farmland and possible Snipe outside the breeding season, waders are unlikely.

Keep an eye open for woodpeckers along the more wooded western and southern banks of the lake, all three of which have occurred in the area, as well as Nuthatch and Treecreeper and, in summer, commoner warblers including Reed and Garden, and also Spotted Flycatcher. As recently as the late 1980s both Willow Tit and Tree Sparrow were regular here, but neither of these two declining passerines is now likely to be found on a chance visit. More typical are flocks of finches and buntings on the adjacent farmland in winter; these may include Yellowhammer and, more rarely, Brambling. Reed Bunting is resident in the area. Other wintering species include Fieldfare, Redwing and Siskin.

Aldenham Country Park is unlikely to reward the one-off visitor, but could certainly be taken in on a morning's trip to Hilfield Park Reservoir. Directions are as for that site, but at the roundabout on the A41 turn east onto the A411, follow it past the southern end of the country park and then turn left into Aldenham Road, following signs left again after a third of a mile (0.5 km) to the car park (£2 fee) and picnic area at the north end of the water. There are a number of paths and nature trails allowing access to the area, some of which are suitable for wheelchairs. The country park is open daily throughout the year except Christmas Day, from 9.00 am to one hour before dusk.

40 BRENT RESERVOIR   OS ref: TQ 215870

Habitat

Brent Reservoir flanks the North Circular Road in the midst of suburban northwest London, a short distance northeast of Wembley Stadium. Known locally as the Welsh Harp, it was constructed in the 1830s to feed the Grand Union Canal and subsequently enlarged in the 1850s, by which time it covered some 197 acres (79 ha). At this time, well before the spread of suburban London, the reservoir's rural setting and extensive wetland habitat made it a magnet for birds. In those early days Victorian naturalists collected a wide range of species at the site, including exotic visitors such as Squacco Heron, Little Bittern and even Pallas's Sandgrouse.

Today, as a result of infilling, the reservoir covers around 130 acres (52 ha). It is fairly shallow, rarely exceeding eight feet (2.4 m) in depth, but this increases to more than 20 feet (6 m) at the western end by the dam. There is a sailing base in this corner. The water level occasionally fluctuates, though is rarely low enough to expose mud for long periods. When it does interest often centres on the Eastern Marsh, an area in the southeast corner of the site which can attract waders and at most times offers suitable breeding sites for grebes and wildfowl, as well as feeding Grey Herons, Cormorants and good numbers of gulls. Two hides provide good views across parts of this area from the north bank.

A small 'finger' of the reservoir extends northwards underneath the bridge at Cool Oak Lane towards West Hendon. This area is the Northern Marsh, bordered by a good-sized reedbed to the north and allotments and an elevated area of rough ground and scrub, formerly a rubbish dump, to the west. This part of the reservoir is also the base for a canoe club, though by agreement neither canoes or boats from the sailing club enter the shallows in either the Northern or Eastern Marshes.

There are several stretches of woodland around the reservoir, with extensive areas of willow bordering the Eastern Marsh and to a lesser extent the Northern Marsh, and mainly oak woodland around the field studies centre at the western end of the northern bank of the main reservoir. The site has received SSSI designation for its breeding waterfowl, which find the well-vegetated banks much to their liking. Brent Reservoir can provide some very productive birding in an otherwise unrewarding part of the capital; around 125–135 species are recorded annually by the active local bird group, and during spring and autumn up to 70 or so species may be possible in a day.

Species

Divers occur very rarely at Brent Reservoir, perhaps because of its relatively shallow depth, and though Slavonian, Black-necked and Red-necked Grebes have all been recorded these species too are distinctly unusual here. The reservoir holds nationally important numbers of Great Crested Grebes in the breeding season, with up to 50 pairs nesting in the early 1990s; success is very variable, however, as fluctuating water levels may submerge nests, and in 1993 only three pairs managed to breed successfully. A few pairs of Little Grebe also breed. Cormorants are frequent in small numbers outside the breeding season, and Shag has become almost annual in recent years. Grey Herons are constantly present, often in numbers. Bittern was formerly more regular in winter but is now less likely. Rarer still were the Spoonbills in May 1993 and July 1997, and the Night Heron in May 1994.

The Northern and Eastern Marshes between them hold reasonable numbers of Mallard and other dabbling duck in winter, including Gadwall, Teal and Shoveler; these species are occasionally recorded in summer, and the last two have bred. Garganey sometimes use this site on passage, particularly in autumn, and in December 1995 a late-staying bird could be seen in company with the local Teal and a vagrant Blue-winged Teal – perhaps a unique opportunity to see these three species side-by-side together in Britain. Pintail and Wigeon are scarce here but both are recorded annually. Rafts of Tufted Duck may number up to 300, with lesser numbers of Pochard. Aside from the resident Ruddy Duck, some six or so pairs of which breed, other diving species such as Scaup, Goldeneye, Goosander and Smew are rare here – this last species in stark contrast to

Great Crested Grebe and Common Terns

past years, with flocks regularly reaching 80 birds in the 1950s and peaking at 144 in February 1956.

Kestrel and Sparrowhawk are resident, and between spring and early autumn there is always a chance of seeing one or two Hobbies hunting over the reservoir. Other raptors are unsurprisingly rare, but in recent years have included Marsh Harrier, Osprey, Common Buzzard and on two occasions Honey Buzzard.

Brent supports good numbers of Moorhen and Coot, with 500 of the latter not unknown at peak times, and the Eastern Marsh in particular provides excellent habitat for Water Rail, small numbers of which are constantly present between September and April. Counts of Snipe can reach 30 or more on passage and in winter, and Jack Snipe is reported annually, usually in the damp grass around the edges of the Northern Marsh. In spring and autumn Common Sandpipers may be present in numbers, and Little Ringed Plovers sometimes drop in and stay for a few days. Other waders are rather less predictable, mainly because of the lack of extensive suitable habitat. Dunlin, Greenshank and Green Sandpiper are among the more likely species to call in, while others such as Curlew, Whimbrel and Golden Plover usually move straight through. Less common species such as Little Stint, Wood Sandpiper, Curlew Sandpiper and Ruff have occurred, and are particularly likely on the rare occasions when the water level is lowered for maintenance work.

Large numbers of Black-headed Gulls use the site, particularly in late summer when several thousand may be present, and outside the breeding season Common, Herring and Lesser Black-backed Gulls are regular in lower numbers, along with the occasional Great Black-backed. Yellow-legged occurs annually and there are several records of Kittiwake, but other species including Little, Mediterranean and Iceland Gulls are all local rarities. Common Terns are present from mid-April, and by May some 15 or more pairs may be breeding on the rafts in front of the main hide overlooking the Eastern Marsh. Black Terns are logged most years on passage, and there is a chance of Arctic Tern, particularly in autumn.

Stock Dove, Tawny Owl and Green and Great Spotted Woodpeckers are resident in the area, and Lesser Spotted is also recorded annually though no longer seems to breed at this site. Turtle Dove and Cuckoo occur on passage, especially in spring, while Kingfishers are present year-round and a pair breeds in the vicinity of the Eastern Marsh. Skylark, Meadow and Tree Pipits and Yellow Wagtail are all migrants here, but Pied and Grey Wagtails both breed. The playing fields and scrubby slope beyond the old dump can be productive for Whinchat and Wheatear in spring and autumn, and more rarely Redstart, Nightingale and Ring Ouzel have also been recorded. In winter Redwings can be numerous, but Fieldfares are usually noted only on passage.

Common bird censuses over many years have shown good numbers of warblers in the summer months, with birds on territory augmented by numerous passage migrants. There are healthy populations of Reed and Sedge Warblers around the margins of the reservoir, and the scrub and woods hold breeding Whitethroat, Lesser Whitethroat, Garden Warbler, Blackcap, Chiffchaff and Willow Warbler. Occasionally a migrant Grasshopper Warbler can be heard reeling during spring, while rarer warblers have included a singing Cetti's, two overwintering *tristis* race Chiffchaffs in 1990–91 and a Yellow-browed Warbler in September 1994. Spotted and the occasional Pied Flycatcher may appear on passage, and Firecrest should be looked out for among migrant Goldcrests in spring and autumn. Nuthatch is rare, and Treecreepers have not been proved breeding for a decade. The commoner tits all breed. In past winters parties of Bearded Tit have occasionally appeared in the reedbeds. In addition to Reed Bunting and the commoner finches Siskin and Redpoll may both be present in winter, while a singing male Serin was present in the allotments by the Northern Marsh for two days in April 1991.

Other rarities have been thin on the ground in recent years, but regular coverage over a long period since the 1950s has been rewarded with records of numerous regionally rare species including Leach's Storm-petrel, Purple Heron, Spotted Crake, Stone Curlew, Hoopoe, Wryneck, Richard's Pipit, Aquatic Warbler and Ortolan Bunting.

Timing

There are enough regular species of interest to justify a visit at any time of the year, though spring and autumn offer the greatest variety of birds and winter the highest numbers. The reservoir is a popular public amenity site and can suffer from disturbance, especially at weekends. Angling is not permitted but the activities of the sailing and canoe clubs can push waterbirds around the reservoir, although the Eastern and Northern Marshes are generally free from such disturbance. Early morning visits are recommended throughout the year, and if time is short coverage of the Eastern and Northern Marshes alone should pick up most of the interesting birds present; for a fuller route around the banks allow up to half a day, bearing in mind that the paths are very muddy in winter.

Access

There is unrestricted public access to the banks except at the dam wall,

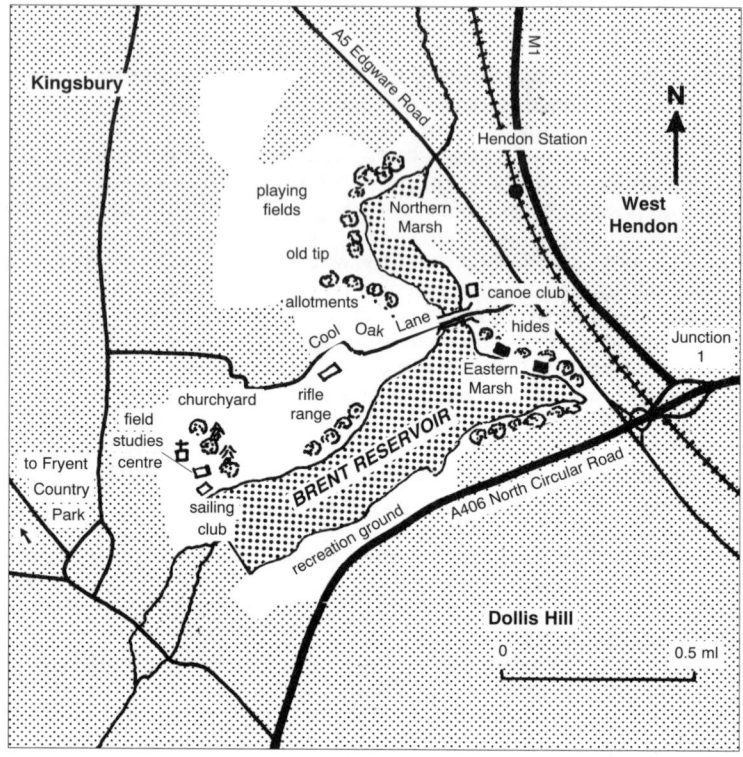

though note that the reservoir is not visible from the well-wooded paths along much of the south side. The Field Study Centre is not usually open to the general public, and use of the hides is subject to the presence of a keyholder on site: weekends are likely to be the best times. Keys can be obtained for a nominal sum from the Welsh Harp Conservation Group.

Brent Reservoir lies just northwest of the junction of the A406 North Circular Road and the A5 Edgware Road near Hendon and Brent Cross, immediately west of junction 1 of the M1. The most convenient access point for the best birding areas is by the narrow road bridge that separates the Northern Marsh from the main reservoir; to reach this part of the site turn north off the A406 onto the A5 (signposted Edgware and Colindale), and left after three-quarters of a mile (1.2 km) into Cool Oak Lane NW9. Park in the second road on the left, Woolmead Avenue, and a few yards further down Cool Oak Lane take the public footpath around the back of the canoe club car park which leads down onto the bank and eventually to the hides and the Eastern Marsh. For the Northern Marsh, continue over the bridge in Cool Oak Lane and turn right along the bank for the best views of the area. Alternatively, for the dam end turn off the A406 almost two miles (3.2 km) further west and head north on the A4088 Neasden Lane, turning right after half a mile (0.8 km) into Birchen Grove and continuing past the cemetery on Old Church Lane on the left to the Field Study Centre. Park along the road, not in the sailing club car park.

By bus: routes 142 (Mondays–Saturdays only) and 32 run along the A5 for Cool Oak Lane at the eastern end of the site, the 112 serves the A406 for access to the south side of the reservoir, and numbers 182 (Mondays–Saturdays only), 245, 297 and 302 all stop along Neasden Lane at the dam end. *By underground:* the most convenient tube stations are at Brent Cross (Northern line), from where the 142 bus runs to Cool Oak Lane, and Wembley Park (Jubilee and Metropolitan lines) for the dam end via bus routes 182, 245, 297 and 302. *By train:* overground services from King's Cross stop at Hendon station near the eastern end of the reservoir. From the station walk west along Station Road, turn left onto the A5 (here known as The Broadway) and soon after right into Cool Oak Lane.

Calendar

All year: Little Grebe, Great Crested Grebe, Grey Heron, Pochard, Tufted Duck, Ruddy Duck, Sparrowhawk, Kestrel, Tawny Owl, Kingfisher, Green and Great Spotted Woodpeckers, Grey Wagtail, Reed Bunting.

Winter (December–February): Occasional oddities such as scarce grebe or Shag, Cormorant, Gadwall, Teal, Shoveler, Goldeneye (scarce), chance of Smew (very rare), Water Rail, Snipe, Jack Snipe (scarce), Stonechat (occasional), Fieldfare, Redwing, Chiffchaff, Goldcrest, Firecrest (rare), Siskin, Redpoll.

Spring (March–May): Garganey (rare), Hobby (from late April), passage waders including Little Ringed Plover, Snipe, Redshank (scarce) and Common Sandpiper, Common, Black and perhaps Arctic Terns, Turtle Dove, Cuckoo, Meadow Pipit, Yellow Wagtail, Whinchat, Wheatear, commoner warblers, chance of scarcer passerine migrants including Redstart, Ring Ouzel, Grasshopper Warbler, Firecrest and Pied Flycatcher.

Summer (June-July): Occasional oversummering dabbling duck, chance of Hobby, Common Tern, Sedge Warbler, Reed Warbler, Lesser Whitethroat, Whitethroat, Garden Warbler, Blackcap, Willow Warbler.

Autumn (August-November): Chance of Garganey, Water Rail (from September), Hobby (until early September), passage waders including Snipe, Greenshank, Green and Common Sandpipers, Common and perhaps Arctic and Black Terns, Meadow Pipit, Yellow Wagtail, Stonechat (rare), Whinchat, Wheatear, Fieldfare and Redwing (from October), commoner passage warblers, Spotted Flycatcher, chance of scarcer passerine migrants including Tree Pipit, Redstart, Firecrest and Pied Flycatcher.

OTHER SITES IN THE AREA

40A BARN HILL AND FRYENT COUNTRY PARK   OS ref: TQ 194874

This 250-acre (100 ha) tract of remnant countryside lies about half a mile (0.8 km) northwest of the western end of Brent Reservoir. At 282 feet (86 ha) Barn Hill is the highest point in the area, with the suburb of Wembley

Park spreading out from its western slope, but with some attractive deciduous woodland on the eastern side, which includes oak, hornbeam, ash and beech. This gives way to open grassland and scrub, immediately to the north and east of which are the meadows and hedgerows of Fryent Country Park. The whole area is poorly-watched, but has a reasonable range of resident birds and summer visitors.

Sparrowhawk and Kestrel breed locally and, as at nearby Brent Reservoir, Hobbies are not infrequent visitors in the summer months. There is also a record of Peregrine from here in the 1980s, but far rarer was the calling Quail found in June 1983. One or two pairs of Stock Dove appear to breed in the vicinity, Green and Great Spotted Woodpeckers are resident and occasionally Lesser Spotted Woodpecker is also noted. In summer, warblers include Lesser Whitethroat, Whitethroat, Blackcap, Chiffchaff and Willow Warbler, while in winter the odd Goldcrest may accompany tit flocks in the area. Treecreeper breeds, and until fairly recently the area also used to hold Yellowhammer and Tree Sparrow, though these species no longer nest. Reed Buntings may be present alongside the commoner finches, particularly in winter. Migrants have included Pied Flycatcher and, more unusually, Long-eared Owl, though a visit in spring or autumn is perhaps more likely to produce passage species such as Spotted Flycatcher, Whinchat and Wheatear.

The area can be very popular, especially in summer and at weekends, so early morning visits are likely to be best. Barn Hill and Fryent Country Park can be reached from the western end of Brent Reservoir by following the A4088 Neasden Lane/Blackbird Hill northwest, then continuing in the same direction along Salmon Street, becoming the A4140 Fryent Way which separates Barn Hill to the west from much of the country park. Park in the car parks signposted at the latter site and explore the area. To the north, the A4140 connects with the A4006 Kenton Road/Kingsbury Road, which runs east back to the A5 Edgware Road just to the north of the eastern end of Brent Reservoir. The 304 bus runs along Fryent Way past the country park (summer only), the 79 runs along The Mall to the northwest of the site, routes 183 and 204 serve Kingsbury Road just north of the country park, and numbers 83, 182, 224, 245 and 297 stop at or near Wembley Park station. The nearest underground stations are at Kingsbury (Jubilee line), just east of the A4006/A4140 junction immediately north of the country park, and Wembley Park (Jubilee and Metropolitan lines), a half-mile (0.8 km) walk to the south of Barn Hill along a road of the same name and across the A4088 into Bridge Road.

41 TRENT COUNTRY PARK   OS ref: TQ 290970

Habitat

To the northeast of Barnet, the northernmost edge of suburban London at Cockfosters forms the boundary with rural Hertfordshire. On the right side of this divide and just within the M25 lies Trent Country Park, an extensive mixture of woodland, parkland and farmland. This site is essentially to north London what Dagnam Park is to east London: a mature rural setting whose location and mix of habitats and land use make it suitable to some specialist farmland species. Belts of woodland and agricultural land contrast with large areas of short turf in the south of the area which, among other uses, is home to part of the campus of Middlesex University. Several small lakes serve to increase the range of species here.

To the north and east lies Enfield Chase, a broadly similar area of habitat which can be accessed by a network of footpaths and which is also worth exploring. Within this area and a short distance due east from Trent Country Park lies Vicarage Farm (TQ 305975), a spot that has proved productive for migrants and other species in the past; the birdlife of this site is taken into account below.

Species

No one species here is outstanding, but Trent Park has enough ornithological interest to justify attention from the capital's birders at any time of the year.

The lakes are home to a limited range of waterbirds including Great Crested Grebe, Tufted Duck, Pochard, the ubiquitous Coot and Moorhen and occasionally one slightly more distinguished species – Mandarin Duck. At present confined to the status of irregular but not infrequent visitor, it is surely only a matter of time before this 'exotic' becomes a permanent feature: its nearest breeding sites are just a few miles northeast at Wildwoods (TQ 322995) and to the southeast in Southgate at Grovelands Park (TQ 306943), where winter gatherings of up to 50 or more have occurred. At Trent Park ones and twos, on even the smallest ponds, are more likely.

Raptors include the standard line-up of Sparrowhawk and Kestrel, but keep an eye open for the occasional overflying Hobby in summer. The farmland holds small numbers of Grey and Red-legged Partridges and Pheasant, while Stock Dove is resident and Turtle Dove and Cuckoo should be looked for between May and September. Owls in the area have on rare occasions included both Long-eared and Short-eared, and all

Lesser Spotted Woodpecker

three woodpeckers are possible. Skylark breeds on the farmland and, until recently, Tree Pipits were regular in suitable habitat in the park. Stonechat, Whinchat and Wheatear are occasional on passage in the open areas, the last two sometimes in small numbers; the Greenland race of the latter has been reported here on migration. Redstart is not infrequently found during passage times, especially in the Vicarage Farm area in autumn, and Black Redstart has also occurred. Fieldfare and Redwing should be expected in the winter months and, rarely, Ring Ouzel has dropped in during spring and autumn.

The woodland and scrub holds good populations of warblers including Whitethroat, Lesser Whitethroat, Blackcap, Willow Warbler and Chiffchaff. Wood Warbler has been found several times on migration and, proving that even in the well-vegetated cover of sites such as this surprises may be uncovered, a Dartford Warbler was found in song here in May 1987. A few pairs of Goldcrest breed in the conifers, and, more rarely, Firecrest and Pied Flycatcher have put in brief appearances on passage.

The commoner tits are present in good numbers, Marsh Tit also breeds and even the declining Willow Tit is occasionally reported in the area, though sightings are few and far between. Nuthatch and Treecreeper are found in the more well-wooded areas and corvids include Jackdaw. Amidst the usual line-up of finches, which include Siskin and Redpoll in winter, the secretive Hawfinch is very occasionally seen but is probably not regular. There is a reasonable population of Yellowhammers both in the park and on adjacent farmland, where some sizeable flocks have been noted in winter.

Timing

Spring and summer are likely to provide the most rewarding birding, with the wooded areas quieter at other times of year and no particularly likely prospects of note for autumn migration. The park can become quite busy at weekends, even in winter.

Access

The main entrance to the south side of the park is on the A111 Cockfosters Road, just north of the entrance to the London Borough of Islington cemetery at Cockfosters. From Junction 24 of the M25 head south along the A111, reaching the main entrance on the left after 2.25 miles (3.6 km), just south of the junction with Hadley Road.

By bus: route 298 from Southgate via Cockfosters underground passes the park gates. Alternatively, route 384 from Barnet also terminates at the tube station. *By underground:* from Cockfosters station (Piccadilly line) the main entrance to Trent Country Park is a five-minute walk to the north along Cockfosters Road. *By train:* Hadley Wood (overground from King's Cross) is the nearest station, but is a two-mile (3.2 km) walk to the park east along Lancaster Avenue, then right into Cockfosters Road and south to the main entrance.

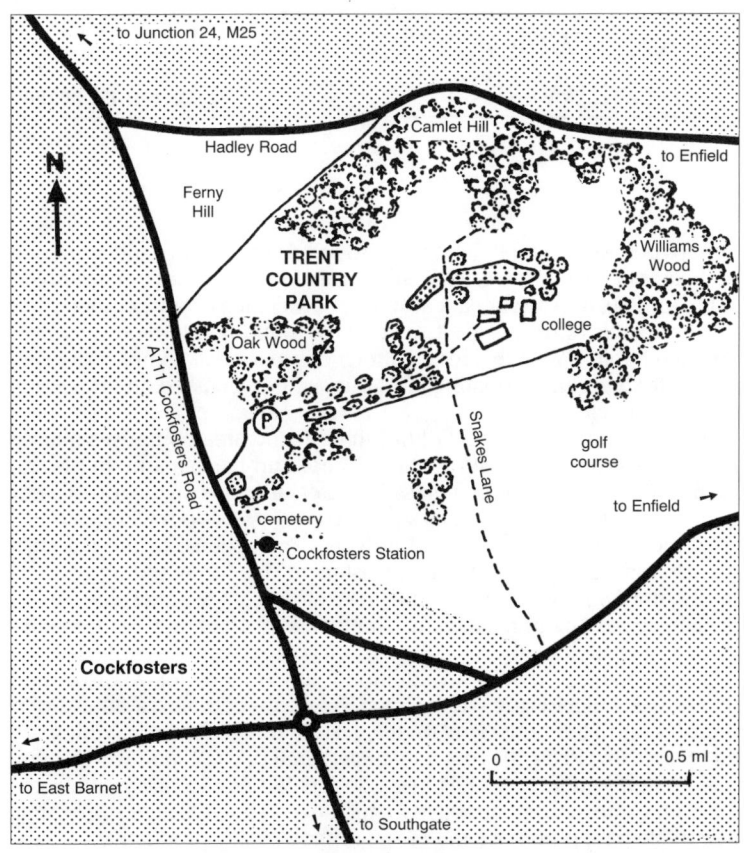

Calendar

All year: Mandarin Duck (occasional), Sparrowhawk, Kestrel, Grey Partridge, Red-legged Partridge, Pheasant, Stock Dove, Green, Great Spotted and Lesser Spotted Woodpeckers, Skylark, Goldcrest, Marsh Tit, Nuthatch, Treecreeper, Jackdaw, Yellowhammer.

Winter (November–March): Redwing, Fieldfare, Siskin, Redpoll.

Spring (April–May): occasional Hobby, Turtle Dove, Cuckoo, chance of Tree Pipit and Redstart, Wheatear, Whinchat, migrant warblers including occasional Wood, Spotted Flycatcher.

Summer (June–July): Turtle Dove, Whitethroat, Lesser Whitethroat, Blackcap, Garden Warbler, Willow Warbler, Chiffchaff, Spotted Flycatcher.

Autumn (August–October): Redstart, Whinchat, occasional Stonechat, Wheatear.

42 ALEXANDRA PARK AND WOOD GREEN RESERVOIRS

OS ref: TQ 302900

Habitat

Perhaps best known for its landmark BBC transmitter aeriel and as the site of Alexandra Palace, the original structure of which was all but destroyed by fire in 1980, Alexandra Park also deserves a place in any compendium of the capital's bird sites for its extensive – and often bird-productive – parkland habitat. With the added attractions of a small complex of reservoirs, filter beds and a boating lake, this site has amassed an impressive list of 153 species.

Covering some 180 acres (72 ha) in total, the area comprises mainly tightly-mown parkland with scattered trees and hedges and, in places, open woodland and rougher grass. The palace stands on the top of a hill in the north of the park, looking south down grassy slopes with scattered trees across cricket pitches and a disused racecourse to the capital's inner suburbs and city centre in the distance. This commanding position has its attractions to birds, with the green slopes of the park standing out like a beacon to migrants passing over the flat plain of the Thames to the south and east.

In the southeast corner an additional lure, chiefly for wildfowl and occasional waders, is the Wood Green Reservoirs complex, a small group of basins and filter beds lying on the eastern fringe of the site which are fed by the New River. Nearby a managed area of woodland with a man-made natural-sided pond has been designated as a conservation area, and with some hedges attractive to migrants on the adjacent slopes, this area of the park is perhaps the most ornithologically productive.

Species

In winter it is the reservoirs that produce most of the interesting birds, with wildfowl and other waterbirds sometimes occurring in good numbers and variety according to the severity of the weather. At this time of year a few Little Grebes join the resident Great Cresteds, and a handful of Cormorants are present outside the breeding season. Surprises are not unknown here: two Shags were notable in March 1988, and in autumn 1991 an immature Gannet circled the reservoirs before drifting off. Among wildfowl Mute Swan, Canada Goose, Mallard and Tufted Duck all breed and Pochard has done so, though both the last two are more numerous in winter. Shoveler is the most likely other duck. Wigeon and Pintail have turned up in recent years, along with other oddities such as Ruddy Duck and Goosander, but the once-regular Smew no longer occurs.

After many years of absence Sparrowhawks have made a welcome return and now breed in the park. Kestrels also nest, and Hobbies have made increasingly frequent appearances on passage.

Aside from a few pairs of Coot and Moorhen, Water Rail sometimes occurs in winter and is best looked for at the pond in the conservation area. Lapwings are occasionally seen overhead in post-breeding or hard weather movements, usually heading southwest. One or two waders occasionally stop off at the reservoirs on passage, with Common Sandpiper the most likely and Little Ringed Plover and Green Sandpiper possible, though other species have included Oystercatcher, Curlew, Redshank, Greenshank and the improbable spring spectacle of a Turnstone flying north in tight formation with four Turtle Doves! Snipe has also occurred and Jack Snipe has overwintered on the sludge beds, but both are highly erratic here.

Gulls are largely unremarkable but have included local rarities such as Mediterranean and Little in recent years, while Common Tern, which bred unsuccessfully here in 1992, is the only member of its family likely to be encountered regularly on migration: Sandwich has appeared three times and Black twice.

Turtle Dove and Cuckoo are occasional on passage, and Tawny Owl and all three woodpeckers breed; Green Woodpecker is one of the more recent additions to the park's list of nesting birds. Migration brings parties of hirundines and Swifts moving through, along with records of species such as Skylark, Meadow Pipit and Yellow Wagtail, which are otherwise not particularly numerous in this suburban part of the capital. White Wagtail has also occurred on passage and Pied and Grey Wagtails breed, the latter around the reservoirs. Whinchat and Wheatear are regular in spring and autumn, Stonechat and Black Redstart less so and Redstart decidedly scarce. Regular searching for migrants here has added Ring Ouzel to the site list, and no doubt more intensive coverage of this well-placed site would produce further records.

Sedge and Reed Warblers used to breed near the reservoirs but are now most likely to be found on migration, while the more wooded areas and hedgerows hold a few pairs of Lesser Whitethroat, Whitethroat, Garden Warbler, Chiffchaff, Willow Warbler and good numbers of Blackcap. Goldcrest and Spotted Flycatcher also nest, and Pied Flycatcher has occasionally graced the park on passage. In addition to the four commoner tit species Willow Tit colonised this site in the mid-1980s, but has since vanished as a breeding species, although individuals have been noted sporadically since then. Nuthatch and Treecreeper both occasionally breed within the park boundary. Among the commoner finches Redpoll no longer nests but is regular in winter, and Brambling is occasionally noted on passage. Reed Bunting is nowadays the only representative of its family to occur regularly.

Considering the small number of local observers the park has a good track record for rarer migrants. Among older records is the noteworthy overwintering of Woodlarks for several consecutive years in the mid-1970s, though sadly none has occurred since, and two records of Mealy Redpoll. More recently, Wryneck has been found three times, Firecrest has turned up in autumn and a Red-backed Shrike was an excellent London record in September 1993. Great Grey Shrike has also occurred, but pride of place must go to the male Ortolan Bunting which frequented the sludge beds in front of an admiring crowd in April 1987, once again demonstrating the rewards of consistent site coverage.

A short distance to the southwest of Alexandra Park, Highgate and Queen's Woods (TQ 283887) hold a similar range of common woodland species including woodpeckers and breeding Sparrowhawk, but have the added possibility of the elusive Hawfinch, which has bred in the area. A wandering Golden Oriole has also been discovered here, as well as locally scarce migrants such as Pied Flycatcher.

Timing
This site can produce good birds, especially during spring and autumn, but it can also be very quiet, so regular coverage rather than a one-off visit is the most productive strategy. An early morning trip during migration times, ideally timed to coincide with winds with at least some easterly component, may well produce some interesting birds.

Access
From central London, follow signs for the A1 and the North through Islington and along Holloway Road to Archway. From here continue north on the A1 Archway Road under the bridge to Highgate underground station, and turn right onto Muswell Hill Road. If time permits, stop off at Highgate and Queen's Woods, which lie on either side of the road here. At Muswell Hill Broadway, turn right at the roundabout down Muswell Hill N10 and then sharp left into the park itself; park as signposted and explore. The park can also be accessed by road from the northeast, via Bedford Road N22 in Wood Green, and there are numerous pedestrian access points.

By bus: the W3 Finsbury Park to Tottenham route is the only service to stop in the park. Buses 43 and 134 via Archway Road and Highgate station (Northern line) will take you to Muswell Hill Broadway; walk a short distance down Muswell Hill and cut through the pedestrian walkway left into the park. Numerous other buses serve the Muswell Hill and Wood Green areas and involve relatively short walks. *By underground:* the nearest tube is Wood Green (Piccadilly line), from where the W3 bus runs to the park. *By train:* Alexandra Palace station connects to King's Cross via Finsbury Park, and lies just outside the park entrance in Bedford Road.

Calendar
All year: Great Crested Grebe, Grey Heron, Tufted Duck, Pochard, Sparrowhawk, Kestrel, Tawny Owl, Green, Great Spotted and Lesser Spotted Woodpeckers, Grey Wagtail, Goldcrest.

Winter (November–March): Little Grebe, Cormorant, Shoveler, Gadwall, occasional wildfowl oddity, chance of Water Rail, gulls, Fieldfare (hard weather), Redwing, Redpoll.

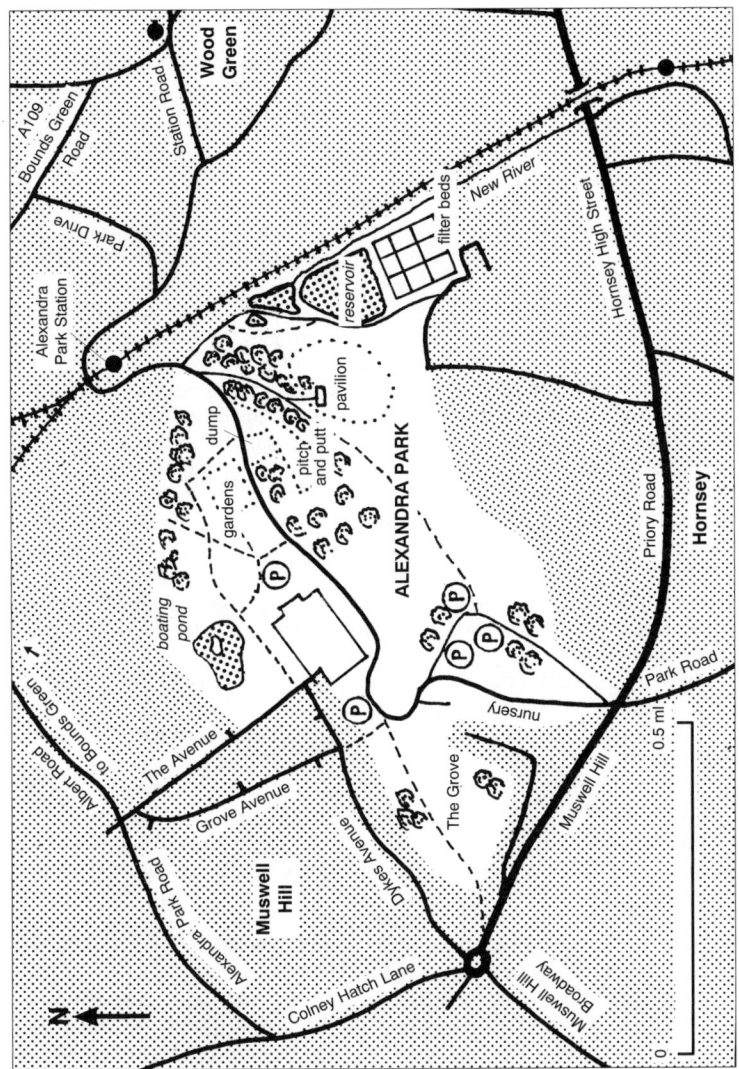

Spring (April–May): Hobby, Little Ringed Plover (rare), Common and perhaps Green Sandpipers, Common Tern, Skylark, Meadow Pipit, Yellow Wagtail, Whinchat, Wheatear, migrant warblers including Sedge and Reed.

Summer (June–July): Lesser Whitethroat, Whitethroat, Garden Warbler, Blackcap, Willow Warbler, Chiffchaff, Spotted Flycatcher, outside chance of Hawfinch in nearby Highgate/Queen's Woods, Reed Bunting.

Autumn (August–October): Hobby (until September), occasional waders including Common Sandpiper, Kingfisher, Skylark, Meadow Pipit, Yellow Wagtail, Whinchat, Wheatear, Fieldfare and Redwing (from October), other migrants including warblers and occasional Black Redstart, Pied Flycatcher and possibly Brambling.

43 STOKE NEWINGTON RESERVOIRS

OS ref: TQ 326876

Habitat

This Thames Water site comprises the East and West Reservoirs, rather incongruously located amid the housing estates and residential backstreets of north Stoke Newington. Perhaps the chief attractions of this site for city-based birders are its proximity to central London and its visibility from a public road. 'Worth seeing but not worth going to see' was how one local birder summed up its staple cast of commoner wildfowl and other expected urban species, but regular surprises among the gatherings of ducks and grebes and the occasional wader are enough to justify inclusion here.

Aside from the reservoirs themselves there is little in the way of additional habitat. A recently rebuilt channel running along the northern side of the site west towards the derelict filter beds at Green Lanes has grassy banks with some vegetation, and around the reservoir perimeter there is a sprinkling of sycamores and other trees. The artificial banks provide resting sites for gulls, wildfowl and the occasional passerine migrant, but their margins more rarely prove attractive to passing waders. The best prospect for the latter is when the water level is lowered on the West Reservoir to expose some of the muddied basin floor: this rare event last happened in 1992–93 during essential pipeline construction, and resulted in a number of interesting wader records.

Following the recent completion of the Thames Water Ring Main the West Reservoir has been decommissioned, and ownership has passed to the London Borough of Hackney which intends to establish a water sports centre. The East Reservoir is still operational, but Thames Water's stated plan is that this basin should serve as a waterfowl refuge, and will benefit from a conservation management plan and improved access.

Species

The historical jewel in Stoke Newington's crown was Smew, and the site was a major stronghold for some years for this delightful but scarce duck in winter. In the late 1960s the species could be guaranteed and as many as 29 were counted, but a decline set in during the 1970s and subsequently there have been no recent records. Nevertheless, there is always a chance of an interesting duck or grebe among the commoner species in winter, especially in hard weather when numbers build up.

The dominant diving waterfowl here in winter are Coot and Tufted Duck, with smaller numbers of Pochard always present; though this last species does not breed here, up to 80 or more can be seen from mid-summer. Mallard are always in evidence but, surprisingly, can be out-numbered by Shoveler outside the breeding season; the latter species sometimes also frequents the lakes in nearby Clissold Park (TQ 332867). Particularly interesting is the site's attraction for Gadwall: up to 40 or more may be present in autumn and winter, the first birds arriving in August and usually staying until early March. Small numbers of Ruddy Duck now seem to be resident, but so far breeding has not been confirmed at the site. Up to seven Red-crested Pochard are often present outside the spring months, but the birds occurring here almost certainly originate from the collection in Clissold Park. Similarly, free-flying Ruddy Shelduck of equal-ly dubious distinction are sometimes seen here.

Other wildfowl are less predictable in appearances, but Mandarin Duck, Shelduck and Wigeon are all occasional visitors. Pintail, Scaup, Long-tailed Duck and Goldeneye are among the true rarities here, as are the Red-necked, Black-necked and Slavonian Grebes which have turned up among the regular Great Cresteds and occasional Littles in the last 10 years.

Interesting wader records are chiefly confined to the period of drainage of the West Reservoir from summer 1992 to summer 1993, result-ing in sightings of Dunlin, Green and Curlew Sandpipers and Ruff, among others. The latter year saw Little Ringed Plovers attempting to breed, apparently the closest recorded nesting to central London, but sadly they were flooded out by summer storms. Other waders are more likely to include just the occasional Lapwing or Common Sandpiper, though a Wood Sandpiper here in August 1994 was noteworthy.

The commoner gull species can be expected outside the breeding sea-son, with several hundred Black-headed sometimes present, and Common Terns regularly fish the basins in spring, late summer and autumn, but other occurrences, like the dazzling party of six Black Terns in early May 1993, are most unusual.

Although the reservoirs focus attention on waterbirds, do not ignore other possibilities. Pied and Grey Wagtails are often present in winter, both having also bred at the site, and Meadow Pipit is likely in spring and autumn; even Yellow Wagtail is occasionally recorded on migration at this built-up site. Reasonable numbers of hirundines hawk insects over the reservoirs during migration times, and House Martin and also Swift breed in the area in summer. Other chance visitors have included Kingfisher (along the channel), Stonechat, Black Redstart and Brambling, and all three woodpeckers have been noted in the surrounding trees, although only Great Spotted is at all regular. Commoner warblers such as White-throat, Blackcap, Sedge and Willow Warblers and Chiffchaff may pass through in spring and autumn and the last species has been noted in win-ter, but more suitable habitat for woodland passerines can be found at Abney Park Cemetery (TQ 334868), half a mile (0.8 km) to the southeast.

Timing

This is essentially a site to check between September and April when the highest numbers of wildfowl bring the best chance of something more unusual. Spring and autumn offer the most likelihood of waders and per-haps wandering terns, and the latter season sees the first major build-up in wildfowl numbers along with the arrival of Gadwall. No more than an hour at most is likely to be required to check the birds present here.

Access

This Thames Water site can be viewed from a public footpath on the north side of the East Reservoir, but much of both basins is visible from the northern end of Lordship Road N16, which runs between them from the A503 Seven Sisters Road to Lordship Park/Manor Road. By car, Stoke Newington Reservoirs can be reached from the West End via Camden Town and Finsbury Park along the A503 Camden Road/Seven Sisters Road. Turn right (south) a quarter of a mile (0.4 km) east of Manor House into Woodberry Grove, which quickly becomes Lordship Road, and park to view the reservoirs over the fence from the north side. Thames Water's strategy for better access at the East Reservoir seems unlikely to be mirrored at the West Reservoir by new owners, Hackney Council, at least in the near future.

By bus: numbers 253, 259, 279 and 359 run along Seven Sisters Road, 106 along Manor Road and other routes including 29 and 141 serve Manor House, Green Lanes and Stoke Newington. *By underground:* Manor House station (Piccadilly line) is about eight minutes' walk to the west along Woodberry Down. *By train:* Stoke Newington station (trains from Liverpool Street) is about 15 minutes' walk away via Lordship Road and Manor Road, and Stamford Hill station, one stop along the same line, about the same distance along Amhurst Road, Seven Sisters Road and Woodberry Grove.

Calendar
All year: Great Crested Grebe, Cormorant, Grey Heron, Mute Swan, Canada Goose, Mallard, Tufted Duck, Pochard, Ruddy Duck, Kestrel, Coot, Moorhen.

Winter (November–March): Little Grebe, Shoveler, Gadwall, feral Red-crested Pochard, occasional wildfowl oddities such as Wigeon and Teal, perhaps Meadow Pipit, Pied Wagtail, Grey Wagtail, occasional Linnet.

Spring (April–May): Departing winter wildfowl, occasional Shelduck, Common Sandpiper and (rarely) other waders, Common Tern, passage hirundines, Meadow Pipit, chance of commoner migrant warblers and other passerines.

Summer (June–July): feral Red-crested Pochard (from July), occasional visiting Common Tern, Swift, House Martin, occasional Sand Martin, common breeding birds.

Autumn (August–October): Gadwall, Shoveler, feral Red-crested Pochard, occasional waders including Common Sandpiper (especially when water level low), migrants including Skylark, Meadow Pipit, wagtails and commoner warblers.

44 HAMPSTEAD HEATH   OS ref: TQ 273866

Habitat
Like many so-called 'heaths', Hampstead Heath bears little resemblance to the kind of habitat which most birdwatchers associate with the bracken-and-pine covered expanses of Surrey, Hampshire or the Brecks. Instead, it comprises largely rolling open parkland with scattered trees and hedgerows in the south, with denser areas of woodland in the north.

The site overlooks the flat plain of central London from the high ground of Parliament Hill, a productive watchpoint for visible migration. From the open grassy slopes of Parliament Hill Fields, the habitat becomes progressively more wooded to the north and in the outlying areas of Sandy and West Heaths, which are separated from the Heath proper by roads. In several areas the closely-mown parkland landscape is replaced by rough meadows fringed with hedges, which together provide attractive cover for passerine migrants in spring and autumn.

The woodland largely consists of mature deciduous trees such as oak, beech and horse chestnut, especially in Kenwood and on West and Sandy Heaths, but there are numerous stands of silver birch, some of them quite extensive, with smaller clumps of alder and scattered conifers. Although Hampstead Heath suffers a great deal of public use, and therefore disturbance, in places the woods and woodland fringes retain some understorey which provides important habitat for breeding and feeding birds.

Wildfowl can find refuge in numerous ponds around the Heath, with most of the waters concentrated in the east (the six Highgate ponds) and the west (the three Hampstead Ponds). Most have margins unsuitable for attracting waders, though the fourth Highgate Pond in particular, designated as a wildlife sanctuary, has reedy fringes and overhanging willows which provide cover for a variety of waterbirds and passerines.

Hampstead Heath is one of the most important areas for birds in urban London. In total around 45 species breed each year and latterly some 110–120 species have been logged annually, with the overall site list standing at 173 species by the end of 1994.

Species

The networks of ponds are home to a range of waterfowl throughout the year. Four or five pairs of Great Crested Grebes find the quieter waters to their liking in summer, and Little Grebes put in irregular appearances on passage. Cormorants have taken to overwintering within the last 15 years, and at peak times up to 20 may be seen wing-stretching on rafts and buoys or fishing in the favoured waters of the lower Hampstead and Highgate Ponds. Grey Herons are regularly seen overhead, usually birds from the nearby heronry at Regent's Park, and are often encountered along more secluded lake margins. Unusually for such a central site, two vagrant herons have also been recorded: a well-watched but brief Little Bittern in June 1995, and a fly-over Little Egret in July 1996.

Mute Swans have recently become resident, and for the first occasion in modern times pairs remained to breed in 1994. A few feral Greylag Geese are recorded each year and Canada Geese are typically present in some numbers, but other wildfowl are poorly represented in summer and not much more numerous in winter. Only the ubiquitous Mallard and Tufted Duck can be relied upon in any number even in the latter season. Unlike many smaller London parks, Pochard are very scarce in winter, and the only other duck that can reasonably be expected is Shoveler: anything up to 15 of the latter may be found in winter, particularly favouring the lower Hampstead pond. Odd Teal and Mandarin Duck occasionally drop in, the latter perhaps most likely on the lily pond at Kenwood, but other species such as Wigeon and Goldeneye remain extremely rare, even in hard winters; records of sawbills are almost non-existent in recent times, with only Goosander at all likely.

In common with many other areas, Sparrowhawks have made a comeback in the last 10–15 years and two or three pairs probably breed annually. Similarly, Hobbies have also become more frequent in recent years, and up to three birds have occasionally been seen hunting over the Heath between May and September; in 1996 a pair even settled to breed. Up to five pairs of Kestrels are resident. Other raptors are very rare but include some impressive species: in May 1992 a male Lesser Kestrel was a staggering find over on East Heath, while other wandering raptors have included Common Buzzard, Osprey, Peregrine and Merlin. In 1995 local observers re-wrote the records books by adding three new migrant raptors to the Heath list – Honey Buzzard, Red Kite and Montagu's Harrier. The only local gamebird is Pheasant, which has strangely established itself only in the last few years, while in most winters a Water Rail is present. Waders are distinctly scarce, the most likely species being occasional Woodcock or Snipe outside the summer months and Common Sandpiper on passage, or perhaps a party of Lapwings overhead, particularly during cold weather. However, recent regular migration watching from the higher points of Parliament Hill Fields, especially Parliament Hill itself (known locally as Kite Hill), has produced some unusual wader finds including records of parties of Golden and Grey Plover, Curlew, Whimbrel and Bar-tailed Godwit. Red-throated Diver and a party of Brent Geese are some of the other recent oddities to have been observed moving over this vantage point.

All five commoner gull species are recorded each year, with highest numbers in winter; Black-headed is easily the most numerous and Great Black-backed the scarcest, with just a handful recorded annually. Rare gulls are exceptional but have included Iceland, Yellow-legged Gull and two birds which may have been rare Common x Mediterranean Gull hybrids. Common Terns are present on the lower Highgate Ponds between May and August and have bred in at least two recent years.

Stock Doves are resident with a very healthy colony of about 15 breeding pairs, the majority in Kenwood, and Woodpigeons are very common; numbers of the latter are boosted in autumn and winter and impressive gatherings of several thousand may sometimes be witnessed. In contrast, Collared and Turtle Doves remain infrequent visitors, and similarly just a handful of Cuckoos are recorded on passage each year – typically in spring, though this species bred in 1994. The only owl here is Tawny, though night-time calling birds are probably more easily located just off the Heath around south Highgate, South End Green or Belsize Park. Short-eared Owl is yet another migrant oddity to have been seen from the Kite Hill watchpoint in recent years.

Kingfishers occasionally grace the ponds, especially in autumn and winter. One of the Heath's biggest attractions, however, is its woodpeckers: all three species breed here and can be seen throughout the year, though early spring, when birds are drumming and there is little greenery on the trees, is probably best. Several pairs of Green are outnumbered by perhaps 10 pairs of Great Spotted, but the real speciality is Lesser Spotted, with the six or so pairs at this site making it one of the best in the London area, if not in southeast England. That fourth British 'woodpecker', the Wryneck, has also appeared on Parliament Hill Fields, most recently during a fall of migrants in August 1994.

Spring and summer sees hirundines moving through to breeding areas further north, with only a few of the locally-nesting House Martins and Swifts remaining during the summer. Pipits are also on the move in spring and autumn, with Meadow the commonest but Tree increasingly recorded in recent years, and October 1996 brought a Richard's Pipit to Parliament Hill Fields. Skylarks are also regular in varying numbers at this time, usually moving straight through overhead, and there have been three recent autumn records of Woodlark. Pied and Yellow Wagtails are passage visitors, with the former also present in winter when the occasional Grey Wagtail may also be found. Other migrants of note include Whinchat, Wheatear and Redstart, all of which occur regularly in small numbers and especially in the southern, more open half of the Heath.

Stonechats have traditionally been scarce here, though more have been recorded in recent years, and autumn also brings passage movements of Fieldfares and Redwings, with small numbers of the latter remaining to winter.

In spring Hampstead Heath comes alive with warbler song, and up to eight species can be expected between mid-April and mid-May as birds move through on passage or set up territories. Reed Warblers are one of the later arrivals, this species having established a breeding colony at the fourth Highgate Pond (from the southern end), and the very occasional Sedge Warbler is also possible at this time of year. The four common *Sylvia* warblers are regular on passage. Whitethroats bred in 1996 for the first time since the 'crash' of 1969, and Lesser Whitethroat and Garden Warbler have both nested recently in the Vale of Health area. This site also played host to the Heath's only recent Dartford Warbler, a singing male in May 1994. Chiffchaff and Willow Warbler breed in good numbers and are even more numerous on passage, and one or two Wood Warblers are likely on migration, typically singing males in spring. Goldcrest is another breeder whose population is boosted by migrants, but particularly noteworthy has been the spring presence of Firecrest in recent years ,which has led to breeding – remarkable for such a scarce species so close to the heart of London.

A little later in spring the first Spotted Flycatchers arrive, and while only

Firecrest

a tiny number of pairs breed this species can be very numerous in the autumn, with passage bringing up to 30 or more to favoured sites: again, the Parliament Hill Fields hedgerows, particularly the third from the south (running east downhill from the Tumulus to the junction of the third and fourth Highgate Ponds), is worth checking for this species and other migrants in autumn. Among them may be a Pied Flycatcher, a species with a chequered history of appearances on the Heath, which has ranged from possible breeding and delightful spring males in some years, to others when none has been recorded.

The woodland bird community is enriched by good numbers of the commoner tits, Goldcrest, Nuthatch and Treecreeper. In three recent consecutive springs, singing Golden Orioles have put in brief appearances in the Kenwood area. Jackdaw, a rare species in built-up London, bred here in 1993. A good range of finches can be expected, though Redpolls have declined as a breeding bird and are now best expected in early spring when perhaps 20 or so may be present. They sometimes keep company with wintering Siskins, up to 200 of which are present in good years among stands of birch and alder; the birches on West Heath are as good a place as any to look. Bramblings are also possible in autumn when birds are most likely to over-fly Parliament Hill Fields, but Hawfinch is distinctly rare with just a sprinkling of recent records. There have been several sightings of migrant Crossbills in recent years. The passerine line-up is completed by Reed Bunting, an occasional migrant and summer visitor which breeds intermittently at the fourth Highgate Pond.

Timing

A visit as soon as possible after first light is recommended to avoid disturbance by dog walkers, joggers and the thousands of other members of the public who use the Heath daily. In spring and autumn diurnal migrants often pass over Kite Hill very soon after dawn; in favourable winds, typically northerly or northeasterly, it can be well worth doing a two or three-hour stint here before undertaking a circuit around the many footpaths across the rest of the Heath. Diurnal migrants may, of course, drop in at any time of the day, so during passage seasons a late afternoon or even early evening visit, when the Heath is less disturbed, can also be productive.

This is a large area so give yourself plenty of time: a whole morning can easily be spent scouring the most interesting areas of habitat, and two to four hours at least is preferable.

Access

Hampstead Heath is easily reached by car or public transport from central London via Camden Town and Kentish Town, with plenty of adjacent parking (though this can be difficult in summer, especially on bank holidays and at weekends). There is open access at all times of year except to Kenwood (locked at night) and some of the enclosed ponds. Most of the latter can be viewed satisfactorily from public footpaths.

By bus: numbers C2, C11, C12 and 214 run to Parliament Hill Fields, 24 and 168 to South End Green for the Hampstead Ponds and H2 and 210 for Hampstead Lane on the north side; bus 268 which runs through Hampstead stops at Whitestone Pond, at the northwest corner of the Heath. *By underground:* Hampstead station (Northern line) is the closest tube; walk up Heath Street to Whitestone Pond (about five minutes) and enter the Heath proper from the south side of Hampstead Lane, or Sandy

Heath from the north side. West Heath lies behind nearby Jack Straw's Castle. *By train:* suburban lines run to Gospel Oak station and Hampstead Heath station from east London via Tottenham, from Richmond via west and northwest London and from Highbury. From Gospel Oak enter the Heath via the Lido on the south side of Kite Hill, and from Hampstead Heath via East Heath Road and the Hampstead Ponds.

Calendar

All Year: Great Crested Grebe, Grey Heron, Mute Swan, Sparrowhawk, Kestrel, Pheasant, Stock Dove, Tawny Owl, Green, Great Spotted and Lesser Spotted Woodpeckers, Goldcrest, Nuthatch, Treecreeper.

Winter (November–mid-March): Cormorant, Tufted Duck, Shoveler, Water Rail, Grey Wagtail, Redwing, Siskin, Redpoll.

Spring (mid-March–mid-May): Little Grebe, Hobby (from late April), occasional Woodcock, Cuckoo, Skylark, hirundines, Meadow and Tree Pipits, Ring Ouzel (rare), Fieldfare, chance of Redstart, Whinchat, Wheatear, warblers including Wood, chance of Firecrest, migrant oddities.

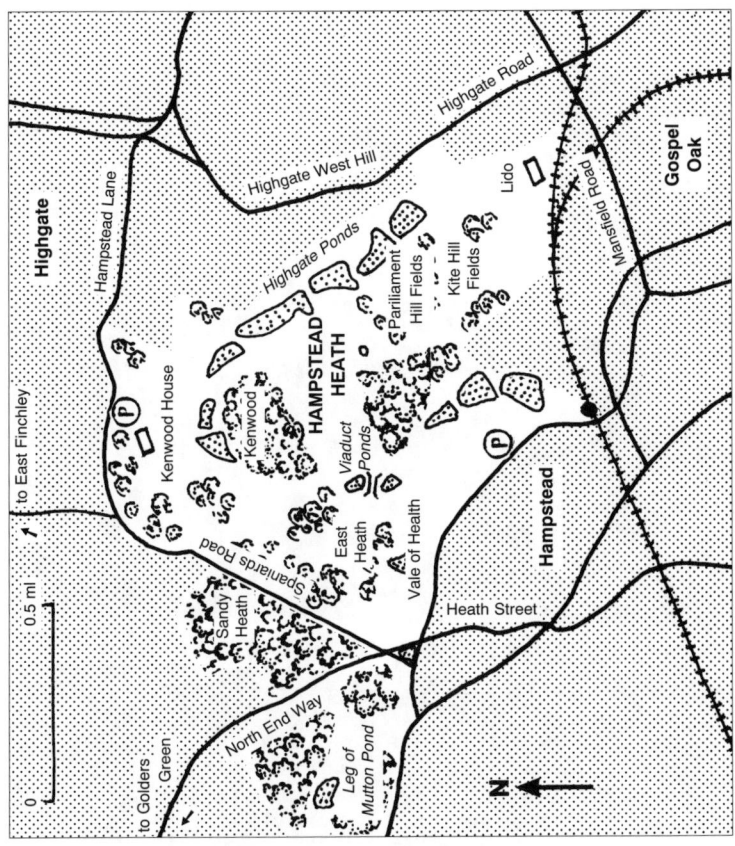

Summer (mid-May–early August): Occasional Hobby, Common Tern, Swift, Reed Warbler, Lesser Whitethroat, Garden Warbler, Spotted Flycatcher, Reed Bunting.

Autumn (early August–October): Little Grebe, Hobby (until September), Meadow and Tree Pipits, Yellow Wagtail, Redstart, Whinchat, Wheatear, occasional Stonechat, Fieldfare, Redwing, migrant warblers, possibly Firecrest, Pied Flycatcher, Brambling, migrant oddities.

CENTRAL LONDON

45 REGENT'S PARK AND PRIMROSE HILL

OS ref: TQ 277830/276839

Habitat

As is the case with most large cities, London's inner areas generally offer little in the way of good habitat for birds, and what migrants and few breeding species there are tend to concentrate in the larger areas of parkland. Inner London has little to offer in comparison with some world-famous city centre sites, such as migrant-rich Central Park in New York, but Regent's Park and Primrose Hill between them can comprise a reasonably productive area for birding in the centre of the city.

Regent's Park lies just three-quarters of a mile (1.2 km) north of Oxford Circus and the West End. It is bordered to the south by the east-west Marylebone Road, and around its other boundaries by the Outer Circle ring road; there is also an inner ring road, the Inner Circle, in the centre of the southern half of the park. On the north and northwest margins, between the Outer Circle and Prince Albert Road, is the Regent's Canal, an extension of the Grand Union Canal which runs through Maida Vale to the west and east through Camden Town to King's Cross. Perhaps the best known landmark in the park is London Zoo, the entrance to which is on the north side of the Outer Circle. Primrose Hill, the first area of high ground on the north side of the Thames floodplain in central London, is a small area of parkland rising to almost 200 feet (61 m) immediately north of Regent's Park, across Prince Albert Road from the zoo.

A significant amount of the habitat is uninteresting 'amenity grassland' – a combination of sports fields and short-turf parkland which is subject to heavy public use. However, there are several areas which offer better quality habitat, including the public and private gardens around the Inner Circle, the boating lake to the west of this area, and the heavily-vegetated environs of the Regent's Canal along the northern edge of the park. It is primarily these areas that are best for birding, especially during spring and autumn when the range of species likely to occur in the area increases dramatically. Over the years Regent's Park and Primrose Hill and their potential for observing bird migration have attracted the attention of several eminent ornithologists, including Eric Simms and Ian Wallace who both made systematic observations over a number of years from the 1950s. As a royal park, the area also benefited from regular coverage by an official observer until the scheme was abandoned in 1979. Today, records come largely from a small number of dedicated local observers who continue to demonstrate the potential of this site for birds.

Species

The greatest variety of species occurs during spring and autumn, when migrating birds can be recorded in some numbers. The right weather conditions, often winds from an easterly quarter with a southerly aspect in spring and a northerly element in autumn, can bring impressive visible movements of diurnal migrants over Primrose Hill and other areas of the park. Skylark, Meadow Pipit, Redwing, Fieldfare and the commoner finches have all been logged overhead in varying (sometimes high) numbers at such times, though often they may move straight through without stopping – familiarity with flight calls of migrant birds can therefore help greatly with identification. Other diurnal migrants, ranging from the odd Hobby, Cuckoo or Turtle Dove to parties of Lapwings and Woodpigeons and large numbers of Swallows, are often also logged.

On good days, when migration is clearly in progress, less frequent visitors are sometimes recorded, including the occasional Tree Pipit and Yellow Wagtail or, more unusually, even Rock Pipit and White Wagtail. Among the commoner finches Bramblings are annual in autumn and Siskins nowadays outnumber Redpolls on autumn passage, though both may also occur sporadically in spring and winter. Perhaps surprisingly, commoner waders such as Snipe, Redshank, Curlew and Whimbrel have sometimes also been noted moving straight through.

At passage times occasional overnight falls can bring other species. Wheatears make regular appearances on the close-cropped turf in spring and autumn, and the larger, brighter Greenland race has been recorded here. Whinchat and Redstart are less regular but have both been noted in recent seasons, as has the odd Stonechat and Ring Ouzel. In this inner quarter of London warblers are almost exclusively passage migrants, but despite this several species may be present at any one time in April and May or August and September. The most numerous species are Blackcap, Chiffchaff and Willow Warbler, but Sedge, Reed, Whitethroat, Lesser Whitethroat and Garden Warbler are all usually noted here on a few dates each year. Wood Warbler is also annual, with records in both spring and autumn in recent years. Goldcrests may arrive in some numbers in the latter season, some perhaps staying to overwinter, while there have also been occasional migrant Firecrests in recent years. Spotted and Pied Flycatchers both occur on passage, the former sometimes in small numbers.

Among such a good range of regular and occasional visitors it is perhaps not surprising that rarer birds are sometimes recorded. In recent years these have included not only scarce species such as Woodlark, Tree Sparrow, Hawfinch and Snow Bunting, seemingly caught up in movements of commoner relatives, but also fly-over oddities such as Shag, Osprey, Common Buzzard, Merlin, Bar-tailed Godwit, Yellow-legged Gull, Sandwich and Black Terns and Short-eared Owl. There are also older records of a Ring-necked Duck on the lake in May and June 1978 and, in the 1950s, fly-through Stone Curlew and Montagu's Harrier. Rarest of all, however, was the fine Black-eared Wheatear found by H C Holme and Eric Simms in April 1951 – still the only example of this Mediterranean vagrant to have been recorded in London.

While most excitement might be provided by spring and autumn migration, there is also a small range of interesting resident and wintering birds. This includes breeding Great Crested and Little Grebes on the lake, which also has a heronry containing some 15 or so pairs of Grey Heron. Small numbers of Cormorants may be present in winter, when wildfowl can include a few Ruddy Duck and the occasional wandering Gadwall,

Teal or Wigeon; a few pairs of Tufted Duck and an impressive 20 or so pairs of Pochard breed. The only wader at all likely to occur is the occasional Common Sandpiper in spring or autumn. There is one pair of Sparrowhawks and up to three pairs each of Kestrel and Tawny Owl, Great Spotted Woodpecker nests and the occasional visiting Lesser Spotted is also reported. Grey Wagtails are present year-round along Regent's Canal, sometimes breeding nearby around Camden Lock, and there are healthy populations of commoner resident songbirds such as Robin, Wren, Dunnock, Song and Mistle Thrushes and Blackbird. In contrast Blackcap is the sole breeding warbler, with just two or three pairs present in areas with denser vegetation. Breeding tits include Coal and Long-tailed, but Nuthatch and Treecreeper are only sporadic visitors to this park. A pair of Bullfinches was also suspected of breeding along the canal in 1993, but this species is more usually a winter visitor.

Grey Heron

Timing

For the chance of seeing migrant birds, the periods mid-March to mid-May and August to late October are likely to be most productive. For diurnal migration the best prospects include a watch from the top of Primrose Hill in the hours after dawn; for other migrants also check the scrub and open areas as early as possible, especially at weekends, as the park is extremely popular and any grounded migrants may move on or will be harder to locate once the crowds begin to assemble.

Access

Entry is straightforward from numerous gates around the perimeter, and there is also a towpath alongside the canal that has open access. Note that the park and the Outer Circle are closed to pedestrians and traffic at night. To reach the area by car, turn north from Marylebone Road into Gloucester Place just west of Madame Tussaud's to reach Park Road, and turn right at the mosque through Hanover Gate into the Outer Circle. From the north the same access point can be reached via the A41 Finchley and

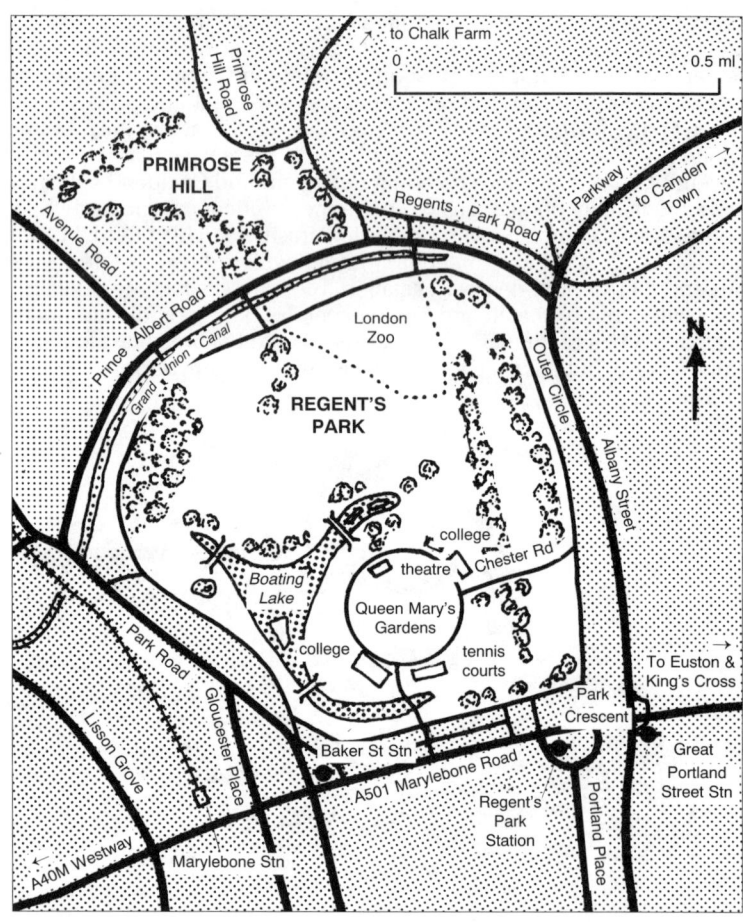

Wellington Roads through Swiss Cottage and St John's Wood to the round-about at the junction with Park Road and Prince Albert Road. From the City and the east, follow Euston Road to Great Portland Street, turning right via the one-way system into Albany Street and left into the Outer Circle through Chester Gate. Follow local parking instructions carefully.

By bus: number 274 runs along Prince Albert Road and Park Road around the northern and western edges of the park, while the C2 from Camden Town stops at Gloucester Gate and Great Portland Street along the east side. Numbers 18, 27, 30 and 135 also serve this point along Euston Road, while further west routes 2, 13, 74, 82, 113, 139 and 159 call at Baker Street; several of these also run up Park Road. *By underground:* the closest stations are Baker Street (Bakerloo, Circle, Hammersmith & City, Jubilee and Metropolitan lines) for the boating lake and southwest corner of the park (turn right out of the station and walk north up Baker Street to Clarence Gate) and Regent's Park (Bakerloo) and Great Portland Street (Circle, Hammersmith & City and Metropolitan lines) for the southeast corner (access from Park Square on the north side of Marylebone Road). Alternatively, Camden Town (Northern line) is 10 minutes' walk east from Gloucester Gate in the northeast corner, and on the northwest side St John's Wood is almost 15 minutes' walk north along Wellington Road from the roundabout at the western end of Prince Albert Road. *By train:* the most convenient overground station is Marylebone, about seven minutes' walk west along Melcombe Street from Baker Street tube.

Calendar

All Year: Great Crested Grebe, Little Grebe, Grey Heron, Pochard, Tufted Duck, Sparrowhawk, Kestrel, Tawny Owl, Great Spotted Woodpecker, occasional Lesser Spotted Woodpecker, Grey Wagtail, Long-tailed Tit, Coal Tit.

Winter (November–mid-March): Cormorant, wildfowl including occasional Ruddy Duck, gulls, Redwing, Siskin, Bullfinch.

Spring (mid-March–late May): Hobby (rare, from late April), chance of Woodcock, occasional Common Sandpiper, Turtle Dove, Cuckoo (from mid-April), Skylark, hirundines, Meadow Pipit (especially March and early April), Tree Pipit (from early April), Yellow Wagtail, occasional Ring Ouzel, Redstart or Whinchat, Wheatear, warblers including occasional Wood, chance of Firecrest, Spotted Flycatcher, migrant oddities.

Summer (late May–early August): occasional movements of Lapwing (June–July), chance of migrant Cuckoo (July), Swift, House Martin, Blackcap.

Autumn (early August–October): Hobby, Lapwing, Common Sandpiper, Turtle Dove, Skylark, hirundines, Meadow and Tree Pipits, Yellow Wagtail, occasional Redstart and Whinchat, Wheatear, Fieldfare and Redwing (from October), warblers including occasional Wood, Spotted Flycatcher, perhaps Pied Flycatcher, Brambling, Siskin, Redpoll, migrant oddities.

46 HYDE PARK AND KENSINGTON GARDENS   OS ref: TQ 270803

Habitat

The royal parks of Hyde Park and Kensington Gardens together form the largest open space in inner London, covering some 630 acres (252 ha) and with a distance around the perimeter of about four miles (6.4 km). The central position of the site, between Paddington to the north, Mayfair to the east, Knightsbridge to the south and Kensington to the west, means that it appears somewhat isolated by built-up areas. However, the expanses of parkland and lakes can be an attractive prospect to overflying migrants, and in fact Hyde Park and Kensington Gardens form a link in a loose chain of sites which extends in the east from the Thames through St James's and Green Parks to Holland Park in the west.

Dominating the parkland landscape is the Serpentine, a large man-made lake on the south side of Hyde Park which continues beyond West Carriage Drive as The Long Water and marks an informal boundary with Kensington Gardens to the west. The latter area also has a small lake, the

Round Pond. At first glance the parks looks generally unpromising for birds, with a flat expanse of short-turf grassland broken up by numerous tree-lined rides and paths. However, there are several interesting pockets of woodland and undergrowth, notably around the Serpentine and The Long Water and along The Flower Walk on the southern edge of Kensington Gardens. Until relatively recently the parks were more wooded, but several thousand elms were reported to have been lost to Dutch elm disease in the 1970s and the great storm of October 1987 took out another 800 trees between here and St James's Park – accounting for the loss of some 15 per cent of the remaining tree cover.

There is a long history of bird recording in these parks, a tradition established both by the systematic observations of the official observers under the royal parks scheme, and by independent coverage from a number of eminent ornithologists including Max Nicholson, whose interest in the birdlife of the area has spanned over 70 years. Since historic times some 177 species have been documented – more than half of all those recorded in the London area – but a good number relate to accidental visitors or very scarce migrants, and a fair proportion of these have not been recorded for some years. The account below concentrates on species occurring in recent times.

Species

Great Crested Grebes bred in inner London for the first time here in 1972, and more than 20 years on two or three pairs can still be found on the Serpentine in summer. One or two Little Grebes pay brief visits in most years, but appearances are highly erratic. Cormorants can be seen throughout the year but are most numerous in winter, and similarly one or two Grey Herons are often also present; platforms have been erected in trees by the Long Water in the hope that this species may be tempted to breed.

Wildfowl include a healthy population of Mute Swans and almost too many feral Canada Geese – numbers of the latter species have exceeded 300, and egg-pricking has recently been carried out to try and control the population. A few pairs of Mallard and a handful of Pochard and Tufted Duck breed, with numbers of the last two increasing significantly during the winter months when immigrants from the Continent arrive. At peak times they may number as many as 70 and 150 respectively; ringing recoveries have shown that the Tufted Ducks originate primarily from Fennoscandia and Russia, while a Pochard ringed in Kensington Gardens was shot in western Siberia, more than 4300 km away. In winter Shovelers also visit the lakes, with perhaps up to 40 present between September and March, but other wild ducks are exceptional: in the last 10 years these have comprised single records only of Teal, Gadwall, Goldeneye and Goosander.

Kestrel is the only bird of prey likely to be encountered this far into the city centre, but with the spread of Sparrowhawks elsewhere, records of this species are on the increase. The site's first Hobby, logged as recently as September 1994, is the only other raptor to have been seen in recent years. Two pairs of Moorhen and about eight pairs of Coot breed, with numbers of the latter rising substantially in winter, especially during cold spells. At such times Lapwings can sometimes be seen on the move overhead, a phenomenon repeated in midsummer during post-breeding dispersal, but otherwise the only other wader remotely likely to occur is a Common Sandpiper around the edges of one of the lakes. Of the few other species recorded, the most outstanding recent record is that of two Avocets circling the Round Pond in May 1992.

Large numbers of Black-headed Gulls can be present outside the breeding season, with more than 1,000 counted around the Serpentine and Long Water at peak times, but Common Gulls rarely number more than 15–30 and Lesser Black-backed and Herring Gulls usually fewer than 10; this last species has twice attempted to nest on the Serpentine island. Four species of tern have been recorded in the parks but even Common is not annual here, while of the three species of auk to have been logged the most recent is a Little Auk which spent half an hour on the Long Water in October 1992.

Aside from the large numbers of Feral Rock Doves found in the park, Woodpigeons are abundant and two pairs of Stock Dove still breed near the western edge of the Long Water, although this species seems to leave the area in winter. At least four pairs of Tawny Owl probably breed though can be difficult to pin down; nest boxes have been erected to encourage this species to nest. Great Spotted Woodpeckers were until recently an uncommon visitor, but a pair appeared to have nested in or near Kensington Gardens in 1994 – the first breeding in the area for nearly 40 years. In contrast, Lesser Spotted and Green Woodpeckers are both rarities here, though the latter species is not infrequent nearby at Holland Park (TQ 248796).

Skylarks, Meadow Pipits, Swifts and hirundines can sometimes be seen on the move over the park in spring and autumn, though birds rarely linger long; a few pairs of House Martins nest close by on the French Embassy on the east side of Albert Gate. Perhaps the most surprising of all recent records was that of a Shorelark feeding on newly-sown grass by the bandstand near the Round Pond one afternoon in October 1996. Both Pied and Grey Wagtails can sometimes be found outside the breeding season, and both have bred in the area. Resident songbirds include reasonable populations of Wren, Dunnock, Robin, Blackbird and Mistle and Song Thrushes, and in autumn and winter, especially during cold weather, small numbers of Redwings may be present. Passage periods also bring the possibility of a Wheatear or two stopping to feed on the short turf and perhaps a migrant warbler in the more wooded areas. Chiffchaff, Willow Warbler, Whitethroat, Lesser Whitethroat, Garden Warbler and Blackcap are the most likely species, but only the latter stays on to breed. Goldcrest is also confined to passage migrant status in the parks, but a pair of Spotted Flycatchers still manages to nest in a private garden in Hyde Park.

Long-tailed, Coal, Blue and Great Tits are all resident and there are a handful of pairs of Nuthatch and Treecreeper. Corvids are represented by the familiar urban trio of Carrion Crow, Magpie and Jay, and those other city specialists, Starling and House Sparrow, are also numerous, although the latter has declined significantly in numbers. Bullfinch, Goldfinch, Chaffinch and Greenfinch all breed, though these last three all appear to vacate the parks in winter. In autumn Chaffinches can sometimes be seen passing over in numbers on migration, but other species such as Brambling, Siskin and Redpoll only very rarely seem to get caught up in such movements.

Timing

This is really a site to come to expecting to see only common breeding birds and visitors, and so it makes an ideal venue for overseas travellers with limited time in the city, or for birders who live or work close by and can make regular visits which may bring other rewards. A visit at any time of year will perhaps find 30 or so species, sometimes more. The park is almost always crowded, unbearably so in summer and on weekends but much less on cold winter days; any birdwatching visit should be as early in the day as possible.

Access

Hyde Park and Kensington Gardens are open from 5 am to dusk, after which gates are locked and West Carriage Drive, which runs north-south through the centre of the park, is closed to traffic. Access is straight-forward from the West End and west central London: there are entrances by road at Victoria Gate on Bayswater Road halfway along the north side; via Cumberland Gate at Marble Arch in the northeast corner; onto South Carriage Drive off Hyde Park Corner in the southeast; and through Alexandra Gate at Kensington Gore on the south side. There are parking meters along and off West Carriage Drive around The Serpentine (charges apply 8.30 am–6.30 pm Mondays–Fridays, 8.30 am–1.30 pm Saturdays) but spaces can often be hard to find; there is also an NCP car park on Park Lane. There are numerous pedestrian entrances around the edge of the park.

By bus: around 40 routes serve the immediate area; catch any bus heading for Marble Arch, Hyde Park Corner or Knightsbridge. *By underground:* Queensway, Lancaster Gate and Marble Arch stations (Central line) are on the northern boundary along Bayswater Road and Marble Arch, and Hyde Park Corner and Knightsbridge stations (Piccadilly line) are close to the south side of the park.

Calendar

All year: Great Crested Grebe, Grey Heron, Mallard, Tufted Duck, Pochard, Kestrel, Tawny Owl, Great Spotted Woodpecker (rare), common tits including Coal and Long-tailed, Nuthatch, Treecreeper.

Winter (November–February): Cormorant, Shoveler, Black-headed, Common, Lesser Black-backed and Herring Gulls, Grey Wagtail.

Spring (March–May): Possibility of Common Sandpiper, Stock Dove, Swift, hirundines, Wheatear, commoner migrant warblers, common finches.

Summer (June–July): Occasional Lapwing movements, Stock Dove, House Martin, Blackcap, Spotted Flycatcher (rare), common finches.

Autumn (August-October): Possibility of Common Sandpiper, Skylark, Meadow Pipit, Wheatear, Redwing, commoner migrant warblers.

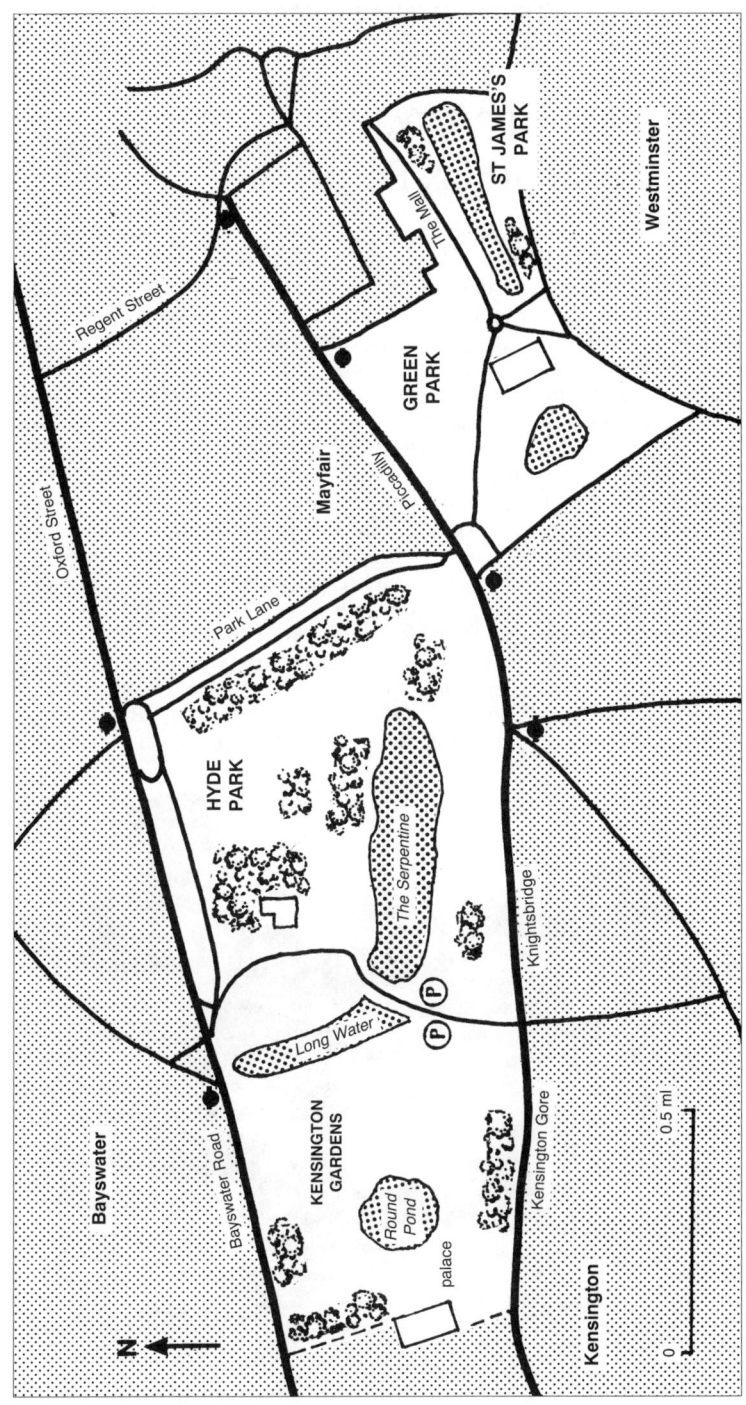

OTHER SITES IN THE AREA

46A ST JAMES'S PARK AND GREEN PARK

OS ref: TQ 294798/290799
Map p. 221

Separated from Hyde Park to the northwest by up to six lanes of traffic at Hyde Park Corner, Green Park and St James's Park combine with the gardens of Buckingham Palace to the south to form another reasonably extensive – though ornithologically less interesting – belt of parkland in the heart of the city. As the palace gardens are private and Green Park has little to offer in the way of interesting habitat and birds, the ornithological focus of this area is centred around St James's Park, and especially its five-hectare artificial lake.

Like Hyde Park and Kensington Gardens, this is really a site for the office worker with lunchtimes to spare or the short-stay visitor from abroad who does not have the time to take in some of the more productive sites in and around London. There are no avian specialities to be found here of interest to anyone with the time to bird elsewhere in the capital – simply a range of common breeding species, and a selection of wintering wildfowl and other waterbirds.

The lake is home to a sizeable collection of captive wildfowl, many species of which are illustrated on noticeboards around the shoreline. Among the 40 or so species noted in the collection in recent years are some, for example Gadwall, Red-crested Pochard and Ruddy Duck, which may tempt unsuspecting visitors into believing they have found an

Tufted Ducks

unusual wild visitor. Most of the captive birds are pinioned; some are kept in pens on the islands. It has long been believed that the presence of these birds, and enthusiasm on the part of the public for feeding them, has helped to attract wild species to the park, sometimes in numbers. These largely comprise wintering Mallard, Tufted Duck and Pochard, in recent years peaking at around 200, 150 and 50 respectively, though Tufted Duck at least was formerly much more numerous; ringing recoveries suggest that a significant number of the wintering individuals of this species probably originate from Russia and Fennoscandia. All three species also breed in small numbers. Shoveler is no longer regular in winter and is now best looked for in nearby Kensington Gardens. Both Little and Great Crested Grebes bred in the 1980s, but again neither is regular at present. There are sizeable gatherings of feral Canada and Greylag Geese, numbers of which are now controlled through egg-pricking in the breeding season. Other waterbirds include up to 11 pairs of Coot and eight of Moorhen in recent years, a few Cormorants outside the breeding season, the occasional Grey Heron and sometimes large numbers of wintering gulls – several hundred Black-headed Gulls can be present here in winter, with highest numbers in cold weather, and among them are often a few Common Gulls and one or two Great Black-backs. Lesser Black-backs are usually noted passing over in spring and autumn, while Herring Gull is often present in the area and at least one pair usually breeds. Interestingly, at least one long-staying individual of the latter species has yellow legs, but in other respects appears to be a Herring Gull rather than a Yellow-legged Gull.

Other species are unremarkable, with just a handful of pairs of species such as Wren, Dunnock, Robin, Blackbird and Song Thrush which are generally much better represented in the other central London parks. There are occasional breeding season records of species such as Long-tailed and Coal Tits, but these and passage migrants of any description are distinctly rare in this busy city centre location.

These royal parks lie immediately south of Piccadilly, with Whitehall to the east and Grosvenor Place to the west. The main access points by road are from Trafalgar Square along the Mall, from Hyde Park Corner via Constitution Hill and Buckingham Palace, and through Buckingham Gate just north of Victoria. No buses run through the parks, but more than 50 routes serve the area and any bus with one of the above destinations displayed will get you close; the nearest underground stations are at Hyde Park Corner (Piccadilly line), Green Park (Jubilee, Piccadilly and Victoria lines) and St James's Park (Circle and District lines).

47 OTHER CENTRAL LONDON SITES

Habitat, species and access

Away from the large green expanses of the royal parks, the main open spaces of ornithological note within inner London are Battersea Park (TQ 282772) and Holland Park (TQ 248796). Lying on the south side of the Thames just west of Chelsea Bridge, Battersea Park is a rather uninteresting public amenity area with an athletics ground, tennis courts and boating lake which has several islands. The park gained notoriety when a proposed cull of the large numbers of Canada Geese attracted outrage in the national and local media. A small heronry here holds 15 pairs of Grey Heron. Tawny Owl and Great Spotted Woodpecker are occasionally noted and may breed in the area, but nesting passerines are unremarkable; Grey Wagtail has been noted outside the breeding season. Most interest is perhaps likely to lie in finding an out-of-place migrant in spring and autumn, and in recent years these have included Hobby, Pied Flycatcher, Brambling, Siskin and Redpoll, with Rock Pipit on the nearby Thames foreshore.

The leafy glades of Holland Park (TQ 248796), situated half a mile (0.8 km) west of Kensington Gardens, have a more interesting range of resident species, but the park has generally turned up less in the way of oddities. Breeding birds include Great Spotted Woodpecker, Blackcap, Chiffchaff, Long-tailed and Coal Tits, Jay and Bullfinch, with other species including Tawny Owl, Green Woodpecker, Goldcrest and Treecreeper occasionally noted. Locally rare migrants over the years have included Woodcock, Wood Warbler, Firecrest, Pied Flycatcher and Hawfinch.

The Thames and its foreshore are worthy of scrutiny for a small selection of commoner waterbirds and the possibility of something more interesting. Although a casual visit is unlikely to be rewarded with anything other than Cormorant, Grey Heron or the commoner species of gulls, Black-headed often being particularly numerous, Yellow-legged Gull is occasionally noted this far upriver from late summer through to winter. Terns are rare but Common is sometimes seen in spring and autumn and both Black and Sandwich have been recorded in recent years. Aside from Mallard, ducks are only likely to occur during weather-related influxes, which have also been known to bring Shags in the winter months and, much more rarely, even ocean-going species such as Fulmar and Guillemot – the spectacular influx of some 40 or so of this last species along the Thames between Tower Bridge and Chelsea Reach in early 1986 was particularly noteworthy.

On the south side of the Thames between Southwark and Blackfriars Bridges, Bankside Power Station (TQ 320806) has recently played host to a long-staying Peregrine Falcon. The bird is usually seen perched on ledges near the top of one of the cooling towers, but is occasionally noted in flight and presumably sustains itself on a diet of Feral Rock Doves. At the time of writing it seems to have assumed permanent residence. More typically it is Kestrel that is the most likely bird of prey to be encountered in the heart of the capital, but Sparrowhawks are now also regularly noted over the City and West End.

There is little in the way of passerine interest away from the main parks except for a chance of one of London's true specialities, the Black Redstart. Numbers are never high, and the species' recently-developed habit of holding territory on new buildings as well as older constructions and derelict sites means it can be particularly difficult to locate. In general terms, however, the area to the north of the City seems particularly favoured, especially around Shoreditch. Birds have also been present in the breeding season at Bankside Power Station and, until recently, around Tower Bridge Wharf (TQ 342802) between St Katherine's Dock and Wapping. The latter area includes London's last undeveloped World War Two bomb site – the artificial habitat which helped to establish the species in the capital during the war – and has also attracted occasional passerine migrants of note, including Wheatear and Yellow Wagtail. Grey

Wagtails are sometimes also seen along the foreshore here, and a few pairs breed in inner London along the Thames and at other sites.

Both Black Redstarts and Grey Wagtails can, with a good amount of luck, also be found in the industrial area immediately north of King's Cross station. Here the Regent's Canal works its way around the edge of the extensive area of railway lines and goods yards among which Black Redstarts sometimes breed. Grey Wagtails are probably best looked for along the canal at Camley Street Natural Park (TQ 300834), a London Wildlife Trust urban nature sanctuary which nestles along the southwest flank of the railway yards. Within its tiny confines the range of habitats includes wet and dry woodland, grassland, areas of fen vegetation and a pond. Tufted Duck breeds here and Redpoll and Siskin are regular in winter, while Reed, Sedge and Willow Warblers and Chiffchaff are among the passage migrants recorded, the latter species also occasionally turning up in winter. In 1992 a pair of Reed Warblers stayed to breed. There is a visitor centre and nature trail with full disabled access; the site is open six days a week (closed Fridays) from 10 am–4 pm, with extended hours in summer. With so much development pressure on sought-after sites such as this in central London, particularly in view of ongoing improvements to the railway infrastructure, there has been a question mark over this sanctuary's long-term survival; at present, however, it continues to form a valuable oasis in the heart of the city.

All of the above sites lie within a relatively small area of central London, and are easily accessed by roads, footpaths, bus services and the underground system. Rather than recommend preferred routes here, use an *A–Z London Street Atlas* and bus and tube maps to decide on the itinerary that most suits you.

USEFUL ADDRESSES

National associations and statutory organisations

- British Trust for Ornithology (BTO). National Centre for Ornithology, The Nunnery, Thetford, Norfolk IP24 2PU.
- English Nature. Northminster House, Peterborough PE1 1UA.
- Forest Enterprise. 231 Corstophine Road, Edinburgh EH12 7AT.
- National Trust. 36 Queen Anne's Gate, London SW1H 9AS.
- Ramblers Association. 1–5 Wandsworth Road, London SW8 2LJ.
- Royal Society for the Protection of Birds (RSPB). The Lodge, Sandy, Bedfordshire SG19 2DL.
- Wildfowl and Wetlands Trust (WWT). Slimbridge, Gloucester GL2 7BT.
- Woodland Trust (WT). Autumn Park, Dysart Road, Grantham, Lincolnshire NG31 6LL.

Regional associations

- London Natural History Society. Enquiries about membership of the ornithology section: P C Holland, Flat 9, Pinewood Court, 23 Clarence Avenue, Clapham, London SW4 8LB. Copies of the *London Bird Report* are available from: H M V Wilsdon, 79 Mill Rise, Westdene, Brighton, East Sussex BN1 5GJ.
  To submit bird records for the area within a 20-mile radius of St Paul's Cathedral, contact the appropriate official recorder – the LNHS area is divided into seven metropolitan counties with their own bird recorders:
  Inner London: K C Osborne, 10 Ellice Road, Oxted, Surrey RH8 0PY.
  Essex: D Lambert, 10 Chandos Road, Tottenham, London N17 6HM.
  Hertfordshire: A D Wilson, 14 Marina Gardens, Cheshunt, Herts EN8 9QY.
  Middlesex: C Lamsdell, 4 Hardings Close, Iver Heath, Bucks SL0 0HL.
  Buckinghamshire: A V Moon, Chalk Dell House, London Road, Rickmansworth, Herts WD3 1JP.
  Kent: A J Morris, 134 Station Road, Crayford, Kent DA1 3QQ.
  Surrey: S J Spooner, 32 Berkeley Drive, West Molesey, Surrey RH8 0PY.
- Berkshire, Buckinghamshire and Oxfordshire Naturalists' Trust. 3 Church Cowley Road, Rose Hill, Oxford OX4 3JR.
- Buckinghamshire Bird Club. Graeme Taylor, Field House, 54 Halton Lane, Wendover, Aylesbury, Bucks HP22 6AU.
- Essex Birdwatching Society. Maurice Adcock, The Saltings, 53 Victoria Drive, Great Wakering, Southend-on-Sea, Essex SS3 0AT.
- Essex Wildlife Trust. Fingringhoe Wick Nature Reserve, South Green Road, Fingringhoe, Colchester, Essex CO5 7DN.
- Hertfordshire and Middlesex Wildlife Trust. Grebe House, St Michael's Street, St Albans, Hertfordshire AL3 4SN.
- Hertfordshire Bird Club. Ted Fletcher, Beech House, Aspenden, Herts SG9 9PG.
- Kent Ornithological Society. Dr Keith Derrett, 14 Chestnut Avenue, Staplehurst, Tonbridge, Kent TN12 0NH.
- Kent Trust for Nature Conservation. Tyland Barn, Sandling, Maidstone, Kent ME14 3BD.

- London Wildlife Trust. Central Office, 80 York Way, London N1 9AG.
- Marylebone Birdwatching Society. Miss Barbara Luke, 9 Princess Court, 74 Compayne Gardens, London NW6 3RX.
- RSPB members' groups. There are 12 local branches of the RSPB in Greater London; for details contact the head office in Bedfordshire (see National Associations).
- Surbiton and District Birdwatching Society. Mrs Nicola K Morris, 155 Walsingham Gardens, Stoneleigh, Epsom, Surrey KT19 0NB.
- Surrey Bird Club. Mrs Jill Cook, Moorings, Vale Wood Drive, Lower Bourne, Farnham, Surrey GU10 3HW.
- Surrey Wildlife Trust. School Lane, Pirbright, Woking, Surrey GU24 0JN.

Other organisations
- Birdline South East. For regularly updated information on the latest rarity sightings and other interesting bird news in and around the London area, contact 0891 700240. To leave details of your own bird sightings, phone the hotline on 01426 933933.
- London Ecology Unit. Bedford House, 125 Camden High Street, London NW1 7JR.
- Thames Water. Amenity and Recreation Officer, Nugent House, Vastern Road, Reading, Berkshire RG1 8DB.

CHECKLIST OF BIRDS OF THE LONDON AREA

The following 345 species have been recorded within a 20-mile radius of St Paul's Cathedral as at 31 December 1995.

Red-throated Diver
Black-throated Diver
Great Northern Diver
Little Grebe
Great Crested Grebe
Red-necked Grebe
Slavonian Grebe
Black-necked Grebe
Fulmar
Manx Shearwater
Mediterranean Shearwater
Little Shearwater
European Storm-petrel
Leach's Storm-petrel
Gannet
Cormorant
Shag
Bittern
Little Bittern
Night Heron
Squacco Heron
Cattle Egret
Little Egret
Grey Heron
Purple Heron
Black Stork
White Stork
Glossy Ibis
Spoonbill
Mute Swan
Bewick's Swan
Whooper Swan
Bean Goose
Pink-footed Goose
White-fronted Goose
Greylag Goose
Canada Goose
Barnacle Goose
Brent Goose
Red-breasted Goose
Egyptian Goose
Shelduck
Mandarin Duck
Wigeon
American Wigeon
Gadwall
Teal
Mallard
Pintail
Garganey
Blue-winged Teal
Shoveler
Red-crested Pochard
Pochard

Ring-necked Duck
Ferruginous Duck
Tufted Duck
Scaup
Eider
Long-tailed Duck
Common Scoter
Velvet Scoter
Goldeneye
Smew
Red-breasted Merganser
Goosander
Ruddy Duck
Honey Buzzard
Black Kite
Red Kite
White-tailed Eagle
Marsh Harrier
Hen Harrier
Montagu's Harrier
Goshawk
Sparrowhawk
Common Buzzard
Rough-legged Buzzard
Golden Eagle
Osprey
Lesser Kestrel
Kestrel
Red-footed Falcon
Merlin
Hobby
Gyr Falcon
Peregrine
Red-legged Partridge
Grey Partridge
Quail
Pheasant
Water Rail
Spotted Crake
Little Crake
Baillon's Crake
Corncrake
Moorhen
Coot
Crane
Great Bustard
Oystercatcher
Black-winged Stilt
Avocet
Stone Curlew
Cream-coloured Courser
Collared Pratincole
Little Ringed Plover
Ringed Plover

Killdeer
Kentish Plover
Dotterel
American Golden Plover
Pacific Golden Plover
Golden Plover
Grey Plover
Sociable Plover
Lapwing
Knot
Sanderling
Western Sandpiper
Little Stint
Temminck's Stint
White-rumped Sandpiper
Baird's Sandpiper
Pectoral Sandpiper
Sharp-tailed Sandpiper
Curlew Sandpiper
Purple Sandpiper
Dunlin
Broad-billed Sandpiper
Buff-breasted Sandpiper
Ruff
Jack Snipe
Snipe
Great Snipe
Long-billed Dowitcher
Woodcock
Black-tailed Godwit
Bar-tailed Godwit
Whimbrel
Curlew
Spotted Redshank
Redshank
Marsh Sandpiper
Greenshank
Lesser Yellowlegs
Solitary Sandpiper
Green Sandpiper
Wood Sandpiper
Common Sandpiper
Spotted Sandpiper
Turnstone
Wilson's Phalarope
Red-necked Phalarope
Grey Phalarope
Pomarine Skua
Arctic Skua
Long-tailed Skua
Great Skua
Mediterranean Gull
Little Gull
Sabine's Gull

Bonaparte's Gull
Black-headed Gull
Ring-billed Gull
Common Gull
Lesser Black-backed Gull
Herring Gull
Iceland Gull
Glaucous Gull
Great Black-backed Gull
Kittiwake
Gull-billed Tern
Caspian Tern
Sandwich Tern
Roseate Tern
Common Tern
Arctic Tern
Bridled Tern
Sooty Tern
Little Tern
Whiskered Tern
Black Tern
White-winged Black Tern
Guillemot
Razorbill
Little Auk
Puffin
Pallas's Sandgrouse
Feral Rock Dove
Stock Dove
Woodpigeon
Collared Dove
Turtle Dove
Ring-necked Parakeet
Cuckoo
Yellow-billed Cuckoo
Barn Owl
Scops Owl
Snowy Owl
Little Owl
Tawny Owl
Long-eared Owl
Short-eared Owl
Tengmalm's Owl
Nightjar
Common Nighthawk
Swift
Alpine Swift
Kingfisher
Bee-eater
Roller
Hoopoe
Wryneck
Green Woodpecker
Great Spotted Woodpecker
Lesser Spotted Woodpecker
Short-toed Lark
Crested Lark
Woodlark
Skylark
Shorelark
Sand Martin

Swallow
Red-rumped Swallow
House Martin
Richard's Pipit
Tawny Pipit
Olive-backed Pipit
Tree Pipit
Meadow Pipit
Red-throated Pipit
Rock Pipit
Water Pipit
Yellow Wagtail
Citrine Wagtail
Grey Wagtail
Pied Wagtail
Waxwing
Dipper
Wren
Dunnock
Alpine Accentor
Robin
Nightingale
Bluethroat
Black Redstart
Redstart
Whinchat
Stonechat
Wheatear
Black-eared Wheatear
Desert Wheatear
Hermit Thrush
Ring Ouzel
Blackbird
Dusky Thrush
Fieldfare
Song Thrush
Redwing
Mistle Thrush
Cetti's Warbler
Grasshopper Warbler
Savi's Warbler
Aquatic Warbler
Sedge Warbler
Marsh Warbler
Reed Warbler
Icterine Warbler
Melodious Warbler
Dartford Warbler
Subalpine Warbler
Sardinian Warbler
Barred Warbler
Lesser Whitethroat
Whitethroat
Garden Warbler
Blackcap
Pallas's Warbler
Yellow-browed Warbler
Wood Warbler
Chiffchaff
Willow Warbler
Goldcrest

Firecrest
Spotted Flycatcher
Red-breasted Flycatcher
Pied Flycatcher
Bearded Tit
Long-tailed Tit
Marsh Tit
Willow Tit
Crested Tit
Coal Tit
Blue Tit
Great Tit
Nuthatch
Treecreeper
Short-toed Treecreeper
Penduline Tit
Golden Oriole
Isabelline Shrike
Red-backed Shrike
Lesser Grey Shrike
Great Grey Shrike
Woodchat Shrike
Jay
Magpie
Nutcracker
Jackdaw
Rook
Carrion Crow
Raven
Starling
Rose-coloured Starling
House Sparrow
Tree Sparrow
Chaffinch
Brambling
Serin
Greenfinch
Goldfinch
Siskin
Linnet
Twite
Redpoll
Arctic Redpoll
Two-barred Crossbill
Common Crossbill
Parrot Crossbill
Common Rosefinch
Pine Grosbeak
Bullfinch
Hawfinch
Lapland Bunting
Snow Bunting
Pine Bunting
Yellowhammer
Cirl Bunting
Ortolan Bunting
Rustic Bunting
Little Bunting
Reed Bunting
Black-headed Bunting
Corn Bunting

GLOSSARY OF TERMS

Carr Woodland, usually willow or alder, growing in waterlogged ground.

Chat Collective name for Robin, Black Redstart, Common Redstart, Whinchat, Common Stonechat and Northern Wheatear.

Commoner gulls Collective name for Black-headed, Common, Lesser Black-backed, Herring and Great Black-backed Gulls.

Corvid Collective name for the crow family. Includes Jay, Magpie, Jackdaw, Rook, Carrion Crow and Raven.

Dabbling duck A duck, such as Mallard or Teal, which feeds while sitting on the water, often by up-ending. Also known as surface-feeding duck.

Diurnal migration Daytime movements of birds migrating overhead, which can be seen mainly in autumn.

Diving duck A duck, such as Pochard or Tufted Duck, which feeds by diving below the surface.

Fall (of migrants) Sudden arrival of migrant birds, usually overnight, that are grounded by adverse weather such as rain or mist.

Feral Birds that have either escaped or been released from captivity and are now living successfully in a wild state.

Grey Geese Collective name for Bean, Pink-footed, White-fronted, Lesser White-fronted and Greylag Geese.

Hirundine Collective name for martins and swallows. Applied particularly to Sand Martin, Swallow and House Martin.

Immigrant A bird moving into the area from elsewhere.

Irruption Periodic (every few years) mass arrival of birds from elsewhere, usually because of high populations and/or food shortages in their normal areas. Applied particularly to birds such as Crossbill.

Larger gulls Collective name for Lesser Black-backed, Herring, Iceland, Glaucous and Great Black-backed Gulls.

Leaf warbler Collective name for Wood Warbler, Chiffchaff and Willow Warbler, and the rarer *Phylloscopus* species.

Loaf/loafing Term applied to gulls and waterfowl resting after bathing or feeding.

Migrant/passage migrant A bird passing through, usually in spring and autumn, en route between its breeding and wintering grounds.

Overshooting Term usually applied to spring migrants which are blown further north than their intended destination by strong winds from the southern quarter.

Passage Movement of birds through an area, usually in spring and autumn.

Passerine Collective term for perching birds. Includes larks, swallows and martins, pipits and wagtails, dippers, wrens, accentors, chats, thrushes, warblers, flycatchers, tits, nuthatches, treecreepers, shrikes, crows, starlings, sparrows, finches and buntings.

Predator Collective name for species which kill and eat live prey, applied usually to raptors and owls.

Raptor Collective term for birds of prey, which includes eagles, kites, harriers, hawks, buzzards, osprey and falcons but excludes owls.

Rarer grebes Collective name for Red-necked, Black-necked and Slavonian Grebes.

Rarer gulls Collective name for Mediterranean, Yellow-legged, Iceland and Glaucous Gulls.

Rarity Used here to refer to birds which are rare either in the London area or nationally.

Reel/reeling The rapid, uniform, sustained trilling song of Grasshopper Warbler, which is reminiscent of an angler's reel.

Rode/roding The display flight of Woodcock at dusk, during which it flies with a peculiar, deliberate wing action and utters a short grunting note.

Roost/roosting Birds gathering to rest communally at a safe site, usually at night.

Sawbill Collective name for Smew, Red-breasted Merganser and Goosander.

Scrape Shallow, man-made excavation in wet ground to provide habitat for wildfowl and waders.

Scrub warblers A collective term for warblers of scrub habitats, especially Lesser Whitethroat, Common Whitethroat, Garden Warbler and Blackcap.

Seaduck Duck normally found in coastal waters such as Scaup, Eider, Long-tailed Duck, Common and Velvet Scoters, and Red-breasted Merganser.

Set-aside Areas of farmland left fallow under the European Union's Common Agricultural Policy. This provides winter food for birds.

Sink-hole A hole into which streams disappear in limestone districts.

Six species of tits Collective term for Long-tailed, Marsh, Willow, Coal, Blue and Great Tits.

Sylvan/woodland warblers Collective term for warblers that inhabit woodland, especially Garden Warbler, Blackcap, Wood Warbler, Chiffchaff and Willow Warbler.

Three woodpeckers Collective term for Green, Great Spotted and Lesser Spotted Woodpeckers.

Vagrant A bird many miles from its normal range, such as seabirds inland.

Wader Collective name for oystercatcher, plovers, sandpipers, snipe, godwits, calidrids, phalaropes and so on that generally feed in mud or shallow water. Also known as shorebirds.

Waterfowl Collective name for birds which have evolved to an aquatic lifestyle. Includes divers, grebes, swans, geese, ducks, Moorhen and Coot.

Wildfowl Collective name for the Anatidae family, *i.e.* swans, geese and ducks.

Wild/winter swans Collective name for Bewick's and Whooper Swans as opposed to the introduced Mute Swan. Also referred to as migrant swans.

Winter(ing) thrushes Refers mainly to Fieldfares and Redwings, but also includes Blackbirds and Song Thrushes arriving for the winter.

Wreck Term used to describe seabirds, such as Shag, which are driven inland by gales or storms.

BIBLIOGRAPHY

A–Z London Street Atlas. 1990. Geographers' A–Z Map Co.
Alexandra Park and Wood Green Reservoir Bird Report 1990.
Barrett, K. 1995. A Walk Around Dagenham Chase. *Essex Birds* in prep.
Beddington Farm Bird Report Number 6 1992.
Birds in the Lee Valley Regional Park: what was seen in 1993. Lee Valley Regional Park Authority.
Birds in the Lee Valley Regional Park: What was seen in 1994. Lee Valley Regional Park Authority.
Birds on Mitcham Common 1994.
Bowman, N. 1978. *The Birds of Alexandra Park and Wood Green Reservoir.* Published by the author.
Bowman, N. 1992. My Local Patch. *Birdwatch* 6: 21–22.
Burton, J A. 1974. *The Naturalist in London.* David and Charles.
Clarke, P, and Clarke, M. 1995. *Where to Watch Birds in East Anglia* (third edition). Christopher Helm.
Clews, B, Heryet, A, and Trodd, P. 1995. *Where to Watch Birds in Bedfordshire, Berkshire, Buckinghamshire, Hertfordshire and Oxfordshire* (second edition). Christopher Helm.
Cramp, S, and Tomlins, A D. 1966. The Birds of Inner London 1951–65. *British Birds* 59: 209–233.
Dagenham Chase Bird Report 1993.
Department of the Environment. (1973–78). *Bird Life in the Royal Parks,* report published annually. HMSO.
Fitter, R S R. 1945. *London's Natural History.* Collins.
Fitter, R S R. 1949. *London's Birds.* Collins.
Hampstead Heath Ornithological Report Number 48 for 1993.
Hampstead Heath Ornithological Report Number 49 for 1994.
Harrison, J, and Grant, P G. 1976. *The Thames Transformed.* André Deutsch.
Hastings, R. 1992. *Kew Information Sheet 12: Birds at Kew.* Royal Botanic Gardens, Kew.
Hilfield Park Reservoir Bird Report for 1994.
Hilfield Park Reservoir Bird Report for 1995.
Hudson, W H. 1898. *Birds in London* (second edition, 1969). David and Charles.
Lee Valley Park Plan. 1986. Lee Valley Regional Park Authority.
London Bird Reports Numbers 14–58 for 1947–94. London Natural History Society.
London Natural History Society. 1964. *The Birds of the London Area* (revised edition). Rupert Hart-Davis.
Montier, D J (ed) for the London Natural History Society. 1977. *Atlas of Breeding Birds of the London Area.* Batsford.
Nicholson, E M. 1995. *Bird-watching in London: a Historical Perspective.* London Natural History Society.
Pemberton, J E (ed). 1995. *The Birdwatcher's Yearbook and Diary 1996.* Buckingham Press.
Quist, A. 1971. *Epping Forest.* The Sidney Press.
Report by the Committee on Bird Sanctuaries in the Royal Parks (England

and Wales). 1950. *Birds in London 1949*. HMSO.

Report by the Committee on Bird Sanctuaries in the Royal Parks (England and Wales). 1951. *Bird Life in the Royal Parks 1950*. HMSO.

Simms, E. 1974. *Wildlife in the Royal Parks*. HMSO.

Taylor, D, Wheatley, J, and Prater, T. 1991. *Where to Watch Birds in Kent, Surrey and Sussex* (second edition). Christopher Helm.

Thames Water Conservation, Access and Recreation Annual Report 1995–6.

The National Trust Handbook 1996.

Various authors for the London Ecology Unit. *Nature Conservation in ...* series of guides to London boroughs. London Ecology Unit.

White, G. 1993. *An Assessment of the Wetland Resource of the Lee Valley Park*. Lee Valley Regional Park Authority.

CODE OF CONDUCT FOR BIRDWATCHERS

Today's birdwatchers are a powerful force for nature conservation. The number of those of us interested in birds rises continually and it is vital that we take seriously our responsibility to avoid any harm to birds.

We must also present a responsible image to non-birdwatchers who may be affected by our activities and particularly those on whose sympathy and support the future of birds may rest.

There are 10 points to bear in mind:
1. The welfare of birds must come first.
2. Habitat must be protected.
3. Keep disturbance to birds and their habitat to a minimum.
4. When you find a rare bird think carefully about whom you should tell.
5. Do not harass rare migrants.
6. Abide by the bird protection laws at all times.
7. Respect the rights of landowners.
8. Respect the rights of other people in the countryside.
9. Make your records available to the local bird recorder.
10. Behave abroad as you would when birdwatching at home.

Welfare of birds must come first
Whether your particular interest is photography, ringing, sound recording, scientific study or just birdwatching, remember that the welfare of the bird must always come first.

Habitat protection
Its habitat is vital to a bird and therefore we must ensure that our activities do not cause damage.

Keep disturbance to a minimum
Birds' tolerance of disturbance varies between species and seasons. Therefore, it is safer to keep all disturbance to a minimum. No birds should be disturbed from the nest in case opportunities for predators to take eggs or young are increased. In very cold weather disturbance to birds may cause them to use vital energy at a time when food is difficult to find. Wildfowlers already impose bans during cold weather; birdwatchers should exercise similar discretion.

Rare breeding birds
If you discover a rare bird breeding and feel that protection is necessary, inform the appropriate RSPB Regional Office, or the Species Protection Department at the Lodge. Otherwise it is best in almost all circumstances to keep the record strictly secret in order to avoid disturbance by other birdwatchers and attacks by egg-collectors. Never visit known sites of rare breeding birds unless they are adequately protected. Even your presence may give away the site to others and cause so many other visitors that the birds may fail to breed successfully.

Disturbance at or near the nest of species listed on the First Schedule of the Wildlife and Countryside Act 1981 is a criminal offence.

Copies of Wild Birds and the Law are obtainable from the RSPB, The Lodge, Sandy, Beds. SG19 2DL (send two 2nd class stamps).

Rare migrants

Rare migrants or vagrants must not be harassed. If you discover one, consider the circumstances carefully before telling anyone. Will an influx of birdwatchers disturb the bird or others in the area? Will the habitat be damaged? Will problems be caused with the landowner?

The Law

The bird protection laws (now embodied in the Wildlife and Countryside Act 1981) are the result of hard campaigning by previous generations of birdwatchers. As birdwatchers we must abide by them at all times and not allow them to fall into disrepute.

Respect the rights of landowners

The wishes of landowners and occupiers of land must be respected. Do not enter land without permission. Comply with permit schemes. If you are leading a group, do give advance notice of the visit, even if a formal permit scheme is not in operation. Always obey the Country Code.

Respect the rights of other people

Have proper consideration for other birdwatchers. Try not to disrupt their activities or scare the birds they are watching. There are many other people who also use the countryside. Do not interfere with their activities and, if it seems that what they are doing is causing unnecessary disturbance to birds, do try to take a balanced view. Flushing gulls when walking a dog on a beach may do little harm, while the same dog might be a serious disturbance at a tern colony. When pointing this out to a non-birdwatcher be courteous, but firm. The non-birdwatchers' goodwill towards birds must not be destroyed by the attitudes of birdwatchers.

Keeping records

Much of today's knowledge about birds is the result of meticulous record keeping by our predecessors. Make sure you help to add to tomorrow's knowledge by sending records to your county bird recorder.

Birdwatching abroad

Behave abroad as you would at home. This code should be firmly adhered to when abroad (whatever the local laws). Well behaved birdwatchers can be important ambassadors for bird protection.

This code has been drafted after consultation between The British Ornithologists' Union, British Trust for Ornithology, the Royal Society for the Protection of Birds, the Scottish Ornithologists' Club, the Wildfowl and Wetlands Trust and the Editors of *British Birds*.

Further copies may be obtained from The Royal Society for the Protection of Birds, The Lodge, Sandy, Beds. SG19 2DL.

INDEX OF SPECIES BY SITE NUMBER